AIR RAID

The Bombing of Coventry, 1940

Norman Longmate

AIR RAID

The Bombing of Coventry, 1940

David McKay Company, Inc.
New York

AIR RAID

CONTENTS

LIST OF ILLUSTRATIONS

Acknowledgements for Illustrations

Radio Times Hulton Picture Library: 1, 28, 30, 31
Herbert Museum and Art Gallery, Coventry: 2, 17, 24
Bilderdienst Süddeutscher Verlag, Munich: 3
Imperial War Museum: 4, 5, 6, 9
Professor R. V. Jones: 7
Colonel F. H. Lawrence: 8
Fox Photos Ltd: 10, 11, 16, 23
Keystone Press Agency: 12, 14
Camera Press: 13, 31, 33
Coventry Evening Telegraph: 15, 26
The Times: 18, 19, 21, 22, 25
The Birmingham Post: 27
J. Allan Cash Ltd: 32
The map of Coventry shown on pages 6 and 7 is based upon the
Ordnance Survey Map with sanction of the Controller of Her
Majesty's Stationary Office, Crown copyright reserved.

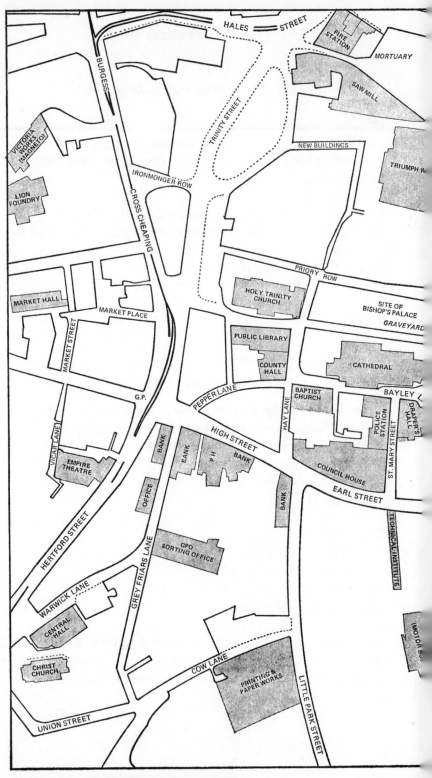

MAP OF THE CENTRE OF COVENTRY, 1940
showing, in simplified form, the main streets and some of the principal
buildings mentioned in the text.

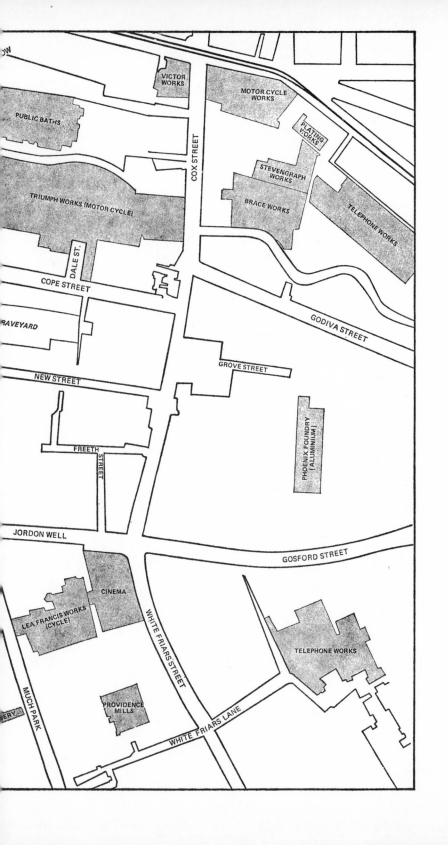

FOREWORD

The present book is one of a number in which I have examined various aspects of civilian experience during the Second World War. Although concerned essentially with only one night in a single city, it deals with a subject that in some way affected most parts of the British Isles. When collecting contributions for my first book about the war, *How We Lived Then*, I found that of some forty subjects on which I had invited recollections air raids attracted by far the largest response, exceeding even that on such evocative subjects as the American invasion and the events of 1940, both of which I have since covered in separate books.

Because a full-scale book on the London Blitz already exists, and because air raids on different places, however interesting to those involved, can easily seem similar to the ordinary reader, I was attracted by the idea of a detailed study of a single air raid on a city outside London, and the attack on Coventry in November 1940 was the natural choice. This made an immediate impact, not merely on the whole country but throughout the world, and was immediately recognized as a landmark in the history of aerial bombardment. Subsequently the warm response to the radio programme *Target 53: Coventry*, of which I wrote the script, transmitted on BBC Radio 4 on 15 November 1973, showed how general was interest in the raid, some of the appreciative letters received coming from listeners too young to remember the war. Significantly, too, the *Coventry Blitz Show*, supposedly set in an air-raid shelter, staged at the Belgrade Two Theatre, Coventry, in November 1974, which I reviewed for the BBC, involved a mainly young cast, few of whom could have witnessed the events they described so movingly and, in some cases, divertingly.

I am grateful to all those who contributed to the radio programme *Target 53: Coventry* for allowing me to draw on their recorded material in this book; to Mr Stanley Williamson, of BBC Manchester, who produced the programme and bore with forbearance my delivery of a grossly over-length script; and to Mr Geoffrey Green, now of BBC Birmingham and in November 1940 of the *Coventry Standard.* I also owe a particular debt to Colonel F. H. Lawrence, C.B.E., M.C., C.STJ., T.D., D.L., who commanded the heavy anti-aircraft defences of Coventry in 1940 and who went to great pains to answer the technical questions with which, as a non-gunner, I bombarded him; and to Professor R. V. Jones, formerly of Air Ministry Scientific Intelligence and the Secret Intelligence Service and now of Aberdeen University, who guided me, in conversations and correspondence, through the intricacies of the 'wireless war' in which he was deeply involved, and also reinforced my own scepticism about recent suggestions that the British government had prior warning of the raid. Mr Alfred Price kindly answered for me questions arising from his interesting history of radar, *Instruments of Darkness*, and Mr Derrick Garrard, formerly of the Royal Aircraft Establishment, Farnborough, made inquiries for me about the salvaging of the crashed Heinkel, described in Chapter 3. On the important question of morale in Coventry, I owe much to the late Tom Harrisson, with whom I had discussed the whole subject just before he left for his final, fatal, trip to the Far East. He had generously made available to me the Mass-Observation report on the raid as well as his own reminiscences of the whole episode, so that the account which appears here is fuller than that contained in his own posthumous book, *Living Through the Blitz*, which I was able to read in proof. His findings, as the leading authority in his field at that time, entirely bear out my conclusions.

Other help was given me by the staff of the Reference Library of the Harris Art Gallery and Museum at Coventry, who answered many questions and supplied many invaluable press cuttings and local publications, and by Miss Josephine Salond of the University Library, Birmingham, who made a number of inquiries for me on the spot. Miss Diana Phillips, of the Ikon group, was responsible for the picture research in Lonbon and Coventry and for obtaining photographs from Germany. Mr Hind and his colleagues at the Imperial War Museum were as helpful as ever in tracing other illustrations. And I am, as always, deeply in the debt of Miss Idina Le Geyt, who tackled the daunting task of working her way through the huge volume of official documents about the raid in the Public Record Office with her usual indefatigable enthusiasm and punctilious regard for accuracy.

My final, but far from least, acknowledgement must be to the many newspapers in the Midlands which carried my appeal for reminiscences of the raid and to the people who responded and often went to great trouble to answer additional questions or suggest other sources of information. The limitations of space have meant that many contributions have had to be heavily cut or omitted, but all the material sent to me proved helpful in providing background knowledge about, and (I hope) an understanding of, a city which, at the time I started work on the book, I had visited only once, very briefly, in the 1950s. It is almost invidious to select one individual for special mention, but I must record my thanks to Mrs Lucy Smart, formerly Miss Lucy Moseley, who not merely sent me an outstandingly comprehensive and useful contribution but subsequently read through the whole manuscript for me with the vigilant eye of someone born and brought up in Coventry, though she has, of course, no responsibility for any of the statements made.

In previous books I have not identified informants by name in the text, believing that this information is of little interest to other readers. In the present book I have followed a somewhat different policy, since the same individuals tend to recur at frequent points throughout the narrative and many will still be readily identifiable from the positions they held at that time. While keeping to the general rule of anonymity, therefore, I have included names in a few cases where this seemed helpful to the reader, and the names of all those who sent me material are also listed, unless they asked otherwise, at the end of the book.

N.R.L.

ACKNOWLEDGEMENTS

Transcripts of Crown-copyright records in the Public Record Office appear by permission of the Controller of Her Majesty's Stationery Office. Grateful acknowledgement for the use of other copyright material is made to the following: to the City of Coventry for the extracts from *The City We Loved*; to Mr Raymond J. Shelton for the passages from *A Night in Little Park Street*; to the British Publishing Co., Gloucester, for *Coventry under Fire*; to Mr Anthony Cave Brown and W. H. Allen and Co. Ltd for *Bodyguard of Lies*; to Mr William Stevenson and Messrs Macmillan, London and Basingstoke, for *A Man Called Intrepid*; to Group-Captain F. W. Winterbotham and Messrs Weidenfeld and Nicolson for *The Ultra Secret*; to the Very Rev. R. T. Howard for *Ruined and Rebuilt*; to Mr Allen A. Richie, Mr Walter Graebner and Messrs George Allen and Unwin Ltd, for *Lights of Freedom*; to the trustees of the Mass-Observation Archive and the late Mr Tom Harrisson for the Mass-Observation report on the bombing of Coventry; to Sir David Hunt, Professor Michael Howard, Group-Captain F. W. Winterbotham and *The Times Literary Supplement* for the reviews quoted in the Appendix; and to Mr E. H. Dean, formerly Head of the Modern Language Department at Coventry Technical College, for permission to use his translation from *The War Books of German Youth*.

Apologies are offered for any inadvertent breach of copyright where, owing to the lapse of time, it has proved impossible to trace copyright-holders, and appropriate amends will gladly be made in any future edition.

I

TOO FAR INLAND TO BE BOMBED

'10th June.   Italy declared war.   Played tennis.'
Diary of a young Coventry Civil Servant, 1940

FEW events of the Second World War have become more encrusted with misleading legend than the German air raid upon Coventry on 14 November 1940. It is an accepted part of the folklore of the period that in this 'terror' attack upon a small and peaceful town, unprepared and with no reason to expect it, the enemy revealed himself in his true colours and justified the long series of steadily escalating reprisals which followed.

The true facts, as will be seen, are very different. Yet the bombing of Coventry *was* a landmark in the history of aerial warfare and the city *was* unique, if not for the reasons commonly supposed. Unlike so many manufacturing centres it was not a former village, swollen hideously into a city within a decade or two by the Industrial Revolution, but an ancient community that could trace its origins back beyond the Middle Ages. The first settlement on the site was a convent, said to have been built near 'Coffa's tree' in the seventh century, and this had been succeeded by a Benedictine monastery founded in 1043 by the Saxon Earl Leofric and his wife, the Countess Godiva, the one citizen of Coventry of whom everyone has heard. The story of the famous occasion when she 'mounted her horse naked, letting down the hair and tresses of her head so that her whole body was veiled except for her very beautiful legs', and rode through the streets in answer to her husband's offer (if she did so) to 'free the town of Coventry from heavy bondage and servitude', may itself be apocryphal. It was not mentioned by a chronicler until more than a century later and modern commentators have suggested it was the horse that was 'naked', i.e. saddle-less, rather than its rider. True or not, however, the story of Lady Godiva had been cherished by Coventry, and the wife of the American Ambassador, unveiling the latest statue of her in 1949 (paid for by a donor who had also given the nation a Spitfire named 'Godiva'), remarked that, like the city itself, 'It was Lady Godiva's refusal to accept defeat . . . that won her fame.' Also destined to go down to posterity was the name of Peeping Tom, the solitary citizen said to have ignored her pleas that everyone should stay indoors behind drawn curtains during the famous ride. Tom's very existence is doubtful, for he did not appear in the story until the seventeenth century, but by 1940 there were no fewer than six busts, statues or carvings of him in existence in Coventry, of which the most famous had become something of a civic talisman and had for more than a century looked down on the traffic of Broadgate until, shortly before 1939, it was banished to a glass case in a hotel.

Coventry first emerged as an important commercial centre thanks to the cloth trade, followed by an associated business, ribbon-mak-ing, and then an even more skilled craft, watch manufacture, the need of these occupations for ample light resulting in the construction of many half-timbered houses with wide upper windows. The men who grew rich from these trades left the city a legacy of schools and almshouses, of which the most famous were Ford's Hospital, founded in 1509 under the will of a wealthy local merchant, and Bond's Hospital, established about the same time by a former draper and ex-Mayor. Their Tudor buildings were among the show-pieces of Coventry, but, apart from its churches, its chief archi-tectural glory was probably St Mary's Hall, formerly the Guildhall, built early in the fifteenth century as a meeting place for the trade guilds and for a time the seat of the town's government. The great symbol of Coventry, however, which gave it the name, beloved of guide-book writers, 'The City of the Three Spires', was provided by its three great churches, which prompted some much-quoted lines by Alfred, Lord Tennyson, writing, inevitably, about Lady Godiva:

> I waited for the train at Coventry;
> I hung with grooms and porters on the bridge,
> To watch the three tall spires, . . .

The spires belonged respectively to Christ Church, which dated back to the fourteenth century, Holy Trinity, and St Michael's, which had been elevated to the dignity of a cathedral only in 1918, when the diocese of Coventry was carved out of the ancient Bishopric of Worcester. Its chief custodian in 1940 was Provost R. T. Howard, who recalls its special appeal:

It was one of the largest and most beautiful of all those churches built in England 600 years ago in the new style in which English builders had broken away from the lavish continental style to something peculiarly English in form. It was very spacious, [possessed] exquisite proportions of slender pillars, broad arches and large windows. It had the equal third tallest of all the spires in the country, perfectly decorated from the ground to the weathercock 300 feet above.

All told there were in 1940 in Coventry twenty-four officially registered Ancient Monuments, plus eight surviving sections of the city walls, but what had made its name known throughout the world were its industrial products, especially those concerned with transport. Its emergence as a centre of skilled engineering and the metal trades had begun in the 1860s, and by 1914 it was already the 'bicycle capital' of the world, and housed the largest manufacturer of machine tools, Sir Alfred Herbert and Co., in the country. Between the wars these activities were overtaken by vehicle manufacture, which in turn were joined by aircraft, and – a natural successor to the old ribbon trade – synthetic fibres, to manufacture which a vast modern factory was built by Courtaulds. Although its population had soared, from 45000 in 1881 to 106000 in 1911, and to an estimated 238000 in 1940, Coventry escaped the worst effects of the Depression. There *were* unemployed, many of them attracted to Coventry by rumours of abundant jobs who found themselves instead joining the dole queues, and even skilled men might find themselves out of work, or on short time, for months on end, but with the start of the rearmament drive in the mid 1930s the city began to become in fact the boom town it had already been painted in legend. While factories were closing elsewhere new ones were being opened in Coventry, like the large new works of the Coventry Gauge and Tool Company in Fletchamstead Highway, in 1936, and the Courtaulds plant just mentioned. Shortly before the war the leading motor manufacturers were summoned to London by the Secretary of State for Air to launch the 'shadow factory' scheme, under which the government would finance and build new armament works, for use if war came, though they would be operated by existing public major companies. All through the bitter winter of 1939–40 work was pressed on for the shadow factories being built for Daimler, Rootes and other concerns, one of which alone, the Standard No. 2 Shadow Factory, covered eighty-eight acres.

Rearmament made Coventry, already prosperous, a boom town. Just as it already had more car owners than most places, so by 1939, although by now overwhelmingly working-class, it had more house owners. Between 1931 and 1939, 25 500 new houses were completed in Coventry, most of them in new, modestly priced estates on the outskirts. One girl, then aged thirteen, can still remember the builder's board standing outside the brand-new 'semi' in Glendower Avenue, three miles from the city centre, to which her family moved early in 1939, advertising that it had cost '£45 down and 13s 9d a week', amounts within reach of her father who held a typical Coventry-type job as an inspector at the Armstrong Siddeley Works in Parkside. To find work was the only reason people moved to Coventry; no one ever retired there. But to another schoolgirl the house into which her father, manager of a shoe shop, moved in Crecy Road, also in Cheylesmore, in 1939, 'was,' she remembers, 'my idea of heaven', with 'to one side of us . . . a field where blackberry bushes grew in profusion'. When in due course she was offered evacuation to North Wales she firmly turned it down.

The unique feature of Coventry was the way in which, thanks to its long history and the refusal for many years of the corporation to authorize building on the common land surrounding the city, sizable factories, small workshops, shops, flats and houses of all kinds were mixed up together around the ancient centre, although the newest industrial plants, like the shadow factories, were mainly to be found on the outskirts. Even within a minute or two's walk of the Cathedral, however, one could find not merely small manufacturing businesses but large concerns which almost anywhere else would have been confined to a non-residential district. Frequently, close to the factories were historic buildings dating back to Tudor or even medieval times.

Most people who moved to Coventry were pleasantly surprised, both at its ancient buildings and at the open space surrounding it. The wife of one engineer, who had reluctantly abandoned life in

London in 1930 at the height of the Depression to find employment at the Morris Works, was charmed to find 'the old City . . . intersected with narrow streets and dozens of little courts and back to back houses all mixed up with the shops and business premises'. By October 1938 this family were doing well enough to occupy 'a newly built house on the fast-growing estate in Cheylesmore . . . overlooking Whitley Common and open country', though 'our happiness at this pleasant move was overshadowed by the news which was coming each day over the radio'.

A Civil Servant then in her late twenties who had been most unwilling to move there in the summer of 1939 from softer surroundings further south also rapidly changed her mind.

I had feared [it] would be a dirty industrial town. It was not. Most of the factories were on the outskirts and the town itself was pleasant, with the lovely cathedral and the other 'two spires', a good shopping centre, gardens, and above all, the easy access to the surrounding countryside of leafy Warwickshire. Kenilworth was not far away, nor was Leamington Spa, where we used to walk in the Jephson Gardens and listen to concerts in the pump-room on Sunday evenings. I had made friends, joined a tennis club. We went about in a crowd, walked a great deal, danced and went to the cinema.

The hostel [the YWCA hostel in Sherborne House, The Butts, where she lived], known to my father as 'the harem', was comfortable and cheap. The food was good, we had our own rooms and for the older girls the restrictions were few. We could always get a key if we wanted to be out late. Our pleasures were simple and innocent.

The heart of Coventry was Broadgate, a short, wide, street a stone's throw from the Cathedral and Council House, which also housed the central police station, and was only a few yards from St Mary's Hall, Ford's Hospital and the charming group of timber-framed Tudor houses known as Priory Row. 'Broadgate was a meeting place,' remembers one resident whose roots went deep in the area – as a choirboy he had witnessed the consecration of St Michael's as the Cathedral and later had been confirmed and married within its walls. 'You could stand there and see people you knew every few minutes.' The outstanding impression of one engineering assistant, who joined the Borough Engineer's Department from Solihull in January 1938, was of 'the armies of cyclists that rode through the city centre at lunchtime and again in the evening peak, often five or six abreast'. Only a minority in this citadel of the motor industry could yet afford their own car but everyone could buy a bicycle. 'The corporation staff car park seldom had more than a dozen or fifteen cars in it, but it contained cycle racks for several hundred bicycles and these were usually full.'

Many people still lived close to the city's ancient centre, as they had done since medieval times. One young woman, then owning her own hairdressing business, who in September 1940 married an apprentice engineer from Armstrong Siddeley, found a flat in Judges Court, a building once occupied by the royal justices when on circuit:

It was right in the heart of the city, a few minutes walk away from the Cathedral. There was an industrial area very close to it, indeed one of the car factories was next door to the old house. But the house itself was very ancient, built of stone, stone staircases, arches into walled gardens, very beautiful, which had been in suites of rooms ... separated for modern use into flats. We had a flat on the second floor, up a stone staircase through a great oak door, into a modern flat overlooking the garden, a walled garden with a mulberry tree and a quince tree – very pleasant.

Not far away was Coventry's solitary department store, Owen Owen, opened shortly before the war, and occupying a special place in the affections of Coventry people, for board after board had turned down the Council's approaches until Owen Owen had finally agreed. Already by 1939 it was a Coventry institution and its manager, Leslie Worthington, still in his thirties, had, he remembers, settled down contentedly in the brand-new buildings and in his house further out.

In Coventry, as everywhere else, Air Raid Precautions had made a slow start. The Council had set up an ARP Sub-Committee on 29 January 1935, but its first report, that June, was not received with much enthusiasm, for Coventry, which had recently become a Labour Party stronghold and had a strong pacifist and international-ist tradition. 'Many of the leading members of the City Council,' one resident remembers, 'were members of the "Peace Movement" who thought that they could get armaments banned.' Another Coventry man, then a schoolboy, remembers how the efforts of his father, a works engineer, 'to interest the City Council' in his plans to protect his factory 'were largely unheeded'.

On 12 January 1937, nearly four years after Hitler had come to power in Germany, the first public appeal for volunteers for the ARP services was broadcast, and in Coventry recruiting posters appeared on hoardings and enrolment forms were distributed to chemists' shops. Among those who came forward was Harold Tomley who, after volunteering for the Army in 1914 and witnessing the carnage of war on the Western Front, had become a Branch Secretary of the League of Nations Union, only to decide reluctantly in April 1937 that 'until the vast majority of mankind had reached the stage of completely renouncing war . . . national defence would have to be retained'. Being blind in one eye, he had no prospect of acceptance by the Army, but he volunteered to join the infant ARP service and rapidly became an ARP instructor, using the experience he had gained in lecturing about peace to teach other volunteers, two evenings a week, about modern war.

On 17 March 1937 the Air Raid Precautions Committee approved an *Outline Scheme of Organization* for the city to be divided into six zones, requiring between them 412 Wardens' Posts, of which 104 would be in the Central Zone. To keep 'Control', the central operational headquarters in the basement of the Council House, in touch with all these out-stations, 50 messengers, 76 bicycles and 161 light cars or motor-cycles would be needed. Sixty-seven depots or bases, with 323 personnel, should be set up to man rescue and decontamination parties and other emergency services, and Coventry would also require 20 auxiliary fire stations, and 60 pumping units served by 537 trained men, plus 120 reserves and telephone operators. The Emergency Medical Services should, it was advised, be even larger, totalling almost 1000, including 65 doctors, 378 ambulance men, 294 nurses, 34 First Aid Parties, and several hundred 'general helpers', distributed between two Casualty Clearing Hospitals (the permanent hospitals in Gulson Road and Stoney Stanton Road), six Base Hospitals and seventeen First Aid Posts. Parallel with this 'Local Authority Organization', a 'Joint Industrial and Commercial Organization', usually known as 'Industrial ARP', was set up, under which every major factory would form its own fire brigade, First Aid Parties and rescue and repair teams, who would also, it was hoped, sally forth when they could to help in the surrounding streets.

By September 1938 only 45 per cent of the wardens needed had come forward, when, as elsewhere, Munich produced a sudden upsurge in recruiting, though one clergyman, who later found himself fighting fire-bombs in Coventry, remembers greeting the occasion with a sermon in praise of Neville Chamberlain. Others had less faith in the Prime Minister's effort. Five hundred more people volunteered for ARP work and training was intensified. One man, previously a plumber, who joined the Auxiliary Fire Service remembers being puzzled later as to 'why we had been given so many lectures on gas . . . when all we were required to know was "Where was the fire?" and even more important, "Where was the water?" ' A commercial traveller who became a War Reserve constable, for whom there was also a recruiting drive, decided most of the training was valueless. What, he decided later, would have been far more useful would have been some practical tips, like how to stop water running to waste from bombed houses by flattening the broken ends of a lead pipe or wedging up the ball-rod of an overflowing cistern with a stick.

Plans for evacuation also went ahead. One clergyman, soon to move to Coventry but then in charge of a small country parish outside Warwick, offered to try to find accommodation for child evacuees in the local villages and 'tramped many weary miles over muddy fields, getting refusal after refusal, especially from many of the richer people', but after 'great persuasion' at last had sixty-four places earmarked, only one short of the required total.

Disillusionment about the prospects of maintaining peace became general in March 1939 when Hitler tore up the Munich agreement and occupied the whole of Czechoslovakia. The daughter of the chief designer of one of the leading engineering firms in Coventry found herself with her father at this inauspicious moment in Berlin, after attending the Leipzig Trade Fair. 'Whenever we were greeted with "Heil Hitler!" ' she remembers, 'he saluted politely, while muttering under his breath, "God save the king!" '

In the spring of 1939 people in Coventry, like those in other target areas, began to be offered Anderson shelters, which were free to manual workers covered by the National Insurance Acts or others earning less than £250 a year. Not everyone responded, though later crowds were to clamour to be offered them. One carpenter living in the Holbrook district, one of the first residents in his road to apply for an Anderson, still remembers 'the discouraging remarks of the neighbours, who "were not going to have their gardens disfigured" ', as he duly excavated the three-foot hole it required in the middle of his small lawn. His work, they told him, was 'a waste of time' as 'you will never need that.' 'I replied,' he recalls, '"You may be glad to share it some day".' A foreman at the GEC works, who had served in France as a gunner in the First World War and knew only too well the power of high explosive, installed in his Anderson 'bunk beds, deckchairs, toilet, and first aid equipment' and provided an escape route, via the adjoining pantry, which extended into the garden of their house in Harris Road. The result so impressed the Council that a 'Home Office official came to photograph it'. The neighbours reacted differently. 'Many laughed at his urgency and said "Windy",' remembers his wife. A laundry worker – who soon afterwards moved into munition manufacture at Armstrong Siddeley – put his Anderson completely underground, installing steps down to it and planting rose trees on top. (Before the war was over they were fully grown.) Inside, long before bunks were officially issued, he installed a full-size bed, kept clear of the floor on blocks. Alderman Jack Moseley, soon to be Mayor, also set an example to his neighbours. His Anderson, in their modest house in Kensington Road, Earlsdon, was, his daughter remembers, covered with 'more than the regulation amount of earth' and fitted 'with a strong wooden door, steps leading down to it', seats on either side, a sump in one corner, easily baled out, and – a final refinement – 'a light from a rechargeable battery'.

Some residents made their own arrangements for sheltering their families. One man living on the outskirts of the city 'lashed out and bought a concrete air-raid shelter', three-quarters sunk in the ground, with a layer of earth on top, in which he grew strawberries. It cost more than £30, and, he recalls, 'my friends and neighbours thought I was mad' – until the raids began 'when they all wanted to use it'. Dr Alan Ashworth, Deputy Medical Officer of Health and second-in-command of the ARP Casualty and Medical Services, who lived in Leamington Road, was also well prepared. 'I made a dug-out in my back garden, lined the walls with . . . the sides of my coal bunker and covered it with earth,' he remembers, though he later replaced this emergency 'dug-out' with a purchased Anderson costing £5. Leslie Worthington, general manager of Owen Owen Stores, also outside the income limit for a free Anderson, who lived in one of a group of six semi-detached houses in Knoll Drive, Styvechale, had one of the most unusual shelters in the city, for he discovered a solid gamekeeper's larder in a neighbouring spinney, which was rented to him for a peppercorn rent of a shilling a year. Here, it was planned, the eight adults and six children living nearby would assemble when the siren sounded, each family providing their own bunks and blankets. Later, anticipating the official 'Morrison' table shelter, which was not distributed until 1941, he constructed a steel shelter in his lounge to prevent the discomfort of the nightly trek out of doors.

The problem of protecting the customers in his store was less easily overcome, until the Council solved it for him, constructing in the basement a 425-place shelter for passers-by, which could also be used by shoppers. Many similar shelters were built near the city centre, where cellars and underground storerooms were still common.

Coventry lacked an underground railway system or a network of caves to provide natural deep shelters, but in June 1939 the Coventry ARP Committee unsuccessfully sought Home Office approval for building two such shelters which could later serve as underground car parks, a forward-looking idea for the time. The Council was never enthusiastic about the official alternative of surface shelters, and in any case no materials for the best type were available and the City Engineer of Coventry disliked the 'second-best' design, which had an arched brick roof, considering it unsafe if erected, as advised, on a non-concrete foundation to save time. But by the time the war began public shelters of some kind had been provided on a reasonable scale.

On the whole factory workers were better protected than ordinary citizens, for the firms concerned had ample resources of materials and engineering skill on which to draw. Coventry Gauge and Tool, for example, created first-class deep shelters just outside the factory perimeter with concrete roofs several feet thick, which were later to provide a refuge for 2000 schoolchildren. In the Courtaulds viscose factory in Foleshill Road the cellars were rapidly converted into shelters, and the factory's raw materials were also pressed into service. 'Compounds of wood-pulp bales were constructed,' remembers the works chemist and ARP controller, 'which afforded complete protection from all missiles except direct hits.'

Shelters were, however, only one of the requirements laid upon managements by the government as war drew closer, and an architect working for one large Coventry company remembers having to submit for approval of the Admiralty, for which his firm worked, plans to set up a strongly protected ARP headquarters, to divide up vulnerable sections of the plant with fire-walls and steel fire-resistant doors, and to build concrete blast walls round the most essential machinery – preparations which were to pay a rich dividend later. The camouflaging of the whole works proved less successful, doing little except use up a prodigious amount of paint, for aerial reconnaissance revealed that converging roads and railway lines still betrayed its presence.

In June 1939, Dr Ashworth noted, a curious rumour began to circulate through the city that local firms had been warned to order any goods delivered through the port of Danzig by 28 August, after which it would be closed by war, a remarkably accurate prediction. When the fatal date arrived the international scene was so threatening that he sent his own daughters away to stay with their grandparents in Worthing, anticipating the start of the official evacuation scheme by three days.

Coventry was not even allowed to go to war in peace. In the summer of 1939 there were a number of IRA outrages in the city, leading up to the leaving of a bomb in a tradesman's bicycle in Broadgate, which killed five people and injured many more. The explosion, heard all over the city, led many citizens to conclude that the war had already started. One woman then living in Harris Road, who was near enough to the scene to see 'a small girl carried away dying', remembers being 'far more horrified and shocked' by this senseless crime than by anything that happened later. Another woman recalls casualties 'lying about and people crying. I couldn't get on the bus fast enough to get home', and she almost fainted on seeing one of the badly shocked victims getting on her bus, with his trouser leg cut from knee to ankle by debris. The Broadgate murders provided police and ambulance workers with a preview of the horrifying wounds high explosive could inflict on the human body and almost overshadowed the greater events elsewhere.*

Evacuation officially began on Friday 1 September 1939 and it

---

*One Special Constable recalls that it was desire to take some positive action against those responsible, not hatred of Hitler, that led him to volunteer.

was even less successful than in many other places. In Coventry only about 20 per cent of those eligible actually left for the country, half the rate for London and a third of that for Manchester and Merseyside, and few stayed very long. One first-aider, helping to evacuate two hospitals of their hundred elderly patients at this time, recalls reflecting that few of them were likely ever to see the city again, but he was almost certainly wrong. Most adults and children were back long before the leaves, much less the first bombs, had fallen.

The start of the war meant less of an upheaval in Coventry than in other towns, in spite of evacuation and the black-out, for many people were already on war work. For some citizens, in the AFS (Auxiliary Fire Service) or the Police War Reserve, the declaration of war meant an immediate change of occupation, as from being unpaid part-timers they became full-time professionals. One former commercial traveller, who now became a constable, still admires the courage of his wife who, having never driven before, nobly agreed 'to try and keep a little of my connection together till after the war' and 'after a couple of runs round the square . . . she drove throughout the war, dodging bomb holes in nearly every street, with my six months old son in a carry-cot until he was three years old'.*

One girl then aged sixteen, living in Three Spires Avenue, Coundon, in a typical inter-war semi-detached, also remembers the sudden flurry of activity that September, first to provide makeshift black-outs from blankets, then to construct 'shutters for our front-room windows to protect us from flying glass'. What impressed her most, she found, was her parents' anxiety for herself and her younger sisters, which communicated itself to her, until even the sight of a soldier or a tank was enough to 'send cold shivers' down her back.

Although the Council's full-time ARP organizers – though not the enforcedly idle wardens and firemen – now found themselves busier than ever, their task became easier overnight, for they no longer had to battle against apathy or outright opposition. Harold Tomley, now full-time Staff Officer of the Earlsdon Division, who had for months been trying to take possession of the premises he wanted for his Divisional headquarters and Training Centre, now found himself officially empowered to 'break and enter to requisition the building. . . . The next month or so,' he recollects, 'I had

*It is pleasant to add that 'she has now driven thirty-four years without accident'.

to build up while the builders were pulling down, raising pande-
monium and clouds of dust in their task of changing a house into a
Divisional HQ, with lecture room, store room, offices, etc.'
Ironically just as order was emerging from chaos he found himself
moved to the more vulnerable Central Division, which already had
spacious headquarters in the four-storey former Rudge-Whitworth
Cycle Factory. Here 'the ground floor was used as a store for
medical supplies, above that Warden Service offices, recreation
room, etc. and the third storey as Warden Service stores.' The
fourth floor was empty – but not for long, for it was to prove
invaluable as a warehouse for furniture from temporarily uninhabitable houses.

The unexpected lull in the months after September 1939 was put
to good use by the ARP services. Dr Alan Ashworth, reviewing
the arrangements for dealing with casualties, was not displeased.
'The First Aid Posts,' he remembers, 'were mainly sited in school
premises and were strategically placed. . . . Their playgrounds made
good parking for the ambulances and . . . all First Aid Posts were
connected by telephone to the Control Centre. . . . In the early raids
the Control Centre . . . worked quite satisfactorily and . . . coped
with the situation well.' Those on duty, however, even if no bombs
were dropped, faced a tiring routine – Dr Ashworth found himself
in charge of the Casualties Section of the Control Centre one night
in three, which meant at best a somewhat restless night on a bunk.
If the warning sounded, even though no raid followed, one had to
turn out and wait.

Anti-gas training continued with unabated zeal during these
months, but the government's under-insurance against the risk of
fire at last began to be redressed. Sluice gates were built on the
River Sherbourne to form a series of reservoirs, and the Home
Office also urged the building of batteries of steel dams or tanks,
holding 100 000 to 200 000 gallons, although the Chief Fire Officer
in Coventry did not agree, favouring instead smaller, 5000-gallon
tanks in residential areas. The Auxiliary Fire Service was also still
sadly under strength, with, in October 1939, only 110 men against
an establishment of 434, although this was less serious than it
appeared, since over much of the city there were well-trained and
equipped works fire brigades, capable at the very least of protecting
their own premises.

The real danger lay in the threat to commercial and residential property. Although conscription for the Forces had been introduced in April 1939, the government was not prepared to introduce it for the ARP services or even to compel civilians to protect their own homes and workplaces. Fire-watching, as it was called – though fire prevention would have been a better name – was left to private initiative and voluntary effort. Coventry was in this respect no worse than anywhere else and better than most. Her architectural treasures were particularly well protected – or so it seemed. The Vicar of Holy Trinity, already in 1940 approaching sixty, set an example which the Home Office would have done well to take as a model. The church was equipped with modern fire hydrants, ladders were installed against the ancient walls to give the fire brigade easy access to any blaze, and a rota of fire-watchers made regular patrols of the nine roofs, each observation post being linked to its own 'Command Post', a camp-bed in the vestry, by field telephone. The preparations made by Provost Howard to defend the Cathedral were equally elaborate, with buckets of sand and water, stirrup pumps and shovels, distributed at key points all over the building, and a four-man-strong nightly guard. The fire risk here was particularly high, for the cavity between the lead outer roof of the nave and transepts and the inner roof of oak might have been designed as a trap for incendiary bombs, although when it had been built even gunpowder was still a novelty.

In Coventry there was never really a 'phoney war', for, though there were many false alarms, when the siren sounded and no bombs fell, all over the city what was later called the Battle for Production was already being fought. The Vickers Armstrong and Hawker Siddeley Works, and their associated shadow factories, were turning out engines or airframes or both, for Blenheim light bombers, Whitley twin-engined 'heavies', Avro Ansons for Coastal Command, Airspeed Oxfords (the RAF's main twin-engined trainers) and, soon, the four-engined Stirlings and Lancasters which were to replace the earlier types. Coventry was also stripping and reconditioning Rolls-Royce engines, including the famous Merlin, which powered the Spitfire and Hurricane. From the works of British Thomson-Houston (BTH Ltd), Ford Street, flowed a stream of aircraft magnetos and other vital parts. Daimlers were beginning to produce scout cars – one was paid the back-handed compliment of being taken for his private use by Rommel when captured in the desert – and GEC were manufacturing, along with more traditional munitions, VHF radio sets, then a novelty, for use in fighter defence. The Dunlop company were making wheels and tyres for aircraft, as well as barrage balloons and anti-gas clothing and would later be turning out 'frogmen' suits for underwater saboteurs. The artificial fabrics produced by Courtaulds, to which in 1939 nylon was added, were now being made into parachutes. Coventry Climax was manufacturing Civil Defence trailer pumps as well as emergency landing-field generators for the RAF.

Although for obvious reasons their work was little publicized, Coventry contained, too, many 'panacea' targets, as they were later known, whose loss could inflict a crippling blow to the whole war effort. The former watchmaking firm of Fred Lee, for example, small by Coventry standards, now made industrial jewels essential to many processes and used directly in compass bearings. The output of Coventry Gauge and Tool Ltd was eventually to provide three-quarters of all the gauges used in the nation's armaments industry, as well as a number of specialized tools. The role of Sir Alfred Herbert Ltd, the country's chief machine-tool manufacturer, was equally crucial. More far-sighted than the government, its president and chairman had had his own factory blacked-out and working a night shift since Munich, but under the notoriously inept Chamberlain government there was still slack to be taken up. In the spring of 1940 Sir Alfred was moved to protest publicly in the *Machine Tool Review* that half the available machines in his works were still lying idle every night. There was as yet no conscription of female labour, so that, despite the vast pool of women who were either not working at all or were employed in luxury trades, only fifty-eight of his night workers were women and his whole vast concern employed only 310.

With men it was different, for skilled craftsmen exempted from military service were already being directed into essential jobs. Typical of them was a thirty-three-year-old tinsmith or sheet-metal worker from Birmingham, previously employed on manufacturing mudguards, who in March 1940 was ordered to report to an aircraft components factory in Coventry. The official hours were long enough, from 7 a.m. till 5 p.m., with a twenty-three mile journey at each end of the day, but soon these were regularly being exceeded.

'7 a.m. till 7 p.m. came to be classed as normal,' this man remembers, as did a seven-day week, though 'on Saturdays we
worked from 7 a.m. to 4 p.m. and on Sundays 9 a.m. till 1 p.m.
Both my wife and I knew that our quiet evenings together after the
children had been put to bed had gone. . . . I had to leave home at
5.30 a.m. to catch the 6.10 a.m. train and might arrive home anytime
after 8.30 p.m., but certainly not before.' Soon the only meal the
family had together was a late tea on Sunday, and this man found
himself desperately tired. More fortunate than most, he was able to
solve his problem by obtaining petrol for his car, in return for
transporting three workmates as passengers. He now left home at
the more gentlemanly hour of 6 a.m. and was home by 7.30.
'Another asset,' he reflected wryly, 'was that I couldn't see Jerry
detail a plane to bomb me, whereas with a train, I couldn't be so
sure.'

In this firm at least ARP was taken very seriously and when it
was discovered that this new recruit was already a trained warden
he found himself 'given the job of recruiting a staff of about a
dozen men [with] a free hand to order what I wished', the board
room being placed at his disposal for training lectures and the
typing pool instructed to give priority to any work he sent them.
There were soon regular lectures, in working time, from experts
from the fire brigade, St John Ambulance Brigade and WVS.
Anti-gas detectors stood ready in the yard – metal plates, on a post,
which 'looked very much like a bird house' covered with detector
paint, which changed colour if liquid gas fell on them – and one
proud day the ARP squad were asked to stage a demonstration
for the benefit of the Chief ARP Officer of a much larger factory.

When our works hooters sounded, to simulate the siren, we went into
action. . . . In less than ten minutes the yard looked like a battlefield. Two
men were rescuing a woman supposedly trapped under rubble, a man and
a girl had put splints on a man's leg and were now strapping his feet together, two more girls had bandaged a man's jaw and were leading him
to a chair . . . four men had formed a chain, and were passing buckets of
water and two more men were up a ladder, rescuing a man who had been
stunned by a falling beam. One man came out of a doorway carrying a
stretcher and I remember two young girls coming out into the yard,
pushing a tea trolley. I also remember thinking that the tea was the only
real thing in the whole exercise.

With the collapse of France in June 1940 the prospect of heavy air raids increased. That month two Ministry of Home Security scientists produced a report entitled *An Investigation of Probable Air Raid Damage*, which predicted the likely effects of various raids on an industrial city, assuming different aiming points and margins of accuracy, and a weight of attack varying from 500 bombs aimed at a particular factory, to 1000 directed at the city centre. By the application of elaborate mathematical formulae the likely damage to property and the estimated number of casualties were calculated and detailed maps were drawn up showing the anticipated distribution of bombs, provided they behaved according to the laws of chance and the expectations of the statisticians. The results of all this effort were somewhat disappointing, the authors of the report merely concluding that 'in day raids . . . by far the greatest number of casualties would be in factories and that even in night raids it would be a very substantial portion of the whole. It would appear from this that in industrial towns a great saving of life could be brought about by improving the standard of factory shelter.' This was not perhaps, very surprising; what was far more significant was that the town selected for study was Coventry, 'chosen as being an attractive target on account of its numerous aircraft factories'.

With the Germans now on the other side of the Channel the evacuation map of the country had to be redrawn and Dr Alan Ashworth recalls fetching home his son and daughter from their grandparents on the south coast; Worthing was now more dangerous than Coventry. The Rev. W. B. Sells, who had recently become curate of St Thomas's Church in The Butts, remembers an adventurous holiday at Middleton-on-Sea in Sussex that summer. 'We watched the dog-fights going on unconcernedly', he recalls, 'but when Ford Aerodrome, just behind us, was badly bombed, we thought we had better go home.' The impact on those working in the factories of Coventry was even greater. A twelve-hour day, seven-day week, already in operation in some key plants, became common everywhere. One man in the metal processing plant at Armstrong Siddeley recalls working every night that summer from 6 p.m. to 6 a.m. with only 'an occasional Saturday night off'. The hours of another worker in an aircraft components factory were 7.45 a.m. to 7.45 p.m. though, if the Section Leader agreed, one was allowed – apart from Saturday and Sunday when work finished at four – 'one early night' a week, which meant leaving at 5 p.m.

For those outside the factories life was still not over-demanding. '10th June: Italy declared war. Played tennis,' wrote the young Civil Servant previously mentioned, now happily settled in her hostel in The Butts, in her diary. '17th June: France ceased hostilities. Tennis.' On 27 July there was something more exciting to record, the sounding of the air-raid sirens, though no bombs followed: the first of many such occasions.

The succession of false alarms that summer led to a revival of pre-war complacency. One seventeen-year-old, living in Coundon, remembers being told reassuringly that 'there were six lines of defences to get through before the Midland area was reached' and that Coventry itself was 'surrounded by barrage balloons and gun installations'. Dr Alan Ashworth, only too well aware that he was partly responsible for protecting 'a compact city' which 'could obviously be put out of action completely by a concentrated attack', recalls friends telling him that 'it was too far inland for a daylight attack'. The Rev. W. B. Sells, still new to the city, found that 'everyone was saying that Coventry would never be bombed as it was surrounded by trees and the bombers would never find it in the dark'. A newly married metallurgist living in Rosslyn Avenue, Coundon, was also assured that 'Coventry was in a hollow . . . the enemy would not be able to find it,' and by an even more comforting rumour 'that anti-Nazi workers in the German munitions factories were filling bombs with sawdust'. Perhaps the most artless reaction of all was that of one small boy, a year old when the war began. He revelled in the sight of 'the barrage balloons gleaming high in the sky on a brilliant day' and, drawing on his limited stock of images, remarked a little later that 'they are just like the silver balls on my birthday cake'.

2

JERRY'S LATE TONIGHT

*'27th October.   Sat on couch with boy-friend listening to
bombs dropping.'*

Diary of a Coventry girl, 1940

WHEN in June 1940 the first bombs dropped at Ansty aerodrome
just outside Coventry they were regarded as an intriguing novelty.
One builder, then working for Garlicks of Gosford Street, remembers being asked to drive an architect associated with the firm
out to see the 'ruins', a few 'demolished hedges and railings'. His
passenger, 'intent on finding a fragment of bomb', was delighted to
be handed one by a roadman, who remarked, with considerable
prescience, 'You'll get a lot more later.' An electrician's mate,
living close to the Morris Engines factory in Durbar Avenue, made
a similarly pessimistic comment when his workmates 'dashed off
in their cars to see the crater' after a later incident, near Tamworth.
'I said at the time,' he remembers, 'that there was no need to rush.'
Also among the sightseers was an apprentice jig-and-tool draughtsman at the Humber works, who went by cycle with a party of
fellow-members of his youth club, to see the 'target', a single
cottage. 'Little did I realize,' he admits, 'that I would experience
this sort of thing on my own doorstep.' This was the general
attitude, even when the bombs came closer, and one woman then
working as a janitor at the Earlsdon library and living in Canley
Road, remembers that after a house there had been demolished 'the
buses were doing quite a trade' as 'the people of Coventry made an
outing of it on the Sunday afternoon, coming to see the damage'.

On Sunday, 25 August, a German bomb wrecked the Rex
Cinema in Corporation Street, near the centre of the city, launching
a typically grim wartime joke: the cinema had been about to show
Gone With the Wind. One seventeen-year-old, who had travelled
in from Leamington to see this famous film with a girl-friend and

'two young Air Force cadets', remembers how the same bomb also
ended a promising romance. The four young people were 'walking
in Spencer Road some five minutes' walk away. We all ran for our
lives, the boys one way and us the other. . . . We never saw them
again.' By now warnings were becoming an almost daily, or nightly,
occurrence, some lasting no more than two minutes, some dragging
on for six hours. Between 18 August and the end of October
Coventry was attacked on seventeen occasions, the most spectacular
raid being by a solitary bomber which defied both the anti-
aircraft balloons, landing a single bomb, spectacularly and accur-
ately, on the paint shop of the Standard Motor Works at Canley.
All told, in this period 198 tons of bombs were dropped, made up of
938 high explosives and 8400 incendiaries, and though nothing like
as bad as the pre-war forecasts, the damage done, and casualties
caused, were formidable, the latter amounting to 176 dead, 229
badly injured and 451 minor injuries treated at first-aid posts.

While the attention of the press was focussed on London,
Coventry in these weeks was far from enjoying a period of peace;
few places, in fact, were suffering such constant attention from the
enemy. But, just as in London, people there were already adjusting
to the ever-present threat from the skies. A seventeen-year-old girl
living near Stoke Park, whose family owned a flourishing signwriting and black-out-shade-making business, still noted each new
attack in her diary, but already they were beginning to make
monotonous reading:

August 25th-26th. Nerves a bit [disturbed]. Spent night on floor of living
     room . . .
16th September. Sixteen killed . . . three balloons lost . . .
12th October. Twenty to nine bombs started dropping and sirens went
     afterwards. A bad night.
20th October. Very little sleep and great fires . . .
27th October. I felt really happy for the first time for ages and we sat on
     couch listening to bombs dropping while four listened to music in other
     room across the hall. Bed at 2.30.

For this more cheerful entry there was a simple explanation. Her
boy-friend had arrived on leave from Scotland.

For somewhat similar reasons the apprentice draughtsman
quoted earlier found that the siren provided a not wholly unwel-

come interruption each evening at his youth club, for the clergyman
in charge invariably sent the members home, making each young
man responsible for one of the girls. Once out of sight, however,
one of these far from unwilling escorts remembers, 'all we did was
stand around and watch the "fireworks" ', and he can still recall
one particularly fine one, 'my first parachute flare, hanging over the
G E C Works. The girl I was taking home insisted on stopping to
watch, despite air-raid wardens warning us not to look up, as the
pilots would see the reflection from our faces.'

For those in charge of the protection of vulnerable factories,
like the A R P Controller of Courtaulds in the Foleshill Road, the
raids brought more serious problems. It was impossible, he knew,
for the whole plant to shut down whenever the siren sounded, for

the process of making viscose fibres is a continuous one and . . . apart
from the fact that the production is completely spoiled by an appreciable
stoppage, at one stage of production there was a hazard of spontaneous
ignition. This had in fact happened when we had stopped production on
previous occasions and the raids had only been slight and not in close
proximity to the factory.

Like many other firms, Courtaulds found the answer in roof-
spotters, posted on a tower, and work only stopped when they gave
the 'Imminent danger' signal.

The thirteen-year-old schoolgirl quoted earlier, whose family had
been delighted with their new home in Cheylesmore Avenue,
remembers how they now looked at the location with new eyes, for
'we were only about a quarter of a mile from the main Standard
Factories and the No. 2 Shadow Factory, so the feeling was that if
Jerry wasn't a very good shot – we were for it'. As yet, however,
she found the constant warnings, like most teenagers, 'more
interesting than frightening'.

I did not feel much about the raids, except that they were a nuisance
interrupting one's sleep. . . . We had a suitcase packed with necessities,
underwear, flasks of hot drinks, food, warm clothing and small treasures
like grandfather's watch chain. . . . We didn't like the shelter very much
because you couldn't get any sleep at all, so that if there wasn't much
activity we stayed in the house. . . . A feather bed was put into the stair
cupboard for me to sleep on . . . and I took the family tabby cat with
me. . . . At school [Centaur Road] the cellars were well sandbagged but

we didn't like going there much because we had to run down all the stairs from the second floor . . . when the warning bell went and when we got there it smelt of old coke, damp and mice.

Life at home can have been little more peaceful, as the memories of another woman living on the Cheylesmore Estate (her husband had come to Coventry to work at the Morris factory) make clear. Following the 'daylight sneak raids', she remembers, with 'lone planes machine-gunning people in the streets' came 'the more severe raids in October when many properties near the railway were bombed. . . . By the end of October we brought our mattress down from the bedroom and a small one for Irene (aged ten) and we went to bed downstairs.'

The young woman Civil Servant quoted earlier, who lived in a hostel in The Butts, had few private anxieties, for her home was not in Coventry, and the life she recorded in her diary that autumn, if clearly unusual, was not wholly disagreeable:

On 8th October a bomb dropped before the sirens went at a dramatic moment in the film *Rebecca*, which we were seeing at the Gaumont. The lights went on, we were all asked to file out quietly, but my new shoes were hurting so I'd taken them off and couldn't get them on again. Down to the street and shelter in my stocking feet – and I never did see the end of *Rebecca*.* On the 12th October I recorded . . . 'Fun and games started at 8.45, thirty planes over, lots of bombs.' On the 14th October: 'Sirens at 8.30, incendiary in front garden. Fireworks till 1.30.' . . . On the 21st: merely 'Work and cellar' and on the 22nd 'As above'.

Already, however, the authorities at the hostel had equipped the cellar as a shelter and 'we'd been advised to pack a suitcase with essentials and leave it there in case the worst happened'. But their charges, being largely young, felt less apprehension. 'None of us really believed the worst *would* happen, and gradually my stock of clothing had been depleted as I ran out of stockings and other items and raided the suitcase so that all that was in there at the end was a new raincoat, a suit and one pair of shoes!'

The wife of a GEC foreman, living in Harris Road, was at first also more conscious of 'the nuisance of the early raids . . . than fear', for they meant her husband, in the works fire brigade, was on duty

---

*This informant adds that she at last saw the end of the film when it was shown years later on television 'and I could still pinpoint the exact moment when the bomb dropped'.

almost every night, until after one lunchtime raid she returned to her job in the wages department of BTH 'shattered to find machine-gun bullet holes through our desks and my teapot broken'. Further realization of the real meaning of air warfare came when she provided temporary shelter for 'two very distressed old people . . . bombed out of their home in which they had spent all their married life'. Those nights there were no 'silly jokes about "Old Moaner" [i.e. the siren] and "Don't worry, it's one of ours". What Jerry would do was all too plain in their faces, the old lady clutching her handbag closely to her chest all night long.'

A Special Constable, living in Villiers Street, Ball Hill, was finally convinced of the dangers to come during a 'spectacular raid' in late October, when gas and water mains were fractured and his own home was damaged by debris from a wrecked building and blast from a 'DA' (Delayed Action) bomb in Walsgrave Road. 'It had a profound effect upon us,' he remembers. Soon afterwards he sent his children to stay with friends in Leicester – an industrial city itself, but clearly far safer than Coventry. Leslie Worthington, who had reached a similar decision, found his ten-year-old son 'disgusted at having to "leave the fun"' when sent away with his five-year-old sister to his grandparents. 'He insisted on taking with him a carrier bag full of tops from the bombs to show them in Blackpool.'

Mr Worthington soon had confirmation that he had been right, for in the heaviest raid yet, on 14 October, one of the 140 bombs dropped hit the corner of his store, exploding on the first floor and causing part of it to collapse, although those sheltering in the strength-ened basement survived. Among them were many of the audience from the nearby Coventry Hippodrome, who paid their hosts a tribute such as few businesses had ever received: 'Your store saved our lives.' About the same time a solitary bomb had dropped near St Thomas's Church in The Butts while the Rev. W. B. Sells and 'the vicar were saying matins as usual at 7.30 a.m. . . which shook our church and our complacency'. Wasting no time 'that morning I bundled my wife and son and all our furniture into an open lorry I had borrowed and in pouring rain, drove them to Leamington, to my sister-in-law's house. After that I left our house in Winifred Avenue and lodged in the attic in the vicarage on a camp-bed.'

Mr Sells had no difficulty in filling his spare time as a 'bachelor', for three evenings a week were devoted to an ARP training session at the church hall, where the other members of his fire-guard party, 'a big, fat baker, a bricklayer and two others, were highly delighted to have a parson among them and pulled my leg without mercy about saving them from hellfire and everlasting damnation'. At this stage, however, the team clearly needed practical rather than spiritual guidance:

One night at the beginning of November, cold and clear, we got an urgent call from neighbours in the next road to say that a chimney was on fire there, a real flamer, and that planes were flying about. So out we rushed with buckets, ladders, etc. . . . We put up the ladders to the roof of the house, filled the buckets with water and prepared to carry them up to the roof to pour them down the chimney. One man stood at the bottom of the ladder to stop it slipping. I was halfway up, another at the top, and one on the roof and we began to get the buckets up. As we did so a plane began to zoom down toward us. We were sure it was a German and we panicked. The man on the roof dropped his bucket of water all over us below him and slid down the roof towards the top of the ladder. The man at the top of the ladder slid on to me and he and I on to the man at the bottom, so that there was a heap of cursing, terror stricken men on the pavement, all watching the plane roar away again. It was one of ours . . .

Fire was not as yet regarded as a very formidable adversary. 'As long as we had stirrup pump and bucket,' remembers Civil Defence Staff Officer Harold Tomley, 'the ordinary incendiary bombs we came to regard almost with contempt.' Their sheer number, however did come as a surprise. An AFS man, sent to help another bombed city, remembers how 'on our first night out, as we sped towards the centre of Birmingham my team were *shovelling* incendiary bombs from the rear of our vehicle'.

Morale in the Civil Defence forces in Coventry that autumn was high; certainly higher than it had been during the long months of waiting for the war to begin, and at least one old soldier, who had volunteered for the infant LDV (Local Defence Volunteers) early in the summer, now resigned to join the ARP as an ambulance driver as 'he required something more active'. He was highly impressed with his First Aid Post, 'a large day school, fully equipped with six ambulances, all converted from large cars or vans and a single-deck bus (with driver called Bill) for use in case of evacuation', and eagerly looked forward to his first night on full duty, scheduled for 14 November.

For existing members of the ARP services the early raids on Coventry provided an invaluable 'shake-down' period in which they discovered the wide gulf between theory and practice. For one War Reserve constable in 'B' Division, covering the area between Holyhead Road and Ansty Road, the first lesson came while he was taking down particulars of an accident caused by two vehicles, both unlighted on police instructions, running into each other in the black-out. Engrossed in his note-taking, he ignored the noise of a falling bomb until a nearby Home Guard, a veteran of Flanders, 'got hold of me by the scruff of my neck and pulled me into a ditch'. The policeman's battle inoculation continued at another incident near Wallace Road, when, after finding himself first on the scene at a shelter which had suffered a direct hit, he dutifully cycled as instructed to the nearest police box, in Jubilee Crescent, to report the incident and call for help, only to find the line was dead and he had to cope on his own. 'The official procedure,' he decided, 'was proper Army style "bull". All theory and no good in practice.'

During these increasingly noisy and dangerous weeks many wardens and other ARP workers learned, like soldiers, to harden themselves to coping with sights and emotions for which no lectures could prepare them. One first-aider, working at Sir Alfred Herbert Ltd, remembers the morning when 'coming back from duty at Stoke School I saw a trail of blood leading into a brick shelter,' and, following it, discovered 'a dead man lay inside'. The same policeman, after a bomb had 'dropped on an ice-cream shop in Clay Lane', found himself not merely called on to drag the four dead or dying victims from the rubble but to break the news of his bereavement to a close relation of one of the deceased.

Also like front-line soldiers, many ARP workers who had privately worried how they would behave under fire were reassured by experience, though occasionally natural instincts still took over. The first-aid worker just quoted recalls, how, while a small group were tunnelling into the debris of a bombed house, another bomb was heard whistling to earth. 'We all lay down, all but one police inspector who took to his heels down the road. Someone said he was trying to catch it.'

By now the evening siren had become so familiar that people joked about setting their watches by it. The tinsmith from Birmingham, mentioned earlier, remembers how, as he set off each night with his carload of workmates, it became a nightly race to get away before the warning sounded.

It got to be taken for granted [he remembers] so that if the sirens hadn't gone when our car moved off, someone would be bound to say 'Old Jerry's late tonight' or 'Jerry's having a night off, mate'. . . . Just before 7 p.m. we would hear them and we'd say, 'Oh, blimey, he's here again' and once I heard a mate say, 'I'll have to drop Adolf a line and tell him to give old Jerry a night off, he ain't had one this week.'

Although a few bombs did fall in it, the surrounding countryside was still clearly safer than the city itself and as the nights lengthened there was a rush every evening to get as far away from Coventry as possible. This 'trekking', which had begun after the August raids, was by early November well established, as Dr Alan Ashworth observed.

At dusk there was a rush to get out of the city. People took buses to the surrounding towns – Leamington Spa, Rugby, Kenilworth, Warwick, etc. and settled for the night in the public air-raid shelters, much to the annoyance of the locals. Others took buses out of the city, to sleep in them. . . . Others who couldn't afford to do this streamed out of the city with perambulators, bedding, children, to sleep under bridges or anywhere that there was shelter. From my house in Leamington Road, they appeared like war refugees – which I suppose they were.

Dr Ashworth found the spectacle 'very disturbing', deducing from it that 'morale was obviously failing', but to a schoolgirl living in Glendower Avenue on the outskirts of the city the noise of the 'tramping' outside, accompanied by torches piercing the winter darkness, created a more cheerful impression, since it 'sounded like people going to work or a football match'.

Trekking soon became part of the daily life of Coventry and affected every part of the city. The caretaker at the Food Office in Warwick Row, 200 yards from Broadgate, watched night after night for several weeks before mid-November the sad procession forming up: 'Anything that had wheels on it was utilized to carry the bedding: prams, bikes, wheelbarrows, boxes on old pram wheels, and the oldest method of all – carry it.' Between three o'clock and six, he estimated, '5000 people passed the doors of the FO going out to sleep under hedges, in barns, when lucky, burrowing under ricks of hay and straw . . . anything to get away from what they feared might happen.' Another man, whose own nights were spent on duty at the Observer Corps Report Centre under the GPO, remembers seeing the pathetic groups returning to the city each morning, 'pushing perambulators and handcarts', after nights spent, it was rumoured, 'sleeping under trees beneath tarpaulins'.

The most visible trekkers, who went on foot, were the poorest, but trekking affected all classes, until, it was later estimated, at least a quarter of the population, and perhaps as many as a half, joined in the nightly exodus. The better-off went by car, and often had accommodation arranged at the other end of their journey. One apprentice remembers how 'some of my senior colleagues at Humber bought or rented wooden chalets in the surrounding countryside, such as Binley Woods. While we turned up in the morning after a raid a little tired they were relatively refreshed. Sometimes a mild resentment was expressed with a comment like, "We were left to look after their houses, while they slept in comparative quiet."'

Among the working-class parishioners of the Rev. W. B. Sells in The Butts, resentment was considerably more vocal and many, he remembers, who slept downstairs in rat-infested rooms, rather because the upstairs rooms had leaking roofs than from fear of the bombs, considered 'the better-off people who went out at night to friends in Kenilworth and roundabout . . . very cowardly. . . . We heard rumours of trekkers who bought black-market petrol so that they could drive out to the country and sleep safely in their large cars.' Personally he admired more one 'old ex-prostitute' who replied to his polite inquiry about what she did during raids 'I go to me bloody bed, mate,' and there, a few weeks later, she was to be killed.

The *Coventry Standard* that October and November carried alongside offers of such contemporary essentials as 'ARP Stirrup Pumps (Not a squirt, a real pump)' at £1 3s 6d, 'ARP Sandbags. Genuine Government size and quality' at 36s 6d per hundred, and 'Heavy corrugated steel sheets, for protection against shrapnel, blast, etc.' at various prices, a range of advertisements which must have made bitter reading for those who had no option about staying in Coventry:

Comfortable, private, pleasantly situated COUNTRY HOME; safe; Coventry buses pass daily, 20 miles, two or three adults. Moderate terms, Braunston, near Rugby.

COUNTRY COTTAGE. Safe area, Coventry 12 miles. Two reception, Four bedrooms. Main water and E.L. Price £500, Apply Jones, Styles and Whitlock, Rugby.

The demand for overnight accommodation within daily travelling distance soon swamped the supply. One farmer's wife, who lived at Honiley, near Kenilworth, remembers how 'our farmhouse, like most, housed a Coventry family, who evacuated each evening at dusk and slept in safety at the farm'. A Coventry housewife remembers how 'many just took food and drink and blankets and slept in their cars', as 'it was very difficult to find places to stay'. She experimented with trekking, however, only for a single weekend. 'Having no car of our own we were taken by friends but failed to find anywhere to sleep on the Friday night' and 'spent a most uncomfortable time parked in a wood while the German bombers droned overhead on their way to attack Birmingham'. Next night, however, 'we were lucky enough to find rooms in an old country cottage and it was absolute bliss to sink into a large feather bed and sleep peacefully all night'.

Another woman who was then a fourteen-year-old schoolgirl recalls the family friends 'who used to go to Stoneleigh Park by coach every night and sleep there in the coach. The cost was 2s 6d per night. Some people we knew used to go to Westwood Heath and sleep on the floor of the parish room.'

One ten-year-old trekker, like so many returned evacuees, found her family's nightly coach excursions to villages ten miles or so away far from enjoyable, however. Once 'several women met the coach with offers of accommodation' but 'my mother was annoyed by one lady greeting us with the question: "Would you like a bath?" and went off in a huff to another woman's house'. Far worse was the occasion when 'we were taken to Meriden and spent the night on mattresses laid out on the floor of the Archery Hall at Packington Park. . . . I lay there listening to people snoring and coughing into the early hours.'

Many families were desperate to get away: where and how were immaterial. One man who built greenhouses at a works in Harefield Road, Stoke, and delivered them himself all over the Midlands, found that strangers regularly climbed on his lorry in the evening, indifferent to his destination. A woman at Lillington, eight miles away, remembers the nightly stream of callers, whom 'sometimes we could help by sending them to various neighbours', the standard local fee for providing a roof, but nothing else, being a shilling a head.

Among ARP workers, who had often sent their own families away to friends and relations, reaction to the trekkers was mixed. Every absent household meant fewer potential casualties, but it also meant an unguarded house. One woman, who every night made tea for the two local wardens* as they called on their rounds, remembers 'they were annoyed because many in our Avenue [Woodside Avenue, Green Lane] went out at nights'. Each empty house was marked with the chalk mark on the gate 'S.O.' for 'Sleeps Out', since 'they didn't wish to risk their lives looking for people not there'. One Special Constable, whose own family had been sent to stay with his sister in Kenilworth, recalls how that autumn 'the city became progressively more deserted, until I doubt whether 10 per cent of the population were left'. In St Pauls Road, where he lived, only about a dozen houses, out of eighty, were now occupied at night. As October gave way to November apprehension increased – for raids now seemed to be continuous. There were in fact seven between the 1st and the 12th of the month, affecting every part of the city, though only one, in which thirteen people were killed and thirty badly injured, could be considered serious, and in four there were no casualties at all. During the whole period 138 high explosives were dropped, 900 incendiaries, and four oil bombs, a total of 29 tons. The casualty figures, fourteen killed, thirty-six admitted to hospital, forty-six treated at First Aid Posts, seemed bad enough at the time but were soon to appear un-believably light.

One reason for the low death rate, apart from the widespread trekking, was undoubtedly that most families had now perfected a routine of taking shelter in good time and a whole new way of life developed, with the sitting-room or shelter serving as a bedroom. The experiences of one woman living in Highland Road, whose husband and son both worked at the Daimler factory, were typical:

We spent most of the time under the stairs or out in the brick shelter outside the front door. We would hurry our meal and then I would fill the flask with tea and make some sandwiches in case we could not get

*Both men were later killed in action.

back to the house. We did not undress for about six weeks. We had a bed
in the sitting room, my sons would sleep in the big armchairs, daddy and
I would lie on the bed, and when we heard the siren we would go to the
shelter or under the stairs. We would take candles with us to the shelter
and put them under plant pots turned upside down. . . . It was surprising
how much warmth came from them.

One woman living on 'the old aerodrome estate' in Treherne
Road remembers the successive stages of her involvement in the
air war. First, 'we would stand on the front doorstep to see all the
searchlights when Birmingham was being raided'; then, when the
enemy bombers came nearer, 'I used to stay awake so that my
husband could get some sleep' and finally 'when the raids got worse
and my husband couldn't get home from the town' (he was working at Metcalfe's Ideal Products) she went to shelter without him.

The lady at No. 60 used to bring her little dog and we used to sit together
until the All Clear sounded. We had one of those fenders with a coal or
wood box at each end and we used to sit on these in the pantry under the
stairs. One night when she came into No. 62 a jar fell on her head from
the vibrations. We were worried in case the sticky feeling was blood,
but . . . it turned out to be mincemeat. After one of the raids one of our
neighbours found a back axle of a car in his back garden. 'Well,' he said,
'I always wanted a car, but I didn't think I'd start with a back axle.'

This was a time when many conventions crumbled. The Harris
Road housewife quoted earlier recalls how, after a friend had sent
his wife and child away and her own husband was on duty at the
fire station, 'for several nights he slept in the shelter as well as
myself. We joked afterwards of our "sleeping together" but that
poor man needed his rest.'

Bombing also produced some unforeseen reactions. This same
woman admired her father's foresight in fitting 'a heavy shutter of
half-inch board' behind the windows, which he laid down 'should
be kept open top and bottom for the duration', to reduce pressure
from blast, precautions which proved so effective that when 'a
bomb fell fifty yards up the road we lost only one window'.
Curiously enough, however, he forbade his family to keep their
gas masks handy, on the ground that 'when life degenerated to such
an extent that men gassed each other then life was no longer worth
living'.

Life for this family was as peaceful as it could be in the circumstances, which included several bombed-out people as long-term guests. When little was happening, this woman remembers:

My mother used to read aloud to us . . . [and] my elder brother had friends in for musical evenings which extended into the night if warnings were on. Often we'd have several girls sleeping in one living room, the boys in the other. Sometimes they'd be so tired we'd roll them up in rugs after they'd fallen asleep and leave them snoring through the raids. This was called 'Making Jim Pie', etc., according to the name of the sleeper.

Children found this period exciting rather than frightening, like one then aged ten who remembers burning her fingers when she rushed out to collect newly scattered 'shrapnel', and, because her hearing was so acute that even a distant warning roused her, she became unofficial 'shelter warden' to the family. 'The first my parents heard would be my banging on their bedroom door, with my bolster under my arm, and as they got up the sirens would go.'

Only once did she experience real fear when, after the All Clear had gone, an unexploded bomb was discovered in the market garden behind their house and while her parents collected their valuables she was instructed to take four smaller children, two of them under five, to relations fifteen minutes' walk away:

It was still dark, we had to go across an area of rough ground . . . which as yet had only a rough road and some house foundations. The little ones thought it a great adventure and were laughing and singing, but I was terrified in case there were other unexploded bombs on the route that we might step on. . . . When we reached my aunt's house my sister banged loudly on the door and shouted. My uncle was annoyed, as they had a young baby.* All five of us then spent the rest of the night sleeping in one double bed, along the side of it.

For adults, knowing more of the dangers, fear lay nearer the surface. One woman still blushes at the memory of the night when, having hurried indoors from the shelter 'to visit the bathroom' and groping through the kitchen by the light of the tiny red pilot light on the electric cooker, she 'stood rooted to the spot as the door very slowly opened. Thinking it must be a German parachutist I let out a piercing scream and fled as fast as my trembling legs would carry me, frightening everyone within earshot. No one could get out of me what had happened as by that time I was practically inar-

*This informant's mother adds a detail omitted by her daughter: 'Much to the consternation of their uncle they started singing Christmas carols in the middle of the night.'

ticulate'; the 'parachutist' was her husband, coming in search of her.

Animals were as varied in their reactions as humans. One architect and works engineer found that his black Scotch terrier took raids in his stride and 'the noise of guns or bombs exploding did not affect him', but he 'objected most strongly to being awakened by air-raid sirens in the middle of the night and being dragged to the bottom of the garden', showing 'his displeasure by applying his "four-wheel brakes" all the way'. The collie owned by a fireman's family in Cedars Avenue had, however, more concern for his own safety, and 'whenever he set off suddenly in the direction of the shelter, we knew what was coming and he was always right'. This phenomenon, observed by many dog-owners, was, of course, explained by the ability of dogs to hear sounds as yet indistinguishable to the human ear and provided in the city centre almost a second alarm system. 'The first warning,' found a senior member of the City Engineer's department, 'usually came from the barking of the dogs.' Cats on the whole treated air raids with their customary disdain, like Sparkle, who lived in Ramsay Crescent, Allesley Village, and, his owner remembers, 'always disappeared somewhere' when a raid began, invariably returning at daybreak 'with never a scratch'.

As the weather grew colder, conditions in Coventry hotted up, as the diary, already quoted, of a seventeen-year-old girl living in Stoke Park duly recorded:

1st November: We had our first incendiaries . . . all round house, one broke through roof but didn't do more than break four tiles.
4th November: Bomb landed in garden up road and blew in glass behind the boarded bay window onto couch where wife [of the bombed-out family they were sheltering] was sleeping . . . Bits of trees, sand and stone all over everywhere. Wife upset and taking arrowroot for stomach and nerves, very sick.
9th November: Friend bombed out and came to us for help in moving his furniture into one room to cover with tarpaulins till he could find new home. Spent night with us.
11th November: Heavy gale, bombed out friend now washed out, but gale force winds soon dried things on the 12th.

By now most families had evolved their own evening routine. A library caretaker and his wife, living in Canley Road, Earlsdon, had reached an admirable arrangement with the family next door.

They offered the hospitality of their Anderson, on the grounds that 'six was much more fun that three anyway', and in exchange had an understanding that, if conditions became intolerable, they would all 'pile into the neighbour's car and he would take us out into the country'. The family of a girl working in the accounting department of the Daimler No. 2 aero-engine factory, and their two lodgers, had devised the perfect air-raid game, a long session of Monopoly, played to special rules under the kitchen table. The start was invariably enlivened by the arrival of two old ladies from next door, wearing on their respective heads a colander and a washing-up bowl, to prevent their white hair attracting the attention of enemy air crews.

This curious, totally unfounded fear was widespread in Coventry. One woman remembers how her father, a warden, invariably on moonlit nights coated the top of his steel helmet with mud, as he was convinced the reflection would catch some vigilant bomb-aimer's eye. A similar anxiety had already left its mark on the garden of the man soon to become Coventry's leading citizen, Jack Moseley, as his daughter remembers:

For some reason mum, who always kept her worries hidden, became worried if she saw a line of white washing left out shining in the moon-light. Eventually she fastened her dislike on a polygonum creeper which dad had proudly grown from a cutting and which was, in the early raids, a mass of white flowers still, smothering trellis-work the length of the garden. Nothing would convince her the German pilots could not see it. It was no use – in the end it had to be cut down.

The story of the Moseley family that autumn was in many ways the story of Coventry, just as Jack Moseley's background was typical of that of thousands of working men, for his life had been spent on the railways, from which he had retired in 1939 after forty-two years' service. Mrs Moseley was the archetypal working-class housewife, far more at home in her kitchen than on the platform, and one daughter worked in the office of the GEC branch factory in Crow Lane, while her elder sister, Lucy, was a Civil Servant, being Deputy Registrar in the office of the Registrar for Births, Marriages and Deaths. The Moseley family could judge the severity of a raid by the time she arrived home, for 'as the death roll mounted I became later', and though she tried to sit down to supper before the sirens sounded sometimes instead there was a 'hurried dash into the shelter as shrapnel was rattling on the house roof'.

The Moseley family lived, also very typically, in an unpretentious brick-built, pre-1914 terrace house in Kensington Road, Earlsdon, and their reaction to the first raids had sometimes verged on the chaotic:

In the darkness we grabbed what we could in the way of clothing and fled to the shelter. All was quiet except for dad complaining he had forgotten his dentures. When the All Clear sounded and we went indoors we looked ... a motley crew. ... Dad, for instance, fumbling in the wardrobe, was wearing gardening trousers and a dinner jacket. That was lesson number one. Ever afterwards we left our belongings, handbags, etc., all ready, in order.

Lesson number two was not long in coming:

There was one September afternoon, sunny and bright, when dad was on his beloved allotment, between Hearsall Common and the main London–Birmingham railway line, up in the pear tree gathering fruit. A heavy plane flew over rather low and he commented to a neighbouring gardener, 'Think that's one of ours, don't you?' As he said that, there was a terrific explosion, clouds of smoke billowed up from the Standard Motor Works (we think it was the Paint Shop), anti-aircraft guns opened up, sirens sounded. ... Dad said he'd never descended that pear tree so quickly. ... The bomber, flying low, got away.

Before long Lucy Moseley and her friends 'soon learned not to go out in the evening' deciding that 'this was the beginning with worse to come'.

There seemed some kind of pattern in the October and early November raids. Sometimes it would be Coventry for two or three consecutive nights and then Birmingham for the next few nights. ... Often we would have a night of 'on-off-on-off' warnings, but we learned to stay put. ... Usually, in the early hours, when the All Clear was well and truly sounded, we would return to the house, remove our outer garments and, in a dressing gown, would try to snatch an hour or two's sleep.

By now being bombed out seemed a real possibility.

We had noticed in early raids that often, however badly damaged a house might be, the staircase seemed to still stand ... so our cupboard under the stairs, known as the 'glory hole', was cleared out and into it went a strong metal box containing papers, insurance policies, etc., and some

e three spires. A photograph taken shortly before the war

e city centre before the bombing

te Although aircraft and guns of these types were used in attacking and protecting Coventry *se* pictures do not show the actual machines or weapons used, of which no photographs are *ilable*

posite above: Destroyers of Coventry: Heinkel 111 bombers

posite below: Defenders of Coventry: 3.7 anti-aircraft guns

ɔve: Junkers 88 bombers

ow: Bofors light anti-aircraft guns

Three against the Luftwaffe

Above left: Dr (now Professor) R. V. Jones, photographed about 1940

Above right: Colonel F. H. Lawrence, photographed about 1940

Below: Councillor (later Alderman) Mrs Pearl Hyde of the WVS, photographed about 1940

boxes into which we packed treasured possessions. Each of us put in there a complete outfit of good clothes and shoes.... Mum, like so many house-wives, developed an early evening ritual. Hot-water bottles were filled and Army-type blankets wrapped around them. . . . A few sandwiches were cut, flasks of tea and coffee were made. Kettles were left filled after the last washing-up at tea time.

The Moseley family had no doubt that talk of deliberate attacks on civilians was nonsense:

One of our ARP wardens always came into the shelter for a cup of coffee before midnight. Dad would usually say, 'Where are they dropping them tonight, Joe?' and quite often the reply would be 'Oh, it looks to be near the Armstrong in Parkside' (or Daimler, or Rootes and so on).

The weekend of 9 November was an important one in the life of Coventry and in the history of the Moseley family.

We were all at St Mary's Hall for the traditional Mayor-making ceremony, when dad was made Mayor. Even air-raid sirens now and again could not spoil that. . . . A small lunch in the Council House followed for about thirty of us, mostly official guests. All went well and my mum, sister and I felt very proud and happy. That evening we had a little celebration in the shelter. We were always joined by the wife and young daughter of one of our ARP wardens . . . in Westwood Road. . . . We waited until he made his usual call and we drank a toast to mum and dad and their year of office. Civic Sunday followed and we all attended the usual mayoral service in the old Cathedral, the last big service to be held there.
Monday brought the beginning of what appeared to be a busy week of engagements for our parents. I can remember Mr Ernest Bevin, Minister of Labour, visiting the city. On Wednesday the Duchess of Gloucester was visiting the hospitals caring for the injured from earlier raids. We had a nasty raid on Tuesday night and a large bomb in the High Street–Earl Street area cut off gas and electricity all round. By mid-morning mum was nearly at her wits' end for the Duchess was to have lunch at the Council House. Visions of soup and sandwiches loomed, but, luckily, order was restored, and with some frantic behind-the-scenes work, all went off very pleasantly and smoothly.

And so, with the royal visitor gone, after being properly enter-tained, 'mum', Mrs Moseley's daughter recalls, 'really felt she was over her first hurdle'. That night the family rejoiced in her triumph and at this promising start to her husband's year of office. It was the evening of Wednesday 13 November 1940.

3
A BLOW FOR HERR CHURCHILL

'On November 4th we were requested to supply extra guns for Coventry. . . . But we just hadn't enough . . . to go round.'

General Frederick Pile, Commander-in-Chief, Anti-Aircraft Command, recalling 1940

THE importance of Coventry as a potential target had been recognized long before the war. In the great air defence exercises of 1934 it had been one of two key targets assigned the 'enemy' bombers (the other was London) and in January 1935 the Committee responsible for the Air Defence of Great Britain had recommended that after 'completing a defensive ring round London' the next priority should be a general strengthening of the protection of the Midlands. In February 1937 came another report, from Air Chief Marshal Dowding, soon to become Commander-in-Chief, Fighter Command, who urged that 'Midland town defences . . . be widened and strengthened', by doubling the number of guns and searchlights allocated to them, but that May, noted General Pile, 'the defence of Birmingham consisted of two guns and six lights'. By the outbreak of war in September 1939 the provision of guns, both as to quantity and quality, was still inadequate. The basic equipment of Anti-Aircraft Command, of which General Pile became Commander-in-Chief in July 1939, shortly after it had been set up, succeeding General Sir Alan Brooke, was the 3.7- and the 4.5-inch gun, supplemented by several hundred 3-inch naval guns, readily distinguishable to experienced ears by their heavier roar, with, as a defence against low-flying aircraft, the quick-firing Bofors gun.

The real problem was the difficulty of aiming the heavier weapons for experience demonstrated that the sound locators in use at the time were totally unable to cope with the high speed of modern bombers. By the time the sound locator had tracked the target and established its course, the predictor had calculated its future position, the gunner had set the fuse and aimed and fired the gun, and the shell had taken a full minute to reach its destination, a bomber could have travelled six miles in any direction. General Pile himself wryly recalled the saying current in the First World War that 'of the three most useless things in the world one was the anti-aircraft gun' – the other two being at that time considered unprintable – and in May 1940 he felt obliged to warn the Prime Minister that once night raids began, 'we should probably get a "pasting"'. Experience soon vindicated this gloomy forecast. When Churchill asked him at the end of September for his assessment of the results achieved since the start of the Blitz three weeks before, 'I had to say,' General Pile admitted, 'that I doubted whether we had got one aeroplane for 15 000 rounds.'

The real answer, everyone realized, lay in radar, but the first crude sets brought into use late in 1939 could only report the *direction* of the enemy, not his height, and though a more effective type of GL – for 'gun-laying' – set was brought into use on 1 October 1940, which could measure the elevation of the target as well as its bearing, it was still nowhere near accurate or reliable enough to enable a shell to be delivered regularly – or even occasionally – within killing distance. As for illuminating the enemy aircraft, so the guns could be aimed visually, this proved worse than useless, reassuring though the sight of the great beams sweeping the night sky was to those on the ground. The most peaceful nights, in fact, during the early autumn, came after General Pile had ordered the searchlights to be switched off. The enemy pilots, who had come to rely on them for navigation, became 'much confused' and 'the result was extraordinarily effective', so that 'both Birmingham and Coventry . . . enjoyed bomb-free nights'.

At this time the defence of Coventry rested on the 4th Anti-Aircraft Division, one of seven covering the whole British Isles, and commanded by Major-General C. A. E. Cadell, who had his headquarters at Chester. In addition to Coventry, the Division had to protect Barrow, Liverpool, Manchester, Crewe, Birmingham and Ringway aerodrome, but in spite of the area's importance it had lost some of its heavy guns during the summer, the total available to protect Coventry having been reduced from forty-four in July to twenty-four on 11 September. With this number it was still possible to achieve, in theory, the 'sixteen-gun density' aimed at by General Pile, which meant that 'anywhere within a particular defence area the target may be effectively engaged by a minimum of sixteen guns'. In practice, however, with the standard of accuracy then prevailing, 'effective engagement' was rarely possible, as Lieutenant-Colonel F. H. Lawrence, in command of the regiment defending Coventry, was well aware. He recalls being 'ticked off in a major way by a high-ranking officer', after one of the early raids on the city, on the grounds that 'I was not getting enough shells into the air. He said that it was good for the morale of Coventry to hear the guns going full blast. I said that I thought it was a waste of money, firing for the sake of firing.'

Anti-Aircraft Command was well aware that Coventry was inadequately protected. 'On November 4th,' wrote General Pile later, 'we were requested to supply extra guns for Coventry, for the Western ports, for Northern Ireland. But we just hadn't got enough guns to go round, and that was all there was to it.' However he did what he could. A week later, on 12 November the Brigade-Major of 34 Ack Ack Brigade – part of the 4th Division – issued an order from brigade headquarters at 143 Birmingham Road, Sutton Coldfield, detaching one mobile battery, armed with quick-firing 40-mm guns (better known as Bofors) to reinforce the defences of Coventry for the next three weeks. The order continued:

(a) Battery HQ will be located Packington Hall, Meriden.
(b) *Serial 1* Bty will deploy to following VPs* on 12 Nov. 1940:
 'A' Tp† Standard Motor Works
 'B' Tp Coventry Gauge and Tool Co.
 'C' Tp Coventry Goods Yard, LMS
   Serial 2 Bty will withdraw from VPs Serial 1, 1100 hrs, 15 Nov. 1940
   and deploy:
 'A' Tp Rootes
 'B' Tp Humber Motors
 'C' Tp GEC
   Serial 3 Bty will withdraw from VPs Serial 2, 1100 hrs, 17 Nov. 1940
   and deploy:
 'A' Tp Herberts
 'B' Tp New Daimler Motors
 'C' Tp Old Daimler Motors

The defence of Coventry on 14 November rested, however,

*Vulnerable Points.
†'Tp' was a troop, of which there were normally three to a battery.

since the main threat came from high-flying bombers, on the
95th (Birmingham) Heavy Anti-Aircraft Regiment, Royal Artillery
(Territorial Army), raised in Birmingham in April 1939. Since that
time it had served mainly in the Orkney Islands, an unpopular
posting, but one providing a surprising amount of target practice.
'During the ten months in the North,' remembers Colonel Lawrence,
'we had fired in many raids, including a major raid on 17 March
1940, when the first civilian was killed in the country. We were a
trained regiment, with experience.'

Two out of the regiment's three batteries had been raised in
Birmingham and they were delighted to be near home again, within
easy reach for a '24'- or '48'-hour pass, especially as they had been
told that they were being moved to Coventry 'for a rest'. On 14
November 1940 the regiment consisted of thirty officers and
seven hundred other ranks. Its three batteries were each responsible
for two gun sites, on one of which lived the battery commander, a
major, and his staff, on the other his second-in-command, a captain.
The six sites varied in their degree of comfort. Two, at Bedworth
and Binley, had been begun before the war and offered cookhouses
and baths as well as proper mud-free metalled roads. The remaining
four, at Ryton, Tile Hill, Gibbet Hill and Keresley, were of a
slightly lower standard, but still, Colonel Lawrence believes,
adequate and, he remembers, 'we did not have to use schools,
church halls, tents, etc.'

Relations between the gun detachments (the term 'crew', popular
with civilians, was frowned on by the Royal Regiment of Artillery)
and the surrounding families were cordial. 'Many of the chaps made
friends where they had a bath and a meal,' remembers Colonel
Lawrence, while at Ryton 'the local girls sent a number of bags
each week to enable the chaps to put a few smalls in for washing and
mending' and 'many were returned with a note, or a packet of
cigarettes'. The unique, and wearying, feature of service on a gun
site, was the need 'for all to be near the guns twenty-four hours a
day', in contrast to the average Army camp where most weekends
were free. Only a few men could be off the site at a time, although
the owner of the Coventry Hippodrome generously sent the
regiment a regular supply of free tickets five nights a week, which
were allocated on a rota basis.

In mid-November the ground defences of Coventry consisted of twenty-four 3.7-inch anti-aircraft guns, plus the twelve Bofors guns of 157/53 Light Anti-Aircraft Regiment.* These operated independently of the heavier guns, the lieutenant-colonel in command of its three troops having a roving commission to 'show the flag'. 'I did hear,' remembers Colonel Lawrence, 'that on more than one occasion during rush hours in the morning this battery would enter Coventry, take up a position and pull out at night, to enter again the next morning by a different route, so the morale of the people was raised.' A similar purpose would, it was hoped, be served by the even lighter, ordinary machine-guns which GHQ recommended in a signal on 14 November to Western Command, covering Coventry, should be installed on factory roofs, and manned by Home Guards. The War Office, it was stated, had already been asked for 100 Lewis guns with mountings, with 1000 rounds per gun, while the Ministry of Aircraft Production – ever the first to look after its own – had installed other machine-guns at several Coventry factories, among them British Thomson-Houston, in Alma Street, the Daimler No. 2 Factory, Singer Motors, Armstrong Whitworths at Baginton, and Rover Ltd. The officer sending the signal candidly admitted, however, that the guns were not expected to do much good, but were 'primarily to raise the morale of the workers'. Colonel Lawrence is doubtful if, in any case, they had arrived by nightfall on 14 November, though a few were available at the Longford Power Station for its employees.

No less reassuring to the citizens than the sight of the anti-aircraft guns gleaming behind their sandbagged walls, were the balloons catching the autumn sunshine in the sky above, or providing an absorbing spectacle for passers-by when they were hauled down to earth. Coventry possessed fifty-six balloons manned by men of No. 916 and No. 917 Squadrons, RAF, directed from No. 6 Balloon Centre, at Whythall, which was in turn part of No. 31

*The paper *Note on German Operation 'Moonlight Sonata'* quoted in Appendix B refers to the 12 Bofors guns, but states that '40 high angle guns were deployed for the defence of Coventry'. Colonel Lawrence is clear, however, that he had only 24 guns under his command and I can find no reference elsewhere to the additional 16 guns. According to the official historian, writing after the war, there *had* been 44, not 40, heavy anti-aircraft guns at Coventry on 11th July, but the total had been reduced to 32 by 21 August and 24 – which confirms Colonel Lawrence's recollection – by 11 September. The Vice Chiefs of Staff claimed in a report to the Prime Minister on 10 November that Coventry possessed thirty-two 3.7-inch and eight 3-inch guns but I can find no evidence to support these figures.

(Balloon Barrage) Group – one of five in the British Isles – with its headquarters at Birmingham.*

The existence of radar was at this time unknown to the general public, but the third strand in the local defences, of which they *were* aware, was the Observer Corps, whose visual and aural 'sightings' of enemy aircraft supplemented the invisible protective beams of the Chain Home radar network. The Observer Corps' main task was to alert the defences to raiders which slipped in beneath the radar screen, to provide accurate estimates of numbers and to identify the type of enemy aircraft being used, in which its members soon became almost uncannily skilled. The work of the Corps' members, on duty day and night round the clock in all weathers, was little publicized, but deeply satisfying to those involved.

Among them was a local architect, Mr A. W. Staniland, who in addition to being 'CO Buildings' in his Works ARP organization 'also felt strongly the need to do something personally to try and prevent the enemy from reaching the target.' After joining the Corps early in 1938 he was assigned to No. 5 Group, then in process of formation and before long was helping to man the local Centre, 'situated at that time on the top floor of the main General Post Office building', in the middle of the city, and linked by land lines to the Observation Posts, which supplied it with information, and to the Regional and National Centres. Living conditions, even at headquarters, were far from comfortable, for the removal of the Centre from the top floor to 'the rear ground floor, under the floor containing the telephone automatic switching racks', meant the loss of daylight and dependence on artificial 'ventilation pumped in through trunking'. From Munich onwards the Centre was manned continuously, with three crews sharing the day watches, from 8 a.m. to noon, noon to 4 p.m. and 4 p.m. to 8 p.m. and three 'night crews' taking over from 8 p.m. to 8 a.m. Mr Staniland, because of his key daytime job, joined No. 6 crew, assigned to night duty, and soon became grateful for the 'rest room where one or two could snatch a brief snooze as conditions permitted'. Because the observers

*The *Note on 'Moonlight Sonata'* previously quoted states, somewhat ambiguously, that 'The Coventry barrage of 56 balloons was reinforced on the 14th November by 16 further balloons, 8 of which were deployed on the night 14–15th'. (The remaining 8 had presumably arrived but were not yet ready for use.) The official historian agrees with the figure of 56 balloons, on 31 August, but makes no mention of subsequent reinforcement. Nor did any of my local informants refer to it.

in the reporting posts scanned the skies continuously, however, quiet periods were fewer than in most ARP work, and there were also frequent exercises, 'dummy runs in co-operation with other Regional Centres', and, very occasionally, 'darts contests by land line with other Regions'.

The authorities in London were on the whole a good deal less confident about the immediate future than those on the spot in Coventry, knowing that, until Air Interception radar could be fitted to British night-fighters, enemy aircraft would continue to roam the night skies of Britain almost at will. All the defences could as yet do was hope to confuse the enemy crews by radio counter-measures, and this was the special concern of a young ex-Oxford scientist, Dr (now Professor) R. V. Jones, who, at only twenty-eight, had already attracted the favourable attention of Winston Churchill, and was soon to become Assistant Director of Air Intelligence (Science) and Scientific Adviser to M I 6, the Secret Intelligence Service.

Dr Jones had discovered and, almost as important, had convinced the Prime Minister at a famous meeting in June 1940 of the existence of, a system of German navigational beams which not merely led the enemy pilot to his target but even released his bombs for him. Most high-ranking R A F officers, Dr Jones recalls, 'believed that pilots could navigate by the stars with almost infinite accuracy and . . . didn't like to admit that the Germans really had moved one up on us', but fortunately the Prime Minister's mind was less closed to disagreeable truths and with Churchill's support behind him and that of Churchill's Scientific Adviser, Professor Lindemann – Jones's former professor at Oxford – the young man was authorized to go ahead and plan ways of 'bending the beam'. While a series of jammers blotted out the true signal another group of transmitters put out a number of slightly misleading ones, sufficiently close to the original not to arouse a pilot's suspicions, and sufficiently varied to lead him astray even if he did begin to distrust them, as Professor Jones has since explained:

You could not fool an omniscient pilot who had all the time in the world and all the apparatus at his disposal. But in the middle of a war, over enemy country, when you are being shot at, or liable to be shot at, and your judgement inevitably goes a bit, it isn't all that difficult to mislead a pilot . . . which causes him to move over from the true beam on which he is flying to some other position . . . which is going to cause him to miss the target.

So the aptly named 'Operation Headache' was launched, and twenty officers and 200 men of No. 80 Wing, RAF, responsible for Radio Counter-Measures, started putting out false signals on the basis of information provided by Dr Jones and his colleagues. Some encouraging successes were rapidly scored. London, with the Thames pointing the way to it, and the larger coastal targets remained impossible to miss, but the enemy squadrons never achieved anything like the accuracy of which in theory their *Knickebein* beam-guidance system was capable, that is of landing all their bombs in an area 300 yards square. Many bombs were dropped miles from their proper destination and even those which did hit the intended city tended to be scattered instead of being concentrated on pin-pointed objectives. But the principal bonus was probably psychological, for the German crews began to lose faith in *Knickebein* and to blame it for their navigational troubles; and some were so spectacularly misled that they force-landed in Britain in the happy belief that they were on the other side of the Channel.

While the scientists rejoiced, the senior commanders on both sides were curiously reluctant to accept the unwelcome truth. On the German side, Dr Jones later discovered, 'although the pilots knew they were jammed no one quite had the courage to tell Göring this. But in the end the German Air Staff had to face up to the fact that we were effectively dealing with it.' The British commanders were meanwhile struggling, against all the evidence, to rehabilitate the reputation of conventional navigation against the upstart radio. When in mid-October a recently identified German squadron, Kampfgruppe 100, 'started to drop flares some of our senior officers argued that this was because their aids were so inaccurate that they couldn't see the targets and this was to enable them to bomb better'. The true explanation, Dr Jones suspected, was very different. 'What,' he believed, 'they might well be doing was practising a pathfinding technique of lighting up the target, not for themselves but for the main force to bomb, an absolutely logical step, once the main force was as it were blinded because its own beams weren't working.'

Gradually, as the clues were put together at the headquarters of Air Ministry Scientific Intelligence at 100 Broadway, close to St

James's Park underground station in London, this shrewd guess was confirmed: the Germans had installed in the Heinkel 111s of Kampfgruppe 100 a far more sophisticated device than the original *Knickebein*, which had, Dr Jones discovered, 'the gloriously mysterious name of the "X" apparatus'. This, as so often in German code-words, was itself a clue, for the *X Gerät* depended on a succession of cross-beams, which intercepted the main approach beam at various points, the first twelve miles from the target, the second six miles away, and from then on the bombs were released automatically at precisely the right moment.

Dealing with the 'X apparatus' was far harder than coping with *Knickebein*, but then, almost as if in answer to prayer, one was delivered undamaged by the enemy close to the door-step of the Telecommunications Research Establishment at Swanage, where radar research was then concentrated. On 6 November 1940 an enemy bomber crash-landed on a beach at West Bay, between high and low water mark, and as the tide receded the emblem painted on its nose, a Viking long-boat, became visible, and less dramatic, but far more exciting to those in the know, the letters 6 N + B.H. on its tail, which identified it as an 'X apparatus' Heinkel of the new élite pathfinder force, KG 100.

The chance to acquire this priceless treasure intact was then thrown away by an idiotic example of inter-service rivalry, from which the Royal Navy emerged the victor and the British people the loser. As the soldiers who had reached the scene first were waiting to drag the aircraft ashore, a naval vessel appeared off-shore and the captain, asserting the Navy's right to the wreck as it was in the sea, towed the Heinkel into deeper water, where the rope broke and it sank. The two *X Gerät* receivers aboard were later recovered but 'it was only about ten days afterwards when we finally got the sand out of the equipment'.

While the vital receivers were still being cleaned up the scientists and intelligence officers piecing together the jigsaw of information about German intentions realized how little time there was to spare.

On 11 November news reached the Air Ministry that a prisoner of war had told a room-mate (though whether the latter was a planted 'stool-pigeon' or the room had been 'bugged' with a listening device was not revealed) of plans for a larger-scale raid than any so far attempted, involving every available bomber, and scheduled to take place during the period of the full moon, between 15 and 20 November. The targets, he believed, would be Birmingham and Coventry.

The British code-breaking machine installed at Bletchley Park in Buckinghamshire, which was able to read many of the most secret high-level German signals, enciphered on their 'Enigma' machine, revealed the same day that the Luftwaffe was planning a major operation in the immediate future. Its code-name, 'Moonlight Sonata', seemed to confirm what the over-talkative prisoner had let slip, that the attack would take place on, or very close to, the night of the full moon, on 14/15 November, but about its nature the British could only specualte. 'There were,' Professor Jones remembers, 'many, many wild theories as to what it was, including even a full-scale night air-landing operation, [but] no one actually up to the time the bombs dropped could be absolutely certain.'

What was known, or at least guessed, however, was that it would involve KG 100 and one of three possible targets, for ULTRA, as intelligence emanating via the Enigma machine was called, had revealed 'that the X beam stations had been instructed to prepare for three targets, Wolverhampton, Birmingham and Coventry'. In their tidy way the Germans had given each a number:

> Target 51: Wolverhampton
> Target 52: Birmingham
> Target 53: Coventry

but, most unhelpfully, Luftwaffe signals, regularly decoded at Bletchley, instead of also using these numbers, referred to possible objectives by code-names. During those anxious days of mid-November two names constantly cropped up in the reports which reached Dr Jones' desk – *Regenschirm* and *Einheits Preis*. The German officer who coined them had, perhaps, allowed himself a smirk of satisfaction at his ingenuity, but if so it was misplaced. '*Regenschirm* we got straight away,' remembers Professor Jones. 'It means "umbrella" and we could see their minds working. Mr Chamberlain carried an umbrella and Mr Chamberlain came from Birmingham.' *Einheits Preis* proved a shade more difficult, but a translation rapidly provided a clue. The nearest English equivalent was 'single price' which the Air Ministry scientists rapidly associated with Woolworths, whose famous slogan was still 'nothing over sixpence' – and interpreted as Wolverhampton.

There had so far been no obvious candidate meaning 'Coventry' among the intercepted place-names and the British experts, although looking for it, failed to find it. 'We had actually had the code-name beforehand,' Professor Jones recalls, 'but didn't realize it was a code-name at the time. We had just seen one mention in a message to *Korn* [which means, as well as sounds, the same as English 'corn'] and at that stage we really didn't know whether this might have been some kind of jamming of anything'. This seemed by far the likeliest explanation, bearing in mind the penchant of the Germans for revealing code-words and the fact that the thoughts of the British scientists were already turning to the scattering of tinfoil strips to confuse the enemy radar; significantly when the Americans later adopted this device, they called it 'Chaff'. But the unknown German who had devised the list had this time abandoned all attempts at ingenuity and had fallen back on simple alliteration. *Korn* had in fact, nothing to do with jamming, but was the missing code-name for Target 53. And, translated, it tidily rounded off the German list and identified the objective for 'Moonlight Sonata':

Target 53: Coventry

Coventry's fate was finally settled on the night of Friday 8 November 1940 when RAF bombers attacked Munich. The raid achieved nothing, but had one totally unforeseen consequence: it infuriated Hitler, who regarded any attack on the town, the birth-place and shrine of the Nazi movement, as a personal insult. As Dr Jones and his colleagues were still puzzling over the meaning of *Korn* and the captured 'X apparatus' still lay in sea-stained, sand-clogged pieces on a technician's bench at the Royal Aircraft Establishment, Farnborough, the orders were already clattering out over the Luftwaffe teleprinters announcing that 'Moonlight Sonata' was definitely 'on' and demanding a maximum effort from every squadron on the night of the full moon.

While the Germans had been perfecting their preparations the British Air Staff had not been idle. By 12 November, although the precise target had not been finally identified, a detailed appreciation of enemy intentions had been made, which assumed that KG

100 and *Knickebein* would both be employed, along with the maximum number of first-line aircraft the German commander-in-chief, who was expected to take charge in person, could scrape together, although the number available was grossly over-estimated at 1800 bombers. The British commanders ordered 'the maximum scale of night-fighter and anti-aircraft artillery to be concentrated against the enemy raiders' but must have been well aware, from recent experience elsewhere, that neither was likely to make much difference to a determined attack. They therefore placed their chief faith in radio counter-measures, involving 'continuous watch on German radio activity and maximum radio interference with enemy navigational beams and beacons', though this, too, was already being done as a matter of routine, and in a series of spoiling attacks by intruder aircraft and specially-assigned bombers on the principal airfields likely to be used, especially by KG 100, and on the radio-beam transmitters. The whole plan was known as 'Operation Cold Water', a fitting companion to 'Operation Headache'.

Thursday 14 November was a pleasant late-autumn day, sunny, though with a brisk wind. In France the ground crews started work early, overhauling the aircraft dispersed round the airfields, tuning up those where any defect had been reported for a flight test that afternoon, and preparing for the last-minute flurry of bombing-up and refuelling: the Germans always delayed putting bombs and petrol aboard till the last minute. Already the word was that 'something big' was on that night, although only a few favoured officers yet knew the target.

Confirmation of its identity reached the headquarters of the 6th Air Signals Company at Boulogne early in the afternoon. Soon afterwards the Company's transmitters code-named 'Weser', 'Rhein', 'Elbe' and 'Oder', after major German rivers, were switched on. Weser, at the tip of the Cherbourg peninsula, transmitted the main approach beam which crossed the English coast near Christchurch in Hampshire and then, striking to the east of Salisbury and Swindon, pointed straight, like an invisible arrow, to the heart of Coventry. The beams from Rhein, Elbe and Oder, clustered close together in the Pas de Calais, crossed the main approach beam at various points, fifty, twenty and five kilometres from Coventry, the first intersection being somewhere in the vicinity of the peaceful little Cotswold town of Moreton-in-Marsh, the second not far from the village of Barford in Warwickshire and the third midway between Leamington and Coventry, a mile or two from the ancient fortress, powerless tonight against these airborne invaders, of Kenilworth Castle.

According to Group-Captain F. W. Winterbotham, then head of the RAF section at SIS headquarters, news of the coming attack reached there in the afternoon:

At about 3 p.m. on November the fourteenth someone must have made a slip-up and instead of a city with a code-name, Coventry was spelt out. This was something we had not met before. Churchill was at a meeting so I spoke direct to his personal secretary and told him what had happened. I pointed out that whilst the signal had gone to Fighter Command, I had little doubt there would be reference back to the Prime Minister for a decision as to what to do. . . . I asked the personal secretary if he would be good enough to ring me back when the decision had been taken. . . . In the event, it was decided only to alert all the services, the fire, the ambulance, the police, the wardens, and to get everything ready to light the decoy fires.*

The recollections of Professor R. V. Jones, who was at work that afternoon in an office only twenty yards from Winterbotham's, are very different. Although he was responsible for predicting the Germans' intentions and advising on the disposition of British night-fighters he has no recollection whatever of the arrival of any ULTRA information naming Coventry as the night's target. *His* belief is that what warning of the raid there was came, as usual, as a result of the routine activities of the RAF's Counter-Measures Unit, and this is borne out by the *Note on 'Moonlight Sonata'*, already quoted, which refers to 'German radio beam activity' having been detected by 'about 1300 hours', and to a further report, from the Radio Counter-Measures headquarters 'by 1500 hours . . . that the enemy "River Group" beams were intersecting over Coventry'. Further confirmation came a little later, as Professor Jones had described, the occasion being fixed in his mind because, most exceptionally, it involved two successive miscalculations.

Somewhere about six o'clock that night the Group Captain who was in charge of counter-measures telephoned me in some bewilderment because the listening aircraft had been up, it had heard the German beams . . .

---

*For a fuller discussion of this point, see Appendix A.

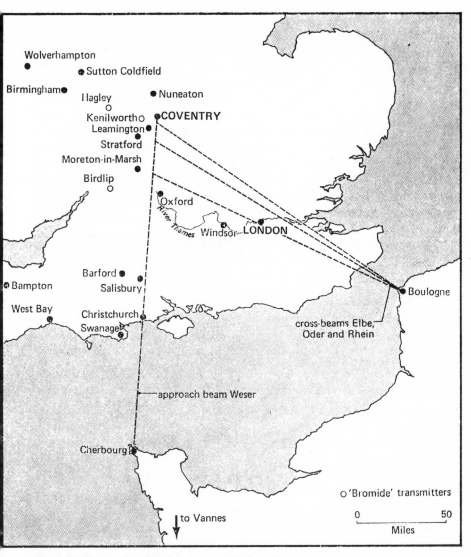

How the German pathfinders were guided to Coventry

Kampfgruppe 100 took off from Vannes, about 150 miles south of Cherbourg, and picked up the main approach beam, *Weser*, over the Channel. On reaching the point of intersection with the first crossbeam, *Rhein*, they settled on to a more precise course, directly on the beam. 30 kilometres later their route intercepted the second crossbeam, *Oder*, a signal to start the special bomb-release clock; 15 kilometres further on they crossed the final beam, *Elbe*, and a second pointer on the clock was started. Fifty seconds after this the two pointers came together and closed an electrical circuit and the aircraft's bombs were relased automatically. The *Bromide* transmitters put out a misleading signal to try to disrupt the German radio guidance system.

there was obviously a big operation on, and he asked me on what frequencies he should put his jammers. And the evidence, the only evidence he could give me, was the frequency which he had reported. Now, I knew from the other work I had done that the frequency measured by the aeroplane couldn't be right and I therefore had to make guesses about what sort of errors would have been made and try and guess the actual frequencies the Germans would use [and] then the three key ones because we only had three jammers. . . . I made the best guesses I could, the Group Captain said he would try and get his jammers on to those frequencies and I then went home to Richmond . . . and spent a distinctly unhappy night realizing that if I had guessed wrong there was going to be some hundreds of people dead the following morning.

The lack of satisfactory information from the 'listening' aircraft was no reflection on anyone. 'We had not sufficiently accurate measuring instruments to be able to record those frequencies,' Professor Jones points out. And its absence had been made good for he had guessed right about the frequency to be jammed. But there now followed a second and calamitous blunder, compounding those which had already occurred.

As it turned out we had got the carrier frequencies [i.e. the wavelength on which the jamming signal would be transmitted] completely right. . . . That was really pure luck. I was just doing the best one could in the circumstances. But what was unfortunately quite wrong was the audible note that we had put on our jammers thinking that we were making them sound like the Germans'. The reason was that someone, I think in Farnborough, having listened – whether he had been tone deaf or what I don't know – made an error, and instead of getting an audible frequency of 2000 cycles per second, he had said it was 1500. All the jammers were put on 1500 when they should have been on 2000. At the time I made myself a little unpopular by saying that someone ought to have been shot but that may have been too hasty a judgement. Everyone was doing his best. It is very difficult to get everything right in war.

From this judgement no one could dissent. But the consequences of this particular error were to be calamitous indeed, for as the German pilots flew across England they were easily able to distinguish in their earphones the correct note of their own transmitters from the very different one put out, on the same wavelength, by the British.

While RAF air crews were being briefed on their part in the

'Operation Cold Water' missions designed to disrupt the German attack, the first dozen crews of Kampfgruppe 100 were already boarding their aircraft and soon after darkness had fallen their Heinkel 111s began climbing into the darkness above their airfield at Vannes on the Bay of Biscay, not far from St Nazaire, and set course almost due north on the 200-mile flight to the coast of Dorset, keeping slightly to one side of the approach beam for fear it had been detected and was being patrolled by British night-fighters. At 6.17, local time, dead on schedule, the first aircraft crossed the Dorset coast and turned slightly north-east, towards Coventry. After crossing the Thames near Bampton, about fifteen miles from Oxford, the river sparkling far below them in the brilliant moonlight, they settled down into the main approach beam, which was soon emitting the reassuring note, like a continuous faint shriek, which meant they were dead on track. From time to time, as they neared the Midlands, there broke into the pilots' earphones the higher-pitched whistle of the British 'Bromide' transmitters, one of which, at Kenilworth, lay directly below the final, crucial stages of their flight path, but it was easily recognized for what it was – the English up to their tricks again – and ignored.

The airmen of the main German bomber force, which were to follow when K G 100's pathfinders had set the target alight, were by now already airborne, or preparing to take off. A detailed record of the experiences of one, at least, as they were published to the German people soon afterwards, still survives for they were written up at length by a journalist from Dr Goebbels's Ministry of Propaganda. Flight-Sergeant Werner Handorf was twenty-four, the son of a Berlin factory foreman, and, after serving as a mechanic in the German airline, Lufthansa, he had volunteered for the Luftwaffe in 1935, flying his first operational sorties against Poland. Now, also a veteran of the campaign in France, he was pilot of a Junkers 88, one of five hundred bombers assigned to attack Coventry, the largest force so far mustered against a single city.

Operation 'Moonlight Sonata' had really begun for the men of Handorf's squadron when, after being warned earlier that they would be flying that night, they had assembled at 5 p.m. for the usual briefing from their Squadron Leader.

And now, comrades, you are acquainted with the nature and essentials of tonight's operation. Our task is, with other squadrons, to repay the attack on Munich by the English during the night of 8 November. We shall not repay it in the same manner by smashing up harmless dwelling houses, but we shall do it in such a way that those over there will be completely stunned. Even though the attack on Munich by the 'gentlemen' of the Royal Air Force was a complete failure, neither the Führer nor our Commander-in-Chief, Reichsmarschall Göring, is willing to let even the attempt at an attack on the capital of the movement go unpunished, and we have therefore received orders to destroy the industries of Coventry tonight. You know what this means, comrades. This place is one of the chief armament centres of the enemy air force and has also factories which are important for the production of motor vehicles and armoured cars. Yes, it can be claimed to be the principal centre of the English automobile industry, and in particular, of the commercial vehicle industry. Quite a collection of factories for engines, engine parts and motorcycles are also situated there. Amongst various other aircraft factories, the Rolls-Royce aero-engine works are specially noteworthy. . . . If we can paralyse this armament centre tonight, we shall have dealt another heavy blow at Herr Churchill's war production. And that is not the least important purpose of the operation before us. We take off at 9.30. We shall not, of course, be the first squadron in order of flying, but there will still be enough left for us and the comrades who follow. But tomorrow morning the factories there must lie in smoke and ruins. We rest till 7.30. Then we get ready for the take-off. Well, comrades, good luck!

This officer specifically told his men that 'our bombs are intended for the armament industry' and confirmation that the Germans meant to hit military objectives, not to make a 'terror' attack on the civilian population, is provided by the list of aiming points issued to this and other squadrons.

Letirgeschwader 1: The Standard Motor Company and Coventry
    Radiator and Press Company
Kampfgruppe 27:   The Alvis aero-engine Works
Kampfgruppe 51:   The British Piston Ring Company
Kampfgruppe 55:   The Daimler Works
Kampfgruppe 606: The gasholders in Hill Street

Like the R A F at this time the Germans spread their attack through the whole night, with aircraft arriving and leaving independently, and Flight-Sergeant Handorf, not due over Coventry until nearly midnight, had ample time to look about him.

As dusk creeps on the lights are turned on in the blacked-out hangars.

The dazzling beams of the hand-lamps which ease the fitters' work on the engines glisten on the planes. There's a sound of hammering, rattling, quiet whistling, subdued talking. The time creeps on. The early autumn evening has sunk down over the aerodrome. A few clouds stand in the starry sky. A light south-east wind blows over the broad field. . . . The meteorologists report that the night's weather will allow the attack to be executed smoothly, with some cloud but not enough to obscure the individual objectives. In their quarters the crews are busy slipping into their flying suits. . . . Flight-Sergeant Handorf takes a small photograph out of his pocket-book and slips it with a smile into a breast pocket of his flying suit – a simple photograph of his fiancée, Marielies [a shorthand-typist at the Junkers factory in Berlin]. . . . It is his talisman and has always accompanied him on every previous flight . . . Handorf never flies without this little photograph. He first placed it there in the attack on Radom on 1 September 1939.

For this crew the long hours of waiting ended at 9.30, when they prepared to take off. Contrary to British practice, the pilot was not captain of the aircraft and Handorf, in aircraft 'Bruno', found himself outranked by his commander, Oberleutnant Schmidfeder, though senior to his gunner, Corporal Bergengrun.

The corporal and the flight-sergeant climb through the hatch into the body of the Ju. 88: the Oberleutnant casts a glance over at the other aircraft, then follows his men.

The leading aircraft is air-borne; soon the second follows. And now on to 'Bruno's' turn. The take-off is signalled and with engines roaring... the Ju. 88 shoots, bouncing and staggering over the aerodrome. Handorf . . . gently pulls the control column towards him, the bouncing ceases and the plane is in the air. . . . Bergengrun stands at his combat post at the rear, peering out into the dark night. Stars twinkle between jagged cumulus clouds floating across the sky only a little higher than the aircraft. . . . Far away over the flat land the horizon can be picked out. Below everything is black-out. . . . Now and then a faint shine sweeps over the land marking the straight ribbon of some road, ghostly visible to the airman's keen eye. Then everything is swallowed up again in the darkness. Oberleutnant Schmidfeder squats on his seat examining his map by the light of a small screen lamp. It is a street map of Coventry; all important objectives are marked with red circles. The light is switched off in the pilot's cabin; only the Oberleutnant's lamp and the blue light from the instrument board spread a faint gleam. . . . The guttural tones of the R/T sound from time to time. . . . Schmidfeder acknowledges in slow drawn-out sentences. . . . Otherwise it is quiet except for the steady drone of the two powerful engines. . . . The enemy coast is not far away now; ahead the chalk wall of the steep cliffs shimmer indistinctly below. . . . And now, in the distance, gleams the light of fires. . . . The flight continues over enemy country, with course set for the Midlands. . . . Now searchlight cones flit pointedly and hastily across the sky illuminating the cloud cover with a bluish tinge, stopping here and there, searching for minutes on end. From time to time they cling for a few seconds to one of the attacking aircraft, but the German aircrew bring them quickly and skilfully out of reach of the dazzling beams. A searchlight has caught Schmidfeder's aircraft and crew twice already. Each time Handorf pulls the rudder round with a quick jerk, works the ailerons putting the aircraft on its wing tips and dives away sharply into the darkness, 600 or 800 feet height are lost. Then, climbing again to over 6000 feet, weaving to and fro, but always getting straight away back on course: the aircraft roars unchecked towards its target. From time to time the Oberleutnant sees from port or starboard one of the other aircraft belonging to his squadron flash suddenly in the cone of searchlights and dive away again just as quickly into the darkness. Irresistibly the aircraft press on towards their common objective – Coventry.

4
AN ORDINARY WINTER'S EVENING

*'The night started for us just like any other winter's evening.
When the sirens sounded we all got into the coal hole.'*
Coventry man, then aged twelve, recalling 14 November 1940

Everyone agrees that Thursday 14 November 1940 was as normal as any day in wartime Coventry could be. Long before it was light the night shift in the Coventry factories had made their weary way home. By sunrise, at 8.18 British Summer Time (reintroduced early in February, it was to remain in force the rest of the war) the day shift were already hard at work, and the firemen, policemen and first-aiders on duty the previous night were enjoying a hurried breakfast before making up for lost sleep, or reporting to their daytime jobs. The tinsmith quoted earlier, leaving his home in Birmingham as usual around 6.30 a.m. to drive three workmates to their Coventry war factory, noted the touch of frost in the air, but decided, despite the slight but keen wind, that they were in for 'a decent morning'. During the dinner-hour he ventured out in the sunshine of a 'beautiful fresh winter's day' and discovered, to his great surprise, a metal scooter, hanging up in a small ironmonger's in Vecqueray Street, the very Christmas present he wanted for his small son. He gladly paid the 27s 6d asked 'and arranged to pick it up in the car, in tomorrow's lunch break' – a plan destined never to be carried out.

A then fourteen-year-old girl, one of seven children, recalls helping her mother that morning to push two of the youngest in the pram the three miles from their home in Wyken to go shopping and passing a former neighbour, 'a very nice young woman', with a young baby, busy 'cleaning her front doorstep' in Hermitage Road where they had previously lived. 'Mum said to her, "For goodness' sake stop killing yourself with work. Your house will be still here when you've gone"', a prediction which they learned next morning had proved horrifyingly correct.

Another housewife, living in a new house on the Cheylesmore estate, spent the morning hanging new green curtains throughout the house. These were to be up for only a few hours and to leave a permanent mark on the family's taste, for subsequently her daughter remembers, they became 'most superstitious and have not had any green furnishings since'.

The scene in a house in Daventry Road was also a very peaceful one, for its occupant had taken advantage of the fine day to clean the windows outside and sweep up the dead leaves that had collected in the garden. By half past four it was growing dark and she did her 'daily round of all windows, making sure there were no gaps anywhere in the black-lined curtains', and reflecting that the main living-room 'looked more like a shambles than the dining room of a young, houseproud wife', with 'the mattress under the table', which doubled as a shelter, though the bed 'was not exactly comfortable as the foot rest about corresponded with our necks'.

The hearth was cluttered with several buckets of coal, a bottle of water, a covered saucepan of milk and, most important, the baby's prepared food. The sideboard was an even worse muddle, candles, torches, the biscuit tin, the cocoa tin, tea-pot, milk, cups and saucers, baby's nappies. By the door was our suitcase ready packed with coats and hats and outdoor boots piled on the top. . . .

I had had my meal and was sitting by the fire feeding my two-month-old baby Judith. My dog Sally and cat Wilf were lying stretched out on the mattress, enjoying the luxury of lying in bed by the fire. Then the siren went. . . . Putting Judith in her basket under the stairs I took my place under the table with the animals. The first thing to happen was the arrival of an out-of-breath husband. He had run all the way from the station, dodging the incendiaries. So there we were, husband, wife, dog and cat and a sleeping baby, just waiting.

Thursday was early closing day in Coventry and 1 p.m. could not come fast enough for one housewife working for the Coventry Co-operative Society, glad to see the end of a 'miserable morning', for after hours spent 'entering customers' accounts in the ledger', a weights and measures inspector had 'complained about my untidy figures on a customer's bill', an incident implanted on her memory by a sharp kick on the ankle from the manager as she prepared 'to answer back'. After devoting the afternoon to cleaning and polishing her 'little house' in Queen Isabel's Avenue, Cheylesmore, about three-quarters of a mile from the city centre, 'I prepared my evening meal, had a quick bath and decided to relax for the rest of the evening'. When the warning sounded 'I had,' she remembers, 'no coffee prepared and no time to change into slacks and woollen clothing', only 'to grab my cat and dash into the shelter'.

Leslie Worthington of Owen Owen's store, which had already suffered from the bombs more than once, had also been grateful that it was early closing. He had spent the afternoon 'digging for victory' in his garden, and attending to the hens they had started to keep to cope with the egg shortage. 'When the raid started we moved into the shelter in the lounge,' he recalls, 'with flasks of tea etc.'

The Rev. W. B. Sells, curate of St Thomas's, had begun the evening with a peaceful and uplifting duty – saying evensong in the darkened church with the vicar – before returning to the vicarage for a meeting of the Youth Club committee, which rapidly moved to the cellar, although the members consoled themselves with the thought that 'it was just bombers going over to Birmingham'.

Thursday was a busy day for many office workers, preparing the wage packets, and for the wife of a foreman, and part-time fireman, at the GEC works, who lived in Harris Road and worked in the Wages Department of BTH, 14 November was no exception. 'During our short lunch break,' she remembers, 'I'd rushed out to buy and post a birthday card to my mother and on it had written: "We are all right, don't worry", as well as birthday greetings', a fortunate addition as it turned out, for 'she received it on her birthday on 16 November and . . . was comforted, thinking I had written *after* the raid. . . . The warning went before I got into the house . . . so I gathered my things together and went into the shelter expecting the usual boring hours.'

For one sixteen-year-old schoolboy it had been an enjoyable afternoon, enlivened by a game of rugger under perfect conditions at the King Henry VIII School, but when the sirens went that evening he was at home in Copsewood, struggling with his 'calculus prep'. A well practised routine followed. His father, works engineer and ARP Controller at the nearby factory, turned off the gas and electricity in their house, and connected the garden hose to the kitchen tap, before going on duty, while his wife and son adjourned to the excellent factory shelters, twenty feet underground.

One fourteen-year-old girl had spent the day in bed in hospital after a minor operation for removal of an ovarian cyst. The nurses, she remembers, had been 'thrilled' by her brand-new 'green pyjamas', and 'nice warm green dressing gown', bought at Owen Owen the day before to cheer her up. At six o'clock her mother and sister arrived to visit her. They 'stayed for about one hour and talked about the very cold weather and what a bright moonlit night it was'.

It had been an equally peaceful day for one ten-year-old schoolgirl, who had that morning, as usual, collected her day's work from her school in Red Lane, which had closed due to the raids, the children being assigned homework under the 'Voluntary System', which most pupils faithfully honoured. Tea was, also as usual, accompanied by *Children's Hour* on the wireless, including that day Episode 5 of *Forgotten Island*, 'The thrilling adventure play by J. D. Strange'.

After tea my mother, father and myself made our way from our house in Oliver Street to the shelters of the British Thomson-Houston Ltd, where my father worked. . . . As we walked the mile or so to the shelters carrying our blankets, flasks, food, etc., we looked at the moon, which was a huge, glowing orange ball, and . . . remarked we hoped there wouldn't be a raid that night, as everything was like daylight. . . . The B T H . . . shelters were, as shelters go, very comfortable, with small, slatted wooden benches, on which we put our bedding and prepared to get some rest. That was soon doomed as the sirens went.

One even younger girl, living in a flat above the furniture shop in Queens Road run by her mother and grandmother, while her father worked at Armstrong Siddeley, remembers a particularly happy family tea that day. She was already excitedly looking forward to Christmas and her fifth birthday due soon after it, while her grandmother and mother had returned triumphant from a furniture sale in Birmingham, and her father was home unexpectedly early to share a festive tea of crab salad, for seeing 'the clear moonlit sky' he had decided not to work overtime. His fears were soon proved justified.

This particular night the sirens sounded much earlier than usual. No preparations had been made. Even the tea things were still on the table. Everything was left hurriedly and we fled to the shelter. My mother and grandmother had new dresses on so went as they were. I was quickly put into my siren suit and a little squirrel coat . . . I can remember my father carrying me in his arms and falling over the sandbags on the way through the yard. I was put on to a bed at the end of the shelter.

The wife of one aero-engine fitter at the Standard No. 2 Shadow Factory remembers taking one precaution not recommended in the official handbooks, 'doping' her two-year-old son and four-year-old daughter with a favourite cough mixture, which invariably sent them to sleep. Tonight proved no exception, even though her husband insisted before long that they all moved out into the shelter in the garden. For one family living in Jenner Street near the Coventry and Warwickshire Hospital 'the night started for us just like any other winter's evening', remembers one man who was then aged twelve. 'When the sirens sounded we all got into the coal hole [where] mother had made a bed on the floor.'

Not all the shops closed early on Thursday. One girl, then sixteen, remembers being anxious to get home from her job at Osbornes, the newsagents, in Jordan Well, to the tiny house in Hertford Square, two minutes from the city centre, where she lived with her four brothers and sisters, for her youngest sister's second birthday party. She stopped only to warn a friend, Dot, who lived in Bull Yard, that she could not meet her that night either to go to 'the pictures' or – their other favourite outing – to a dance at the Liberal Club in Union Street. In the few moments it took to deliver her message she noticed 'how well the barrage balloons stood against the sky as we looked towards the old Food Office by Greyfriars Green', a view etched in her memory because Dot and her family – nine all told – were to die in a few hours' time.

Those who bought the *Midland Daily Telegraph*, an evening newspaper, on their way home, were able to read of the Duchess of Gloucester's visit on the previous day, about the burial of Neville Chamberlain that afternoon, and an encouraging, if misleading, report about the Greeks advancing into Albania. There were pictures of Coventry buildings damaged by bombs and an editorial pouring scorn on the Italian Navy. But the most useful item of information in the paper was black-out time, which that Thursday fell at 5.46 p.m. following moon-rise at 5.18.

No one seems to have had any premonition of what was soon to happen, though the same newspaper reported that a giant question

mark had appeared in the sky over Coventry that morning, supposedly sketched by a solitary German raider. One man, however,
alarmed by recent events, did make his will that day, and posted it
to a relative for safety, giving the recipient a disagreeable shock
when it arrived next morning, though the sender was unharmed.
One girl then in her early twenties and working as a machine box-
maker at Thomas Bushill and Sons in Little Park Street, moved by
an impulse she could not explain, took with her to the cloakroom
as work finished, her overall and scissors, normally removed from
the workroom only at weekends. When a workmate reminded her
'It's not Friday yet', she dutifully returned them, an action she was
later to regret. Her boy-friend, Len Dacombe, had no anxieties,
subconscious or not, about the coming night and called on her at 6.40
p.m. as usual, on his way to his work as a toolsetter on the night
shift at the Coventry Climax factory in Widdrington Road. She
was apprehensive at seeing him leave, but he reassured her, com-
menting that 'It's so light tonight Jerry won't come because we'll
be able to see him.' The siren, sounding as she was clearing the table
after his departure, rapidly proved him wrong. Meanwhile he had,
like a law-abiding citizen, just stopped and dismounted from his
cycle at the traffic lights at the junction of Barras Lane with
Holyhead Road. 'I donned my fire-watcher's tin hat,' he remembers,
'thinking,"What a charley, waiting at the traffic lights when there
is no traffic and Jerry flying overhead."'

To one girl living in Leamington it began to seem that night
that she and a girl-friend had only to arrange a foursome for the
Luftwaffe to make an unwelcome fifth. Despite the abrupt ending
to an earlier evening out, when the Rex Cinema had been bombed,
as already described, she had called at the same friend's home,
around 6.45 p.m. on 14 November, to meet two more 'Air Force
lads from Baginton camp, who called at the house and we sat talking.
My friend's mother was a keen harpist and had a variety of harps
in the house and the boys were fascinated by them', prompting a
somewhat ill-timed pleasantry when, after the warning, the conversation continued in the brick air-raid shelter in the street outside
and one of the visitors 'remarked we would all soon be playing
harps somewhere in the sky'.

What most people remember best about that night is the moonlight. Len Dacombe had been conscious of it 'glistening on the

house-tops' as he left his girl-friend's home, and the Birmingham tinsmith who had that afternoon reserved a toy scooter for his son was also aware of the 'brilliant moon' as he left his work around ten to seven. 'We could,' he remembers, 'almost have read a newspaper, it was such a wonderful night. The solitary tree, on the waste land next to our firm, which we used as a car park, stood out sharply, and I remember thinking as I got into the car and switched on the lights, how unnecessary they were. It could just as well have been broad daylight.' His feeling that it had been a good day was confirmed when 'we passed the bus *before* we reached the lights'. Normally they only overtook the 6.45 p.m. Birmingham bus from Pool Meadow *after* the traffic lights near the Holyhead Road bridge.

For those caring for the sick every warning brought special problems. One student nurse at the Coventry and Warwickshire Hospital had become used to making the patients comfortable *under* their beds but invariably she found herself 'too busy for fright'. On 14 November, being on night duty, she was at breakfast after sleeping all day 'when the raid started', a meal which ended prematurely. Also to remain unconsumed were the 'beans on toast and a glass of milk', which another nurse, at the Gulson Road Hospital, was eyeing hungrily as the sirens sounded. Matron, fearing trouble later, had got her nurses to supper early, but the Germans had come too soon for her, and the girls were sent off to their pre-assigned posts, this student bearing her supper with her to the Emergency Operating Theatre.

Two 'boaties', father and son, who manned a horse-drawn barge transporting coal to local factories and power stations, had, the son remembers, made a late start that day, for, having spent the night at Nuneaton, *en route* from Pooley Hall colliery to Longford Power Station, Coventry, with a cargo of coal, 'we knew we had plenty of time and it was all plain sailing from there'. So far raids had troubled the 'boaties' little.

We used to go about our everyday tasks [this man remembers] and in the course of our travels we would pass our friends on the canal and they would say 'They were bloody over again' and that is how it would pass. Well, away we go for Longford Stop Power Station. We get there sometime between 1 p.m. and 3 p.m. We had to wait for two and a half to three hours for them to unload us with the cranes. When we were unloaded it was beginning to get dusk so dad and I decided to stop the night at Longford Wharf, a mile this side Coventry. We went to the public house and asked if we could stable the horse for the night, which was all right on the payment of sixpence. I put the horse in the stable, fed and watered him and put the straw for him to lie on. When I got back to the boat dad had got the tea mashed and was cooking a bit of dinner. After we had eaten dinner . . . and had a wash dad said, 'We'll go and have a drink, where we put the horse.' It was a little old-fashioned pub for the boatmen, we were having a drink when someone said 'They're over again, the sirens have gone.'

At the little house in Kensington Road, Earlsdon, where the new Mayor lived, his elder daughter, Lucy, had arrived home earlier than usual and 'was able to have tea in peace', before taking part in the usual evening routine.

Washing-up done, we lifted down, as usual, the two birds in their cages. Joey, the canary in the living-room, was placed on the table nearest to an inside wall, and Billy, the budgie, similarly in the kitchen. Both were covered up for the night and we settled down as we so often did. Someone remarked, 'There's a huge, really horrible "bomber's moon" tonight.' It really was unnaturally light outside; hardly ever before or since have I seen such a brilliant November night. As the sirens sounded dad said, 'Crikey, they're early tonight', and we grumbled as we collected our things.

For Colonel Lawrence, in charge of Coventry's anti-aircraft defences, it had been a busy morning. By prior arrangement he had paid a visit to the Council House to meet the newly elected Mayor and the Town Clerk, who, Colonel Lawrence decided, 'knew little about the situation . . . at the end of the interview they appeared satisfied that all was well'.

Only much later that day did Colonel Lawrence receive any indication that the coming night was to be different from any other. 'At 6.50 p.m. I left my office to go upstairs to the Mess,' he remembers. 'As I opened the door a signaller from the Gun Operation Room handed me a message. "Major raid expected on Coventry tonight." At 7.10 p.m. bombs were coming down in a big way.' Colonel Lawrence, forced to abandon his plan 'to go and talk things over with the police', went instead to the Gun Operation Room. He was not to leave it for nearly twelve hours.

The headquarters of No. 916 (Balloon) Squadron, RAF, at

Baginton, lay, unknown to its occupants, less than a mile from the point where the second, or Oder, German navigational beam, crossed the Weser approach beam. The squadron commander later described the scene at about the same time:

In the Barrage Control Office officers and men watched the plotting table with not a little anxiety for a constant stream of enemy planes were plotted as heading for Coventry. The warning was received at 19.11 hours. In spite of the weather risk, the Barrage Commander ordered that the balloons should be flown at staggered operational height. . . . The first balloon inflated was reported at 19.27 hours. This was quickly followed up by similar reports as each site raised its balloon.

Signals to Baginton were also relayed via No. 18 Operational Training Unit, RAF, at Bramcote, six miles away. The airman who was duty driver at Bramcote that night, Rex Fray, still vividly remembers delivering the signal 'Raise balloons to 12000 feet' for by the time he had returned to Bramcote to await further orders the enemy bombers seemed to be flying 'over Bramcote in formation and we could actually see the flame from their exhausts'.

Only just ahead of them at 7.07 p.m. 'Air Raid Message Yellow', meaning 'Raiders approaching your area', had reached the ARP Control Room in the Council House, followed three minutes later by 'Air Raid Message Red', which meant the sounding of the sirens. Their eerie scream was still dying away, with its characteristic strangled wail, as the first bombs began to fall.

5
TONIGHT HE MEANS IT

'I said, "We have never been in one of these raids like this before." She said, "Yes, he means it tonight." '

Conversation in Coventry, 14 November 1940

THE unexpectedly early warning had taken everyone by surprise and so did what followed. Leonard Dacombe, patiently waiting at a red traffic light on his way to the Coventry Climax Works 'in a rectangle between Widdrington Road and the canal', pedalled off as soon as the green light appeared and had hardly reached the factory shelter when 'we were showered with incendiary bombs', as Kampfgruppe 100 scattered them over the city. Previously these had proved an easily quenched adversary – but not tonight. 'I well remember putting a bucket of sand on one, and as I turned away,' remembers Mr Dacombe, 'it exploded and I glanced back to see what looked like a Christmas tree of sparks cascading down.' Before long, work abandoned for the night, the small night shift were fully occupied fighting the fires raging in and around the works.

The Rev. W. B. Sells's fire-watching party near St Thomas's Church in The Butts, whose attempts to put out a chimney fire had proved a fiasco, now coped manfully with a far greater challenge. 'Incendiaries were falling with a smacking sound on the pavement all round us from the start and I remember shovelling up half a dozen in the vicarage grounds and putting them in water buckets even before the [H.E.] bombs began to fall.' But some of his party still had much to learn: 'one chap got badly burned when an incendiary which he had picked up in his hands exploded in his face.'

The siren caught Civil Defence Staff Officer Harold Tomley at the Central Division headquarters in the Old Rudge Works, puzzling over

the allocation, with particular regard to sizes and sexes, of 150 pairs of rubber boots and anti-gas suits just received for issue to the ten Posts....

When a few minutes after the warning, Eric Jordan, Head Warden of Post 105, rang up to say explosive incendiaries were being dropped, I decided to go out and see for myself. . . . We made our way along Spon Street and I soon saw what I was looking for. Just as we got to the bend in the street it dropped on the piece of vacant ground about twenty yards from us and I decided that incendiary bombs must no longer be treated with contempt, but with great caution. Continuing to the end of West Orchard we were confronted with the spectacle of . . . Owen Owen Ltd, no longer a store but a huge bonfire.

Already it was clear that Owen Owen was not going to be the only Coventry landmark to disappear that night, as Harold Tomley discovered on leaving the blazing store behind:

From there [we walked on] to the Market Square, just in time to see an incendiary drop on the pub known as The Hole in the Wall. A soldier in uniform joined us and we dashed into the pub and told the landlord, who said, 'We have just put one out', so I said, 'Well, this is another one.' We found it had got through to the billiard room so we formed a bucket chain and put that one out* . . . The Market Square communicated with Smithford Street, which was part of the medieval street which ran between the Spon Gate and Gosford Gate, and another fire awaited us immediately we passed through the short junction, a furniture shop blazing like a furnace, but the flames had not reached the large display windows so we smashed them and pulled the furniture into the street.

Mingled with the incendiaries and designed to force the firemen into shelter, and to break the water mains, were a few high-explosive bombs and it was these which caused the first casualties. Student Nurse Kathleen Colwill, who as the sirens sounded had, as already described, headed for the Emergency Operating Theatre of Gulson Road Hospital clutching her plate of baked beans on toast, soon found 'life too hectic' to remember her hunger. 'The next thing we knew blasts were rocking the hospital [and] the first casualties began to arrive [caught in the open] on their way home from the surrounding factories.'

Before long, apart from those whom duty kept there, few people were left on the streets. Among those whose intended evening out had already been ruined was Marjorie Whittaker, then a young, unmarried office worker.

*Mr Tomley adds: 'It was only a respite because next morning there were only a few bits of walls standing in the Market Square surrounds'.

I was taking some letters to the General Post Office . . . and then I was going to the pictures with a boy. We got as far as the Empire about seven when the sirens went and at the same time the bombs started dropping. So we decided to go home. We got as far as High Street and Anslow's [a large shop] when a warden ushered us into the shelter.

The evening also failed to develop as planned for the sixteen-year-old girl living in Hertford Square, previously quoted, who, her small sister's birthday party being over, hurried round to collect her friend Violet, her chosen companion for the evening.*

We were only as far as Crow Lane, outside the A R P headquarters, when we were yanked in, because bombs were already dropping. I can remember hundreds of gas-masks lying there in little boxes, and can still see the babies' big ugly masks which looked like something from space. Not being allowed to stay there we were taken across the road to the old Rudge shelter which consisted of two or three rooms. There were dozens of people in there. We could only squat. People were in there with babies, prams – I remember a black and white cat in a lady's arms. And Mrs Brown was there, as she was most nights, with her big basket of chips. She used to keep the fish and chip shop in Spon Street. Very often during a raid she would defy all and bring down those gorgeous smelling chips. . . . Those days I had to be home by 9.30 p.m. Mother must have worried about me that night, but no one would let us leave the shelter.

Soon after the raid began most buses stopped running as one Warwick man who worked as a millwright at a factory in Pool Meadow discovered when, as usual, he reached the adjoining bus station at 7.45. Never had the prospect of spending the night in Coventry seemed less attractive. He found that he was in luck for 'one driver said he was going home to Leamington and would go via Warwick. He told us to jump in, and shot away, with no lights on, but you could see so clearly by the flare lights we read the *Telegraph* on the bus.'

Another Midland Red driver, Mr E. R. Nicks, was meanwhile trying to get into Coventry, conscious of his 'full standing load', including an airman riding on the platform, and of the flares hanging threateningly in the sky only two miles ahead, at the end of their run from Birmingham. Hardly had the R A F man remarked, 'You're not frightened, are you?' when:

*Violet was destined to be killed in a later raid, when the Empire Cinema was bombed.

a bomb dropped a short way away and . . . on looking round I saw the
RAF fellow jump off and run the other way. . . . Turning into Corporation Street I saw in front of me one of our buses that was running late.
Just then a bomb dropped and . . . the bus in front was just lifted bodily
on to the pavement by the blast. . . . I went to see the driver, who was
shocked, but on looking round not a window was broken. I carried on to
Pool Meadow . . . pulled on to the Birmingham stand and as no one was
about I left the stand at 8.8 p.m. by the clock and proceeded to Birmingham.

The unexpected speed with which the raid developed trapped
many people where they were. One Special Constable on his way
from his home in Villiers Street, Ball Hill, to report at the Central
Police Station at 8 p.m. found himself turned back by a senior
officer in Far Gosford Street, 'who informed me that it would be
hopeless to attempt to go farther' and suggested that 'there would
be plenty to do before long' in his own district, a prediction that
proved only too accurate, for his own house, already damaged in
an earlier raid, was among those soon to be destroyed.

At about this time another constable was setting out from the
Central Police Station on a more adventurous journey. After a
pleasant afternoon, swimming at the City Baths, he had seen his
mother and sisters safely on their way to their night-time retreat at
Berkswell, turning back at Hearsall Common in order to report in
good time. Like his swim – the last for a long time as 'within a few
hours the Baths would be a heap of rubble' – it was to be the most
memorable of a lifetime:

By 7.15 p.m. the men who were usually up at the station in readiness for
the sirens to sound, had been lined up in the corridor. The first incident
to be reported to the Central Control [housed in the same building as the
Police Station] was a public shelter believed to have been hit in Warwick
Road and a number of people trapped. PC Bill Timms and I and two
Specials were sent out to this occurrence. When we stepped out of the
station, even after fifteen minutes, we could see it was going to be a heavy
raid. . . . The air was filled with the crash of guns, the whine of bombs
and the terrific flash and bang as they exploded. The sky seemed to be
full of planes.

We made our way along High Street and down Greyfriars Lane and
as we passed the Midland Bank we could see the roof was blazing furiously
and firemen were trying to get it under control. Before we reached
Warwick Road we must have dropped flat a dozen times and thought our

end was near. However, the report turned out to be false and we began our journey back to the station. We put several incendiaries out and as we passed Greyfriars Green a shower dropped here and we had our first experience of the explosive type. As we rushed in to extinguish one on the Green, it exploded, and blazing metal flew in all directions. A young AFS messenger and PC Timms were badly burned on the face and eyes. We took the messenger boy down Greyfriars Green shelter, rendered first aid and rang for the ambulance. . . . It took three-quarters of an hour to do about a mile, so heavy was the raid by this time.

These were not the last incendiaries to fall on Greyfriars Green that night. A little later, a Home Guard walking down Warwick Road was amazed to see that whole open space blossoming with what looked like 'a garden of Roman Candles'. A whole cluster of incendiaries, probably from a single 'Molotov breadbasket', had fallen on the Green and, by a curious chance, had landed vertically, standing upright on the grass like fireworks until, with three other men, he ran along them, stamping them out with his heavy boots. The men then adjourned to the one bar sure to be still open, at the Queen's Hotel in Hertford Street.

It had also already been a busy night for the members of the Observer Corps in their Report Centre beneath the General Post Office. Mr A. W. Staniland, after his usual busy day as a works chemist, had delivered his wife to friends in Meriden, and then come straight on duty.

Almost immediately after taking up our positions a constant stream of enemy aircraft was plotted, heading in the direction of Coventry, both on the 'long range' plotting table [covering] adjacent Regional Centres, and on our Midland No. 5 Group plotting table. Within minutes it appeared obvious that Coventry was going to be the target and warnings were issued immediately to Observer Corps headquarters, local authorities, large industrial concerns, etc. At about 19.30 hours the enemy began the attack by dropping incendiary bombs in large showers. . . . It didn't take us long to realize that this raid was going to be different from previous ones and far greater in intensity, the plotting tables showing wave after wave of incoming planes without a break and a corresponding chain of planes returning to their bases. All individual aircraft were plotted and the information simultaneously and incessantly transmitted by landline and teleprinter until approximately 20.30 hours when certain lines of communication broke down under the bombardment. This was followed immediately by the failure of the lighting service. Rather dim emergency lighting was brought into use. Unfortunately the fresh air ventilating arrangement also ceased to function, although we were not too sorry about this, because it had been feeding smoke from the burning building to us instead of fresh air. We were forced to open the door to get some air into the room and were immediately inconvenienced by the terrific noise of the bombardment.

Only two or three minutes' walk from the G P O was Mrs Megan Ryan, who, 'after a perfectly ordinary day' in her hairdressing business, had welcomed to supper one of the first guests – and as it turned out the last – to be entertained in the flat in Judges Court in which she had begun her married life only a few weeks before. Her husband was, for once, not on duty as a first-aider at the factory where he was an apprentice.

It was just an ordinary pleasant evening, until the siren went. . . . Just the usual nuisance raid. . . . But . . . within an hour we realized that this was something very different. It was our guest who decided we must go down to the shelter. I didn't think it was necessary because the ancient building – it had stood there for centuries – was so secure. After a few moments [in the shelter] I was thinking of my lovely warm flat with a great big fire . . . so I announced that I was going to go back upstairs and collect the paraffin heater, and an extra can of paraffin.

During this visit, Mrs Ryan was able to see how the raid had developed for she climbed up on to the wooden table-top, which covered the bath in the kitchen, to look out over the city. 'It was an absolutely wonderful sight,' she remembers, 'like the transformation scene in a pantomime. It was magical . . . the wonderful light and Cathedral spire shining in the light over the roofs, a marvellous sight, very exciting.'

But it was also clearly dangerous and, reluctantly, Mrs Ryan returned with the promised oil-stove to the shelter in the garden:

Before long it began to warm up and it was a great deal more comfortable. And then people began to come in, outsiders began to come in, people with trivial little wounds, someone had got a cut on his face, we had got a first-aid kit and I went and fetched that, and then it seemed sensible to get some tea and a kettle and before long we had quite a little Post going, we were serving to anyone who came in, we were coping with minor injuries . . . it was very comfortable and very pleasant down there in fact.

Spirits were not quite as high in the YWCA hostel in The Butts, as the resident who was then a young Civil Servant remembers:

We'd got out of the habit of rushing down to the cellar the moment the sirens sounded and many of us stayed upstairs, knitting and gossiping. On this occasion girls began to go down one by one, as it gradually dawned on us that this was a real raid and that more noise than usual was going on outside. By the time only five of us were left in the sitting room we were too frightened to go down to the cellar, for to reach it we had to go outside and having heard that 'under the stairs' was safer we huddled there. For the first time in my life I knew what it was like to shake with fear. . . . Presently there was a hammering at the front door – and we had to come out of our hidey-hole to open it to the air-raid warden, who'd come across to see that we were all safe. So we had to go out and down to shelter. It was less frightening there, and we joked and ate chocolate and even played silly games – anything to keep our minds from the awful things that might happen to us.

About a mile west of St Mary's Hall was the mayoral Anderson shelter in the garden of 39 Kensington Road, Earlsdon, of which Miss Lucy Moseley was one of the occupants.

Almost at once the city was ringed with parachute flares and activity began all around. Before long the constant drone of heavy bombers in waves, the noise of explosions, the banging of anti-aircraft guns and the tremors under our feet told us this was no ordinary raid. Joe Parker [their air-raid warden] slipped in for a cup of coffee. Dad had hardly said, 'Where tonight, Joe?' when the answer came, 'They're dropping the b—— things everywhere tonight, Jack.'

Everywhere any initial attempt to ignore the raid soon failed as its scale became apparent. One woman then aged thirteen and living in Glendower Avenue, Whoberley, remembers the argument which followed the sounding of the sirens, while she was doing her homework and her parents were listening to the radio. She detested going to the surface shelter on the corner

outside Mr and Mrs Higgs's grocery shop, because you just couldn't get any sleep at all. . . . No amount of pleading with my father would [persuade him to] allow us to stay at home as he felt there was 'something big on' by the sound of it . . . so we packed ourselves off with chairs, suitcases, torches and blankets. . . . There was no suggestion of going home for a sleep as there had been on other occasions. It was obvious that this was something bigger than we had ever experienced before. The sky began to glow. I remember thinking that it didn't seem possible that such a small town could burn for so long.

This was one night when most of those who had vowed they would never abandon their own beds for a public shelter finally relented. One of the last to take refuge that night was a soldier's wife, living alone at Bedworth, on the outskirts of Coventry, while working as a silk wrapper for Courtaulds in the Foleshill Road, whose practice was to stay in bed until the last possible minute and then seize her clothes and run downstairs, dressing as she went. 'On the night of the big raid' she remembers cutting it almost too fine: 'I fell to the ground eight times before I could get my knickers on.'

About three miles due north of the city centre those hard-working 'boaties', William Prue and his father, had been enjoying a quick drink at a pub near Longford Wharf until it was interrupted by 'the bumps and bangs' which followed the siren:

We all seemed to drift out. Not knowing where to go we went straight to the boat. As we were going along the canal towpath we could see red glows in the sky towards Coventry. We got to the boat and shut the doors to keep the firelight from showing. Dad said, 'I think we shall be all right here.' Anyway we sat there, didn't know whether to go and look at the horse or what to do. All of a sudden there was one blast and it blew the doors of the cabin open. Dad said, 'It's got us.' The boat was rocking as if it was on the sea, there were people shouting and running about, we looked out and everything seemed as if it was on fire. The sky was all one red glow. Someone in a uniform came to us and said: 'Come and get in a shelter.' He took us along to it and pushed us in. It was in an old railway arch. As we were strangers we did not know anyone. Some were crying, some were trying to sing to cheer everybody up. I said to myself, 'I don't feel like singing at a time like this.' One woman came up to us and said, 'Don't worry, love, it will soon be over.' I said, 'We have never been in one of these raids like this before.' She said, 'Yes, he means it tonight.'

6

THE GERMANS SEEM STRANGELY PERSISTENT

'Strangely persistent this raid tonight, Kenneth.'
Vicar of Holy Trinity church to his curate, c. 7.30 p.m.,
14 November 1940

THE first reports reaching the Control Centre below the Council House caused no particular alarm. News of the one novel feature, the use of explosive incendiaries, was passed to the headquarters of the Midlands Civil Defence Region at Birmingham and then on to London, where it reached the Ministry of Home Security War Room, the GHQ of the nation's Civil Defence services, at 19.50 hours.

HOME SECURITY FROM BIRMINGHAM
I.B.S. (SOME OF EXPLODING TYPE) DROPPED IN COVENTRY AT 1920.

The earliest indication that anything out of the ordinary was happening came in another signal forty-five minutes later:

REF. OUR 1945. COVENTRY REPORTS A LARGE NUMBER OF I.B.S. OVER A WIDE AREA. FIRES REPORTED AT ROVER CO., COURTAULDS LTD, FOLESHILL ROAD, NAVAL ORDNANCE STORE: STONEY STANTON ROAD, NAVAL ORDNANCE STORE, O'BRIEN'S WORKS FOLESHILL ROAD, LLOYDS AND MIDLAND BANK HIGH STREET, OWEN AND OWENS STORES, CENTRAL HOTEL: GPO ROOF AND WAREHOUSE AT FOLESHILL STATION. H.E. BOMBS REPORTED WITH PEOPLE TRAPPED.

Already at the Central Fire Station it had been noted that, instead of affecting only one area, 'there were fires in widely separated districts', and the number soon began to overwhelm the brigade's resources. By 8 p.m. 240 fires had already been plotted on the station map when the building was itself hit by a bomb and the keeping of detailed records ceased.

THE GERMANS SEEM STRANGELY PERSISTENT 85

Many other fires had not been reported at all, either because they had gone unnoticed or had been dealt with by ordinary citizens on the spot. The clergy of Coventry were already proving particularly doughty fire-bomb fighters – though the phrase had not yet been coined – and none more so than the Rev. G. W. Clitheroe, vicar of Holy Trinity, the original parish church of Coventry and proud possessor of one of the famous 'three spires'. From their post in the North Porch vestry Mr Clitheroe and his curate, the Rev. Kenneth Thornton, had already watched with astonishment, as Mr Clitheroe later wrote, while Owen Owen's store 'immediately in front of the West entrance of the church, took fire, for I knew it to be well guarded', and now, with horror, saw 'several direct hits by explosive bombs' on the blaze. Like others that night Mr Clitheroe was also struck by the grandeur of the spectacle all around him. 'The scene,' he later wrote, 'was one of dramatic intensity. The sound of the water pouring on the flames could sometimes be heard, together with the bursts of bombs, the swish of falling incendiaries and the fire of guns', prompting him to remark to his companion, 'Strangely persistent this raid tonight, Kenneth.'

Then their own ordeal began, with 'another storm of incendiaries and a call from Mr Thornton: "Here we are, Vicar, an incendiary on the Marler Chapel." We got to it with our stirrup pump', and though 'the roof was on fire and the incendiary had fallen through that fire was out in less than five minutes'. Looking out from the roof a little later, however, Mr Clitheroe and his companion realized how rapidly the situation was deteriorating.

Fires were blazing everywhere and H.E. was falling. . . . We observed to our dismay that incendiaries had fallen on the Cathedral . . . I knew they had a strong guard there . . . but the flames appeared to spread. . . . It was maddening to Mr Thornton and myself not to be able to lend our aid, but had we left Trinity that, too, would have gone, for about this time the Priests' Loft . . . was fired and had to be dealt with at once. On our return to the Nave after extinguishing the fire in the Loft, we saw that the City Library, which stood alongside the southern boundary wall was alight. Once again, dare we dash across? . . . But no. Down came an incendiary in the Archdeacon's court, and when this had been dealt with nothing on earth could have saved Coventry Library.

Many incendiaries went undiscovered when they landed and had an unpleasant habit of revealing themselves later, just when one felt one was winning one's battle:

On opening the North Vestry door I saw that the Belfry housing our grand old bells was on fire . . . an H.E. fell alongside the Belfry as we prepared to rush across. When the debris had cleared we dealt with the fire but only just in time: for some of the beams were well alight, though burning slowly as oak does until the heat is intense. On our return to the Vestry another H.E. fell immediately outside . . . smashing up the path we had crossed a few seconds earlier. . . . My colleague heaved a sigh of relief and repeated the remark which was usually his first on awakening in the North Porch. 'My! But it's a funny life!'

To the two clergymen the incendiaries now seemed to be arriving in 'an incessant downpour which fell with a swishing sound like heavy rain', interspersed with the thunder-claps of high explosive. 'The Germans,' Mr Clitheroe decided later, 'were using a large number of smallish fellows, of about one hundred pounds weight', the nearest, which they had so narrowly escaped, having 'only made a hole twenty feet across and perhaps ten or twelve feet deep'. Curiously the weight of the bombs dropped seemed to increase as one went up the ecclesiastical ladder, for the next morning he discovered a really 'impressive' crater in 'the Bishop's garden in Davenport Road'.

By now there was hardly a road or street in the centre of Coventry where a similar battle was not being waged. The wife of one ambulance driver, left to guard the family home in Brookland Avenue, Whoberley, remembers 'running out into the road to a little island in front of the house to put out incendiaries with, of all things, old wet rags'. Her choice of weapon was hardly more incongruous than the outfit worn by 'the young man next door, always immaculately dressed', who could be seen going into action in 'pepper and salt overcoat, dustbin lid in hand', with his head protected by 'a colander, which his new young wife had insisted he wear'. Another woman, married to an aero-engine fitter, and living in Lincroft Crescent, also about one and a half miles to the west, remembers how not long after the first wave of fire-bombs had been extinguished there came 'more incendiaries: the roof next door was alight. I fetched the stirrup pump and buckets of water but the harder I pumped the less amount of water seemed to come out. One brave

person went through the trap door to the roof . . . one good kick –
out came the incendiary, a little water did the rest.' (Next morning
six huge holes in the ceiling marked the intrepid fire-fighter's
progress.)

Also vigorously defending his property that night was a well-
known Coventry character, Mr J. B. Shelton, owner of a house
and stable-yard in Little Park Street, separated from Broadgate
only by the short stretch of the High Street. He was well known
for his dedicated interest in the city's history, which on this night
he played some part in shaping. The first shower of fire-bombs
reminded Mr Shelton of 'the story of an accident in Broadgate
when, at the coronation of George III in 1761, the entire [stock of]
fireworks were exploded by the sparks from a catherine wheel'.*
When 'within a short distance of the stable twenty or more . . . now
fell', he was not particularly alarmed, despite their 'terrific . . .
adder-like hissing', and soon put them out, only to find, when he
had time to look around him, that others elsewhere had not been so
efficiently dealt with.

When the flare of these fire-bombs died down we could see the glare of
burning houses, factories and sheds. The entry from my yard to the street
had two large doors which I had closed in order to keep flying sparks
from entering. I opened them and went into the street, finding the Old
Swift cycle factory, now a storehouse and printer's press, etc., well alight
and a fireman attaching his water pipes to the hydrant near my front door.
. . . As I returned to the stables high explosive bombs began to fall every half
minute or so and made the ground and sheds seem to leap in the air . . . .
Small fires became large ones until they joined and were a four or five acre
flame, and by 8.30 p.m. the flames were licking the property on my side
of the street. Suddenly my doors were flung open and someone . . . hurried a terrified horse into the yard with halter and bridle and closed the
doors again. Mr Shepherd and myself caught the terrified animal and took
it into the stable and looking back down the yard I saw both doors blazing
fiercely. An oil bomb had dropped in the middle of the street and the man
who led in the horse must have been killed by it.

When the bombing, after an hour and a half, showed no signs of
letting up those caught away from home faced the disagreeable

---

*To another man, living in the Holbrook district, the 'whistling sound' of the des-
cending incendiaries recalled the large 'Devil among the tailors' firework familiar
from pre-war bonfire nights.

decision of staying put where they were, perhaps till morning, or making a dash for it. Some had little choice; the wardens, having very successfully got everyone off the streets into shelter, were not letting them go again without at least an argument, but many people only now leaving work had a natural desire to get home if they could, and among those conscious of it was Mr E. A. Cox, caretaker at the Food Office in Hertford Street. Although only two hundred yards from Broadgate, the building was, thanks to its tall and thick sandbag walls, proof against anything except a direct hit. To Mr Cox it seemed that 'the bombs were coming down like hailstones.... The building shook like a jelly. . . . Every now and again it would give an extra shudder', as when a bomb wrecked the 'partly completed extension to the Open Market only twenty yards away from the rear of the office'. By 8.45, with 'things really hotting up' and his tour of duty over, Mr Cox made up his mind to venture out into the tumult outside.

I thought I would wait till 9 p.m. and then try and break the cycle record for the half mile, the distance from my house. . . . Getting my bike out I prepared to do the Balaclava bit. I raced along Warwick Row, turned right into Queens Road and . . . was passing the sports field along The Butts, flat out, when a terrific bang from over the wooden fence deafened me and I almost finished up on my face. They had got an AA battery there and they had just let off a big one. Two minutes later I arrived home and, after putting my bike into the lean-to shed at the rear, looked in the Anderson to find it empty. I guessed the family were in the large surface shelter almost opposite our house. Everybody seemed cheerful, patriotic songs were being sung, [but] some children were crying. . . . If the folks were singing to drown the noise of the guns and bombs they came a very bad second.

Although, inevitably, many incendiaries fell on residential property, the Germans, as those sheltering beneath them were only too well aware, were really aiming at the factories. Among those 'twenty feet below ground' at the GEC factory at Copsewood was the schoolboy son of the works engineer.

A stick of incendiaries was dropped on the road outside and in the grass above the shelters and some of the night shift took shovels and went and covered them with earth. I had a look out at that time to see if the house was all right and could see nothing amiss. However a few minutes later one of the night shift called down for my mother to tell her that smoke was coming out of the roof. I went straight away and into the house where we found that the bedroom was on fire and the top panel of the door was burning through. We ran the garden hose through to the hall but found that we had insufficient water pressure to give a jet. We then fetched a bath tub in from outside, bucketed water into it from the rain water butts and used a stirrup pump, but to little effect, as we then found that the other bedroom on the other side of the hall was also on fire. Fortunately a crew of the works fire brigade had been sent over to check on the effect of the incendiaries on that side of the factory and . . . quickly ran a fire hose into the hall and up into the loft. This quickly doused the fire but also brought down sizable chunks of the ceiling plaster in the hallway and both bedrooms. We found afterwards that . . . having started one fire in the loft over one bedroom, the charge had detonated and blown the remainder of the bomb over to the other side of the loft and started a second fire.

Another factory 'showered with incendiary bombs' was the Coventry Climax Works in Widdrington Road, where the early experiences of fire-watcher Leonard Dacombe have already been described. Hardly had he and his workmates coped with their first explosive incendiary, and a host of the conventional kind, when they found that 'one had got a hold in the wooden bins in the finished part works', this being finally put out by an enterprising man who smothered it 'with his overcoat'.

We went out into the yard to see what was going on and discovered that some of the houses in Widdrington Road were on fire. . . . On the other side of the works, across the canal, an A R P depot stores and a furniture warehouse were well alight. An A F S crew arrived with a small pump and proceeded to knock a wall down so that the suction hose could reach the canal water. . . . Eventually they got the water through the nozzle but the jet didn't reach over the canal. Our firemen laughed and said they would get into trouble for breaking the wall down and told them if they couldn't do better than that they had better clear off, which they immediately did. Our firemen then got their own pump and also used all the pumps in the test shop, as we made fire pumps at Coventry Climax.*

Also under heavy attack was the Armstrong Siddeley factory at Parkside, which lay barely two hundred yards south of the Council House. One metal worker confesses to 'silently saying a few

*The A F S men, however, had the last, somewhat grim, laugh, for some hours later the impressive row of brand-new appliances spluttered to a halt, the factory's petrol tanks having been drained dry.

prayers' as he and a hundred other fellow-members of the night shift waited in the shelter assigned to them, while news arrived of other shelters, housing different departments, being hit. Eventually it seemed their turn had come for 'the shelter was filled with smoke and dust' and he discovered 'brick dust in all my pockets'. Venturing outside he found that the full force of a land-mine had fallen upon the Home Guard observation post, which had been destroyed, leaving 'the guards badly injured'. They were brought into the shelter and there they had to stay 'as no one could get in or out of the works'.

One of the most famous companies in Coventry was Sir Alfred Herbert Ltd, whose Edgwick Works in Canal Road were about two and a half miles north of the city centre in a heavily built-up area. Among its 5000 employees was Richard Baxendale, who was in charge of the works' First Aid Post.

Just after 9 there was a terrific bang close to the works and our own fire station got a direct hit. This was a building designed with load-bearing walls and the roof just resting on the walls. A 500 lb bomb went straight through the roof, straight through the next floor and exploded on the ground. It blew the walls in and the roof came down solid and there were seven people in there. We were fortunate enough to get one of them out alive but it was hard work. It took a long while. We had to smash the roof in pieces. It was all reinforced concrete, we were using crowbars and everything to break it in pieces so we could get clean through them.*

The main Daimler factory, in Sandy Lane, due north of the city centre in the 'V' formed by the Radford and Foleshill Roads, and both its 'shadow factories', in Capmartin Road with 2500 employees, and Brown's Lane with 5300, also attracted the enemy bombers. 'Nothing but a miracle could have protected the whole of the Works', the company's historian considered, and assuredly no miracle occurred, for the main factory alone 'was struck by two land-mines, eight H.E. bombs and a small flood of incendiaries, which completely demolished the Boulton-Paul Shop, the Engine Test Department and the north end of the Foundry . . . . The Body Shop, the Aero Shop, No. 3 Shop, the Scout Shop and the Engineering Offices were all severely damaged.' The Luftwaffe also took their toll of No. 1 Shadow Factory, where two high-explosive bombs

*Similar experiences in other cities led, in May 1942, to the decision to combine Rescue Parties and First Aid Parties into a single Rescue Service, trained for both tasks.

'and several hundred incendiaries . . . caused severe damage to the Offices, the Canteen, the Toolroom, the Garage, the Stores and several bays of the Main Shop'. No. 2 Shadow Factory escaped a little more lightly, merely being hit by two land-mines, 'one of which came through the roof and landed in the Main Shop, causing extensive damage to the roof, glass and some of the machinery'. Whether the recreational facilities which Daimler provided for the employees were a legitimate target was perhaps debatable, but land-mines were in any case incapable of such nice distinctions and at the main factory one 'completely wrecked two of the tennis courts and put a third out of use for a long time', rounding off the task begun by the first ever bomb on the factory, back in August, which had blown a crater in the sports ground.

If factories were a legitimate target hospitals clearly were not, but from the air they often resembled a major industrial plant and their spacious roofs and balconies seemed to attract incendiaries. The Coventry and Warwickshire Hospital, occupying an extensive site in the angle between the Stoney Stanton Road and the Foleshill Road, in a partly industrial area, soon proved no exception. Just as in the factories, preparations had proceeded according to a well-established routine as soon as the sirens sounded. Dr Harry Winter, whose supper had been interrupted by the warning, observed as he set out 'to patrol the wards and corridors', that all the patients in the Maternity Ward, close to the dining-room, 'had been placed under their beds, with their mattresses over the top of them' and that 'nurses were wheeling other beds down from the top floors and lining them along the ground-floor corridors, away from flying glass'. Then he went up three flights of stairs and stepped out on the flat roof of the main building.

I could hardly believe my eyes. All round the hospital grounds glowed literally hundreds of incendiary bombs, like lights twinkling on a mammoth Christmas tree. Down below I could see the men of the hospital staff running from bomb to bomb, dousing them with buckets of sand. . . .

Half a dozen small fires had already started in the hospital buildings: flames were licking through the roof of the laundry and another blaze was going on the roof of the emergency storeroom next door to it. From the roof the hospital superintendent was shouting instructions to the hospital's auxiliary fire crew down below. As we watched, however, flames leapt out from the roof of the main storeroom.

I left them fighting the fires and went down to check up on the reception building where the casualties would arrive. Everyone was waiting, tensely, but the preparations had been completed smoothly. Voluntary stretcher bearers supplied by the St John Ambulance Corps had laid out wooden trestles ready for the stretchers. . . .

I had just about completed my inspection when the real fun started. First an incendiary fell on the roof of the nurses' home. Fortunately, a workman examining the roof the day before had put his foot through a rotten section and . . . a nurse passing along the top-floor corridor happened to look up and saw the incendiary perched on the edge of the hole. The fire was put out before it could get hold, but we decided to evacuate the building. Again we were lucky. No sooner had the last nurse left than a heavy explosive crashed into it and exploded on the thick concrete top floor. That was our first direct hit.

In Hill Street, barely two hundred yards to the west of Broadgate, stood Bond's Hospital, an ancient group of almshouses. That night it housed fifteen elderly men, in the care of the matron, who was assisted by a number of helpers living nearby, one of whom was accompanied by her six-year-old daughter, and another by her husband, the only active, able-bodied male on the premises. The matron recalls:

The old men sat in the smoke-room and played cards. The women and child sat under the stairs. The little cat took refuge with them. . . . An incendiary came down by the front door. Mr V. got the hose ready. We waited until the incendiary had exploded then put out the spreading flames. Very soon blast blew off the smoke-room shutters, but the windows held and . . . no one was injured. We could now see through the broken shutters that the gas holder in Hill Street was on fire, as also was the sweet factory in Bend Street and the garage in Holyhead Road.

The electric current failed. . . . The old men were now in the sandbagged room with the antique chairs and in the corridor by the smoke-room door. . . . The two women and the child were very upset but the child was brave and kept quiet if she could hear me answer and see a light from my torch. There were some very near explosions and chimney pots and glass fell. The blast swept through the house repeatedly. The hours passed slowly. When things got a little quieter, Mr V. fetched over some rum, everyone had some and felt a little warmer.

Right at the centre of the historic heart of Coventry was its chief architectural treasure, the Cathedral. Defending it that night was a four-man team, who had assembled, as usual, at seven o'clock, to find the 'Cathedral roof slippery and white' from frost and with the 'bright light of the full moon . . . reflected on the lead'. In charge was Provost Howard, who at fifty-six was already so well known in Coventry that his title had come to be used almost as a Christian name, though really close friends called him Dick. With Provost Howard were 'two young men in their early twenties' and 'an elderly skilled stonemason', who was 'familiar with every inch of the Cathedral', but at sixty-five was also distinctly old for fire-fighting. For nearly an hour this little group saw from their vantage point the 'horizon ringed with a huge semicircle of light'. Then their own ordeal began.

Towards eight o'clock the first incendiaries struck the Cathedral. One fell on the roof of the chancel towards the east end; another fell right through the floor beneath the pews at the head of the nave, near the lectern; another struck the roof of the south aisle, above the organ. . . . The bomb on the chancel was smothered with sand and thrown over the battlements. The bomb on the pews was large and took two full buckets of sand before it could be shovelled into a container. The bomb above the organ had done what we most feared – it had fallen through the lead and was blazing on the oak ceiling below. It took a long time to deal with. The lead was hacked open and sand poured through the hole, but the fire had spread out of reach. We stirrup-pumped many buckets of water before the fire ceased blazing. Another shower of incendiaries now fell penetrating the roofs of the Cappers' Chapel on the south side and the Smith's Chapel on the north side. These were ultimately subdued. . . . Then another shower of incendiaries fell, four of them appearing to strike the roof of the Girdlers' or Children's Chapel above its east end. From below a fire was seen blazing in the ceiling. Above on the roof smoke was pouring from three holes and a fire was blazing through. These were tackled by all four of us at once, but, with the failing of our supplies of sand, water and physical strength we were unable to make an impression; the fire gained ground and finally we had to give in.

The first warning that the Cathedral was threatened had been given 'by shouting from the battlements', when it was relayed to the police station. On duty as station sergeant that night was Sergeant, later Inspector, Walter Groom.

At a quarter past eight Special Constable Marshall came in. 'Sergeant,' he says, 'the Cathedral's on fire' . . . I was at the desk so I made my air-raid message pad out, picked up the direct line to the fire station, which was on one of the old 'candlestick and snuffer' telephones. . . . The fire station answered straight away.

'Yes, police?'

'Fire at the Cathedral.'

'Right', and then down went the phone. Off went Marshall – I told
him, 'It's been reported, let them know.' A quarter of an hour later he was
back again. 'Sergeant, can you say when they're going to send the fire
brigade up to the Cathedral? The fire's spreading in the roof.' So I rang
the fire station again and spoke to the officer in charge there. 'All our
appliances are out,' he said, and of course that meant the Cathedral was
doomed.

Around 9.30 an appliance did reach the burning building from
Solihull, one of the scores now clanging their way into Coventry
from all over the Midlands, to Provost Howard's immense relief.

Length after length of hose was hauled up the ladder outside the north
door, to the roof. At last a jet of water played upon the fire, which was
raging over a large area of the roof and among the pews below. But,
before it could do much good, the water ceased to run. Another series of
hose lengths was run out to the hydrant by the corner of Priory Row and
Priory Street, but still no water came. . . . The main had been shattered. . . .
At about 10.30 p.m. the water came on again from another hydrant and a
hose was brought up the spiral staircase to the vestries and carried through
the sanctuary door. For a while the water was played upon the Lady
Chapel, but the pressure was low and it soon gave out. . . . The firemen
now left the Cathedral for the last time. . . . We realized with intense
consternation and horror . . . that nothing more could be done.

While they had waited for help to arrive Provost Howard and
his little group had salvaged what treasures they could.

We got out the altar cross and candlesticks . . . from the Smith's Chapel. . . .
It was impossible to rescue from the Children's Chapel the beautiful
wooden cross, with a carved figure of a child kneeling before it.

Next we went to the Sanctuary and vestries to rescue the valuable
ornaments and vessels there; the cross and candlesticks from the high
altar; . . . a silver paten and chalice; a silver wafer box and . . . a wooden
crucifix. . . . Finally we saw the two colours of the 7th Battalion, the Royal
Warwickshire Regiment, hanging on the walls of the Sanctuary, where
they had been deposited for safe-keeping at a great service at the beginning of the war. I wrenched these down and placed them in the vestry . . . I
remained in the vestry long enough to carry out the Warwickshire
colours, the altar service books and the books of the Epistles and Gospels
to safety in the police station.

Sergeant Walter Green witnessed the scene which followed:

A solemn little procession came into the police station. It was [led by] the Reverend Howard, Provost, bearing the flag of the Warwickshire Regiment, and there was another flag being borne in, the Union Jack. In followed Supt. Brennan, Inspector Pendleton and one or two more with pieces of silver which they'd rescued from the Cathedral. The party went through the charge office and down to the CID office in the sub-basement of the Council House. Now, I've trooped the colour on the Horse Guards parade when I was in the Army but never were colours carried more reverently than they were on that occasion when they were carried through from the Cathedral and placed in the safe custody of the police station that night.

News of the loss of the Cathedral spread through the Control Centre, in the basement of the building, as one of their precious hurricane lamps was borrowed to light these treasures, all that survived the destruction of a building which had been a centre of Christian worship for six hundred years, into their new home. Then, their duty done, Provost Howard and his helpers watched helplessly as the building they had striven for so many weary months and so many frenziedly long hours to protect was totally destroyed.

It was now eleven. From then until 1.30 a.m. I was in the porch of the police station in St Mary's Street, along with a dozen of the Solihull Auxiliary Fire Service men. Here we could watch the gradual and terrible destruction of the Cathedral. High explosives were falling continually, but in the porch we were comparatively sheltered. At one point 1 clearly saw the pillar by the bishop's throne and noticed that it seemed to have shrunk at the bottom in the intense heat of the burning screen. . . . The steel girders, which had been encased within the principal beams across the nave, were twisted with the terrific heat and must have helped to bring the wall down. . . .

The whole interior was a seething mass of flame and piled up blazing beams and timbers, interpenetrated and surmounted with dense bronze-coloured smoke. Through this could be seen the concentrated blaze caused by the burning of the organ, famous back to the time when Handel played on it. . . . Burning masses of timber from the roof of the Mercers' Chapel filled the chapel itself and burst through the door into the vestry. The fire could be seen finding its way from vestry to vestry, till they were all ablaze. . . .

All night long the city burned and her Cathedral burned with her, emblem of the eternal truth that, when men suffer, God suffers with them.

7

LIKE A GIGANTIC SUNSET

*'As we got to the top of Meriden Hill it was as if a
gigantic sun had set.'*

Birmingham *AFS* man c. *10 p.m. 14 November 1940*

As the flames from the burning Coventry Cathedral roared skyward they added to the glare which was now spreading a crimson dome over the city, making its ordeal known for many miles around. To a man at Warwick, eleven miles away, it resembled 'a huge pot of molten metal'. Among those who also saw the telltale glow was the Minister of Home Security, who was spending the night at Himley Hall, the country seat of the Regional Commissioner, Lord Dudley, about thirty miles away. Also in the party was the Inspector General of Civil Defence, Wing-Commander (later Sir John) Hodsall, and the party were just sitting down to 'a champagne supper . . . when they heard the first waves of German planes bombing in the distance' and went outside 'to see flames already lighting the clear sky over Coventry'.

The King had been warned of the attack even before it began, for the radio beam pointing towards Coventry lay across Windsor Castle, which it had been feared might also be a target. The ancient building was unharmed, but, the King's biographer records, 'watchers on the battlements saw the enemy aircraft streaming overhead in full moonlight'.

Soon it was obvious over much of the Midlands that somewhere was, in the phrase of the time, 'getting it badly'. A Home Guard manning an observation post above the clock tower in the Council House at Birmingham, eighteen miles away, duly reported by telephone the 'halo of light in the south-east', which recalled to him the glow of 'a distant fun-fair'. In the blacked-out streets below a young Birmingham aircraft worker, enjoying a modest 'pub-crawl' with a friend, was 'about 8.15 . . . in the grill bar of the Waterloo . . . when a man dressed in overalls burst in, saying,

"Gi'e us a pint, missus. I've just come from near Coventry with me lorry, they ain't arf copping it."' Going outside again, the two young men watched, as one remembers:

the planes still coming and the whole northern and eastern sky . . . lurid with that weird flickering brightness, sinister red at the heart, white on the edges, almost like the display of the *aurora borealis* we had seen in 1938. I reached home, said to my mother, 'Come up to the front bedroom,' and when we got to the window I said, 'That's Coventry burning!'

Also in Birmingham that night was the Fleet Street journalist Hilde Marchant, who had been hearing that evening that 'the provinces thought London was being pampered and flattered' by the coverage given to the Blitz on the capital in the national press, in contrast to the minimal space devoted to the frequent, if lesser, attacks on the Midlands. 'We're fed up with hearing about it,' one local newspaperman told her bluntly. Gradually, as the noise from outside grew more and more intrusive, it became clear, however, that tonight it was not London's turn.

We sat in the hotel lounge drinking black coffee as the echoes of the bombardment swept through the lounge like a cold draught. At each fresh gust we shivered, for the cold sound was new to the provinces. The porter came in and said, reassuringly, 'Looks Coventry way.' A commercial traveller answered, 'Just my luck. Got an appointment there tomorrow.' . . . We talked for some hours and there was still that distant rumbling touching the door and windows. . . . We went out into the black streets and as we looked up into the flat, black sky we saw a shadow of light over Coventry. . . .
'You may be tired of hearing about Coventry after tonight,' I said to my friend.

The stream of aircraft droning across the sky, apparently without pause or interference, caused similar reactions for many miles around. In the village of Moulton in Northamptonshire, thirty miles east of Coventry, one teacher, on the staff of the South Hackney Central School evacuated to the village, remembers how 'from the time of the air-raid warning until the dawn All Clear the frightening drone of the bombers passing . . . kept almost all of us awake'. Only next morning did this woman, who had been 'playing badminton in the village hall' when the first bombers arrived, realize that she was 'still dressed in a short white frock, socks and plimsolls', definitely not recommended wear for an all-night shelter session in mid-November.

As the night wore on the distant spectacle grew even more impressive and frightening. Near Stratford-on-Avon, eighteen miles south of Coventry, one ARP worker stood and watched 'the flares burning in the sky' while 'the percussion of the explosions made our doors rattle'. A woman hospital helper at Sutton Coldfield, fifteen miles to the north-west of Coventry, had been engaged in the most peaceful of occupations, packing up 'combs, fountain pens, packs of cards, notepaper, jigsaw puzzles, books and socks' for her patients, until the noise outside drew her out on to the terrace in front of her house. Dominating all as she looked eastward, she remembers, was 'the tremendous glow in the sky' accompanied by 'the vibration of our guns and' – a more homely but more immediately dangerous sound – 'fragments of shell tinkling on to the roof and splashing into the rock-garden pool'.

One draughtsman at a factory in Rugby, twelve miles from Coventry, had, as usual, caught the 7.03 p.m. train home to Leamington. 'Having a compartment to myself I had already put all the lights out and let one blind up.' By 7.30 'looking out on the Coventry side of the train I saw what appeared to be a large fire' and there were 'bright white flashes across the horizon indicating that the guns were blazing away'. The scene which greeted his eyes as he walked home from Leamington station seemed by contrast almost unbearably peaceful. 'Passing over the bridge over the River Leam between the Pump Room Gardens and Victoria Park,' he remembers, 'I looked over the Gardens with the river reflecting the moonlight, the night air absolutely still with not a movement of any foliage', but once indoors he found himself 'listening to the planes . . . and the never ceasing noise which was rattling the windows practically every minute', accompanied every now and then by 'a tremendous crescendo of noise which appeared to shake the house and even the earth'.

Reluctantly this man decided he dare not switch on the nine o'clock news for fear it prevented himself and his wife from hearing an approaching bomb, though he had already 'worked out how long a bomb falling from around 10000 feet would take to fall and comparing it with the speed of sound' had decided that he would have 'a few seconds' to take cover. In fact he heard nothing worse than a distant 'swish' followed by a 'slight dull thud which didn't even shake the windows'. Others in Leamington were less lucky: six mis-aimed bombs fell across the town centre, killing seven people and disturbing the memorial to Queen Victoria outside the Town Hall, as an additional plaque was later to testify:

A GERMAN BOMB MOVED THIS STATUE ONE INCH ON ITS PLINTH ON 14TH NOVEMBER 1940

Although the attack was by the standards of the time remarkably well concentrated, a few bombs, and sometimes whole sticks, were dropped miles from their intended target. At Moulton, not even in the same county as Coventry, the teacher already quoted remembers how sometime after midnight one aircraft mysteriously mistook the peaceful village high street for Broadgate, Coventry, or the Foleshill Road, but only one house was hit, a bed being buried beneath a deluge of rubble. By good fortune the two small evacuee boys who had previously occupied it had been moved only a few hours before, due to their constant quarrelling with their foster parents' children – a clear example of lack of virtue being providentially rewarded.

One of the most unlucky places that night was Nuneaton, eight miles due north of Coventry, where one housewife remembers that the most cheerful person in their crowded shelter was undoubtedly 'a little girl of three. . . . Once when we heard a bomb, my husband said "Duck!" and we all crouched down and then, after we heard the explosion, the child said, "Let's do it again!"' Another Nuneaton woman, living with her parents and an unmarried aunt, remembers what happened after 'the planes had gone over in their droves and the gunfire was shaking the house'.

At 11.25 we heard this bomb screaming towards us, mother came running downstairs, with her document case under her arm, and we all made a dash for the glory hole. It turned out to be a land-mine in the next street. . . . My aunt, always a little on the hysterical side, ran down the street crying 'We've had a direct hit' and someone answered, 'Don't you believe it, lady, you would not be here now.' As soon as the All Clear sounded, we went to survey the damage. We did not have one window left in the house, and when we went upstairs we had no roof.

Although a misplaced bomb could fall anywhere, the nearer one got to Coventry the greater the overall danger and the more striking the evidence of the devastation being inflicted on the city. One woman, then aged seventeen and living in Meriden, six miles to the west, remembers how the 'beautiful silver light' of the early part of the evening rapidly gave way to 'a greasy and smoky atmosphere' with 'a fine ash dropping', until by morning 'large pieces of clocking-in cards from Courtaulds', sucked upwards by the heat and scattered over the countryside, were littering the 'fields, hedges and gardens'. Near Kenilworth, a farmer's wife remembers how 'the German planes came over incessantly [and] it was light enough to read a newspaper in the yard', though the farm animals reacted very differently to the noise and glare, for while 'the three horses were dashing about in the field very frightened, the cows were very little upset'. From her cottage window at the nearby village of Beusale another woman watched a shower of incendiaries descending, clearly by mistake, on a farmhouse, deciding 'they looked exactly like a big firework dropped in a hawthorn bush'.

Perhaps the most unfortunate place near Coventry was Lillington, about eight miles south of the city, where two land-mines descended on an open field close enough to the village street to do substantial damage and give everyone the fright of their lives. One woman then living in the village with her four children has particular reason to remember the incident.

We did not hear a bang at the time but the feeling was similar to being in a vacuum and . . . the chair on which one of my daughters was sitting just disintegrated. My brother-in-law, who lived on the opposite side of the road, came across and shouted to my husband, 'Is everybody all right? You have got b——— all left.' In spite of our distress we all had to laugh. I had that day been getting all my fruit ready to make Xmas puddings. Before going into our little shelter I left dishes of currants, raisins and sultanas, etc., on the kitchen table and on the window sill were all our ration books. None of these things nor any sign of them was ever seen again.

We were then taken to the basement of a chapel where the W V S were getting rugs, etc., ready for the possible advent of victims from the Coventry area. . . . The W V S served us with tea and bread and butter, and were most amused when our small daughter asked for marmalade.

Perhaps the most harrowing situation of all was to be safe oneself while knowing that one's loved ones were still in Coventry. One farmer who lived at Bishop's Itchington near Leamington remembers how that night the father of one of his evacuees had come to visit his son. The visitor's bedroom window faced the city and 'he was pacing back and forwards all night long'. At Stoneleigh Abbey, a girls' convent school only just outside the city, one teenage girl, whose parents had – to her great annoyance – sent her there for safety while themselves staying in Coventry remembers how 'the nuns spent the night praying in the chapel'.

The first calls for outside assistance had gone out from Coventry soon after the start of the raid, and Midland Region headquarters at Birmingham had responded by ordering local fire brigades to send pumps, or to have crews standing by, 'closing up' others further away to take their place, until by 8.25 as the Region's historian recorded, 'First, Second and Third Stage moves had been operated to the extent of 100 pumps', Manchester, for example, having 'arranged to send 25 pumps . . . to Stoke-on-Trent' while Stoke crews moved nearer Coventry. Five minutes later direct telephone communications with Coventry broke down and messages had to be relayed via Rugby. Even the incomplete information arriving made clear, however, that the fire service faced a major catastrophe. By 11.50 Birmingham knew that 'the fire position was serious and a grave shortage of water was being experienced. Mobile water carriers, hose lorries and heavy pumps were ordered into the city to relay water from static supplies', though Coventry's main reserve, in the canal, had already run to waste after a chance hit had breached the bank. 'From this time onwards,' admitted the official report, 'the position remained obscure and no details as to the fire situation were available although it was known to be serious.'

Among the hundred crews sent from within Midland Region itself (eighty came from other areas) was the one for which part-time AFS man John Bowles was the driver. With a full-time job by day and 'out every night for weeks on end' fighting fires around Birmingham he was hoping for a quiet night, but was soon disappointed.

About 10 p.m. the bells went. Dick [a fellow-member of the crew] came back: 'It's a long ride tonight, John, Coventry.' . . . That night it seemed hours. . . . We got to Meriden before we saw the glow. As we got to the top of Meriden Hill it was as if a gigantic sun had set. From one side of the horizon to the other was one big glow. My foot half came away from the accelerator and momentarily we slowed down. And then my foot went down to the boards. As we approached Coventry at speed I noticed people waving us down. This I ignored as often on our way to a fire we had been stopped by someone whose garden shed was on fire.

But the nearer we got the more urgent the waves got. I eventually stopped behind another vehicle and was approached by a policeman. . . . He cried as he said, 'You may as well go back, mate, you can't get in.' We stayed until 2 a.m. and like others we then returned home. No one spoke and I think someone was sick. . . . That was our Coventry.

Also despatched to Coventry that night was rescue-worker Mr A. J. Bagshaw of Stratford-on-Avon, who since volunteering two years before 'had spent many hours training and practising . . . using heavy equipment, shoring up damaged houses and getting people out of badly damaged buildings'. Now at last came the call to action.

At 10 p.m. our man who was in charge called out, 'Right, you chaps, get off to Coventry.' We very soon connected up our heavy trailer, which was already loaded with heavy equipment, we all piled into the lorry and off we went. Before we reached Coventry I noticed huge bomb craters along the side of the road and I remember looking round the side of the lorry and seeing the flares hanging in the sky and the shells bursting and thinking to myself, 'We are going into it. I wonder if we shall come out of it all right.' Some little time before reaching Coventry we heard a huge bomb coming down and one of our lads immediately put his head under the tarpaulin which we were carrying at the back of the lorry. After the bomb had thudded down we pulled his leg and his answer to us was that he did not want it to have his head 'even if it had me here', and he patted his posterior.

Soon there were no more jokes.

We were first of all to report our arrival to the police station . . . very near the Cathedral, which was then a raging furnace. I remember hearing the drip, drip, drip of the molten lead. After reporting we were led to an incident where a land-mine had exploded and trapped people in a shelter. It seemed that the end of a house had come down on a shelter and completely demolished it and there seemed to be nothing but a huge pile of loose bricks. . . . We dared not use picks or shovels for fear of injuring someone, but had to pick up the bricks and throw them to one side with our bare hands. After a time we came to the occupants of the shelter. Some were quite cold and others were still warm, but they were all dead.

8

TOO BUSY TO BE AFRAID

'We had lost all notion of time.'
A F S man operating pump at Owen Owen's store,
midnight, 14 November 1940

LONG before the first reinforcements arrived from outside, everyone in Coventry had realized that the city was experiencing a raid on a scale hitherto undreamed of. Aircraftman Rex Fray, who two hours before had carried the first warning signal to Balloon Barrage headquarters at Baginton, saw instantly, when called on around 8.30 p.m. to deliver another message there, how rapidly the situation had deteriorated. It was only an hour and a quarter since the first bombs had been dropped but already 'Coventry appeared to be ablaze from end to end'. His experience on this journey proved strikingly different from the pleasant drive through bright moonlight along near-empty roads that he had enjoyed two hours before. Passing this time 'across the back of the city and by the Humber Works', he found himself 'obliged to "jump" with my car over dozens of hose-pipes across the road, as the "Humber" was on fire'. Conscious that he was bearing an urgent operational message, he managed nonetheless to speed up to 65 m.p.h., and up to 85 or 90 m.p.h. on the final stretch along the London Road to Baginton, only to have a discouraging reception. The message, he learned, was belatedly informing the officer concerned that a major attack was expected that night, its recipient remarking angrily, 'What a f—— waste of time, telling us something we all know.'

Already the police were trying to prevent people entering the city and on this and later journeys Mr Fray found himself repeatedly 'stopped by a policeman flashing a red light', though he was invariably told, 'Carry on, RAF', once he had identified himself. At last, however, his patience wore thin.

I had been issued with a Smith and Wesson .38 calibre revolver so, after the sixth time of being stopped, when I again saw the red light – I had been doing 95 to 100 m.p.h. – I pulled out the revolver, pulled up in front of the copper and simply said, 'Yes?' to which he replied, at panic stations: 'OK, Air Force, OK, OK, OK.' So I said, 'I'll flash my light the next time so get out of my way. I'm in a bloody hurry.' Needless to say I wasn't stopped again.

People who had been involved in coping with the first shower of incendiaries had often by now managed a brief rest, like the Rev. W. B. Sells, who had paid a short visit to the cellar of St Thomas's Vicarage in The Butts.

When I came up again, it was as light as day, from the fires and explosions. Where the bombs were falling we had no idea. We were all being blown about by blast as though we were in a tornado. A barrage balloon was down on some houses opposite, bobbing about like a huge elephant. Fires were all round us, and there was a huge blaze up on the hill where the Cathedral was. The smell of smoke and ceiling plaster was stifling. We could not begin to tackle the fires around us, except for an incendiary or two which had lodged in the vicarage, church and church hall roofs which we were able to dislodge and quench. Fire engines and ambulances were screaming past. People were streaming out of the courts and alleys in The Butts, panic-stricken, and it was obvious that that terribly crowded district was suffering but we had no time to go and help them.

Meanwhile the staff of the Coventry and Warwickshire Hospital were facing their second major threat that night, as Dr Harry Winter recorded:

About 8.30 another shower of incendiaries started fires on top of the Men's Medical Ward, the Women's Medical Ward, and the Eye Ward. With the other surgeons, the orderlies, and nurses, and even some of the able male patients, I ran across the open space between the main building and these wards and began transferring the patients. The nurses wheeled the beds outside while the rest of us hoisted patients on our shoulders and carried them pick-a-back across to the main hall. As I reached the door of the main building with the last patient on my back a bomb screamed down and plunged into the Men's Ward. I saw the whole wall of the building fall slowly outward and crash across the open ground where we'd been a few seconds before.

We put the patients on stretchers and blankets along the main floor corridors, which were already so crowded that I had to tread carefully to get from one end of the hospital to the other. Then the casualties started to come in from outside.

We had made elaborate preparations about classifying the patients as they came in, but they began to arrive so fast that we didn't have time for detailed examinations. All we could do was to divide them roughly into resuscitation cases and those requiring immediate surgery. The resuscitation patients were whisked into beds and given electric blankets and oxygen to help them recover from the shock of their wounds. The immediate surgery cases were divided among the three theatres. I suppose I did about fifteen operations throughout the night. . . . The other theatres handled about forty. . . .

We couldn't work very rapidly. The majority of cases were of lacerations or injuries to limbs. The complication with bomb lacerations, however, is that you get a small wound on the surface but extensive disruption underneath. Everything is pulped together. It's no use fixing the surface wound without doing a major cutting job on the inside. . . .

Every few minutes the theatre shook with the thud of a nearby bomb. About midnight the electric power went off but I continued with the operation I was on by the light from two small bulbs run by our own emergency lighting system. Every few minutes the nurses and the anaesthetist threw themselves under the operating table as the bombs roared down. I didn't like to follow them, but every time one whistled uncomfortably close I instinctively pulled the knife away and ducked sideways. . . .

Up on the top floor of the Gynaecological Ward we had fifteen women whom we couldn't move. They stayed in their beds through it all without a complaint, although a bomb that smashed the staff quarters next door covered them with glass from their windows and plaster from the ceiling. In another wing we had to leave a dozen fracture cases. All night long they lay on their backs, unable to move, hung up on their frames, and watched the Jerry planes cruising about the firelit sky through a huge hole that had been blown out of the wall of their ward.

The only word of complaint came from a wounded German airman, who'd been in the hospital for a few days. He was on the top floor of the main building, and when the orderlies finally went to him they found him cringing in bed and muttering in English, 'Too much bomb – too long! Too much bomb!'

One fourteen-year-old girl had a patient's-eye view of what was happening.

The sirens went . . . the nurses came and brought us all a drink and said everything was all right. They hadn't been gone very long when we heard the whistle of bombs. The old lady [in the next bed] said, 'Not to worry, put your head under the bedclothes.' Just then all the shutters at the windows blew down and we could see the sky outside which was like daylight. . . . The roof was on fire. The plaster and everything was falling. After that the night seemed endless. Porters, ambulance men and ARP wardens came and moved our beds with us in them into a corridor. . . When we came out the end of the corridor was gone and we had to be moved again, downstairs this time. After a time one of the ARP wardens brought us all a bowl to put over our heads as there was no other protection for us. . . . The nurses came in to see if we were all right and Mrs J. said to her: 'Put that little girl in my bed. If we are going to die we will die together.'

A then student nurse at the Gulson Road Hospital remembers how it, too, felt the developing effects of the raid.

The gun on top of the factory roof [nearby] was soon booming away. The beds began to fill up quickly. The operating theatres began their tasks. Sometimes we would have to clear away thick dirt before seeing the patient: they seemed to have been dug out of the ground. . . . We were using emergency supplies and hurricane lamps. The casualties then became a never-ending stream. . . . We were conscious of the very heavy bombing that was going on around us but . . . most of the nurses felt secure hearing the gun on the factory roof. At one time two floors of the factory were on fire, but the men manning the gun never moved. We heard later that they had promised to protect 'their nurses' at all costs. . . .

Everyone was working as a member of a team. . . . Even the consultants, who were normally treated like little gods and who to us poor nurses never seemed to be in the best of moods, became human. During the course of my training I had always the fear of being left with the limb of a patient in my hand after amputation and had so far managed to be off-duty when amputations were taking place. The blitz on Coventry changed all that for me. I didn't have time to be squeamish. . . .

Thousands of patients passed through the hospital during the night. If a patient died, he was just taken out of the bed and it was remade to take the next person. . . .

The kitchens had been put out of action so a big copper had been set up in the grounds and was like a witches' cauldron. I never have felt quite the same about stews since those days.

Apart from the injuries they caused, the high explosive bombs dropped on Coventry hampered the defences to an extent out of all proportion to their numbers, blocking roads, shattering mains, tearing apart telephone lines and power cables, so that in shelter after shelter the electricity failed, plunging the occupants into darkness, usually relieved within a few minutes by the faint and flickering light of hastily lit hurricane lamps or candles. For the ARP services the wrecking of the communications system was even more serious. 'Due to the total breakdown of communications, there was little to be done in the successive incidents that occurred,' admits one warden living in Moseley Avenue. 'We just hung about talking to one another.' These wardens did, however, have to cope with a bomb on a cinema – fortunately the audience were all in the shelter in the adjoining car park – and later with a parachute mine which totally destroyed two shops and two houses, killing seven people. The wardens recovered six bodies, but the seventh casualty, formerly living in a flat above one of the shops, was never found, though weeks later one of his feet came to light in a warden's garden.

Wardens with time on their hands still clung to the traditional rituals, and Mr E. A. Cox, the Food Office caretaker quoted earlier, recalls being 'told in no uncertain terms to put that b—— fag out', when he left his shelter to soothe his nerves with a cigarette, though 'the air was full of red hot cinders falling everywhere and the city a blazing inferno'.

Sergeant Walter Groom, on duty at the main police station, remembers 'telephones gradually going out of order, lights coming up on the screen that said, "That is out", "This is out", eventually most of them were out'. Soon everyone was relying on an older, more reliable, method of communication, the human messenger. 'We had messages coming in from the air-raid wardens, Special Constables and all sorts of people, which we recorded and sent down to the Control Room below,' remembers Mr Groom. These visits, in which the police 'put the message pads on the controllers' desk' provided an opportunity

to have a quick look at the map where pins were stuck in all over the place indicating that bombs had fallen. We had a number of hits on the police station. Things went thump, thump, thump outside, also the roof on the police station caught fire and there was a smell of burning wood and I began to wonder where we were going, because we hadn't anywhere to retreat to. But fortunately the fire party on the roof managed to quell the flames and that solved that problem.

In the Control Room the emergency lighting had been punc-
tiliously tested every night but when, around nine o'clock, it was
needed in earnest it lasted, one Special Constable (by day a draughtsman at the GEC works) remembers, 'for about ten minutes. We
rustled up a hurricane lamp while a policeman was sent out for
candles', the results adding a curiously bizarre touch to the scene,
for 'he eventually returned with some coloured, twisted fancy
candles' borrowed, as he put it, from a piano shop. The lack of
adequate illumination was 'not too serious, as before ten o'clock
only two phones out of eighteen were still working'. Going outside
for a moment this informant was struck by the contrast with the
gloom within, for the whole centre of the city around the Council
House was ablaze with light. Returning inside, much chastened, he
found among the senior ARP staff 'morale on a knife-edge. There
was that silence and disinclination to talk that can be seen amongst
miners working at the coal-face.'

One of those trying to impose order upon the growing
chaos outside was Dr Alan Ashworth, in charge of casualty
services.

As the high explosive and incendiaries fell on the city, I was sending out
ambulances and stretcher parties to deal with casualties. . . . [By] about
8 p.m. all out-going telephones were out of action, but, for about half an
hour, messages from the wardens were still being received. During this
period, we had messengers who were sent out to the First Aid Posts with
reports of incidents for their attention, but they were few in number
and . . . never returned to Control. At about 9.30 p.m. the incoming
telephones failed. The last message that I received stated that a land-mine
had fallen outside my house, but there was no report of casualties, so I
assumed that my family were safe in the air-raid shelter and unharmed.
From then onwards there was little one could do. Every so often, the
direct telephone line from Regional Control headquarters in Birmingham
was able to get through. It was very difficult, because of the general noise
and the crackling on the line, but mainly what they wanted to know was
how many casualties there were and how many dead. All I was able to
tell them was that both were very heavy.

Just over a mile due south of the Control Centre, in Leamington
Road, Dr Ashworth's wife, herself a doctor, was even harder
pressed. Earlier that evening she had taken her two small children
and fifteen-year-old maid, 'very frightened of air raids', into her

neighbours' brick and concrete shelter. Dr Eveleen Ashworth remembers:

At approximately 9 p.m. there was a shattering noise, a powerful blast and a land wave which rocked the shelter. The light went out. The door blew off and disappeared, also a curtain four feet inside it. . . . My seven-year-old said, 'That nearly blew my hair off'. The three-year-old said, 'It nearly blew my head off!'

Soon the shelter filled up, as her brother, a warden, brought in other people from the surrounding streets.

I put my two children in one bunk, so that one elderly lady could lie down and W. [the maid] shared her bunk with another lady. Two of them occupied the chairs. The other four of us stood or sat in turns on the floor. There was no room for all of us to sit. My brother then came a little later to tell me that all communications were cut, the roads in our area were full of holes and heaps of rubble – and I was the only doctor in the area.

So Dr Ashworth ventured out into the bomb-swept streets to tend the injured where they lay. The mains were broken but water was obtained from 'the rainwater tanks in people's houses'. There was no electricity, but 'the moonlight let us see where we were going'. In place of the normal medical supplies 'there were doors which had been blown off, for stretchers, plenty of wood for splints lying around and curtains to tie them on'. It was, however, im-possible to send the patients to hospital through the rubble-blocked streets so Dr Ashworth and her helpers 'made them as warm and comfortable as we could in the safest places we could find, such as unused air-raid shelters or under staircases'.

Most of the injured, however, were treated in the First Aid Posts, mainly staffed by part-time volunteers, and the large buildings (usually schools) they occupied seemed almost to attract bombs, four being damaged to some degree, two of them seriously. No. 3 Post at the Foleshill Baths was hit by blast from a mine, and lost two ambulances – fifteen of Coventry's total of forty were put out of action during the night – and a corporation bus, but when the lights failed the staff, largely young girls, 'carried on with hand torches'. The Post which saw most action, however, was No. 4, at Barkers Butts School, as its supervisor later described:

By 7.30 p.m. all eight ambulances were manned and five cars ready for calls. There were seven First Aid Party squads, a full staff of nurses and doctors. At 8.5 p.m. the first call was despatched and at 8.45 p.m. the telephone went out of action and a car was sent to Central Control, returning with a batch of orders. At 9.30 p.m. a land-mine nearby shattered the dressing station and all the lights went. Doctors and nurses then had to work in the corridors and other rooms by the aid of two emergency lights and hurricane lamps. Even the ambulance room was turned into a treatment room for minor casualties. At 10.5 p.m. all ambulances were out and the cars had begun to return with casualties. We worked at full pressure till nearly midnight. As soon as an ambulance reported in there was a fresh call waiting.

With the Post full of casualties those tending them now faced a new problem.

About eleven o'clock a D.A. [Delayed Action] bomb was reported almost opposite the gate of the Post and we had to decide how to evacuate nearly eighty casualties. The bus was bogged down in the yard and nothing would move it, but someone remembered two double deckers standing at the bottom of Barkers Butts Lane. Off went Bill the busman with a Home Guard who had attached himself to us and . . . back they came with the two, in went the casualties and off went the buses to Whoberley First Aid Post, piloted by Bill and followed by the Home Guard, who had never driven a bus before. . . . Five vehicles came in with punctures, two had to be parked and left as three wheels were flat and the others had their wheels changed alongside the D.A. bomb. These operations were just finished and a few drivers were standing in a sand-bagged entrance when the Post received a direct hit in the rest room, where only an hour earlier had been about a dozen injured people. No one was hurt, but . . . the Post was a sorry sight. Not a room was left undamaged, the main corridor was blocked and every ceiling was open to the sky.

One ambulance driver on duty at No. 4 FAP that night was the draughtsman living in Brookside Avenue, Whoberley, previously mentioned, who had resigned from the Home Guard to join the Ambulance Service. The raid had hardly started when he and his mate were ordered to transport two casualties in their converted van to Gulson Road Hospital. They found it surrounded by hose-pipes and in process of being evacuated, so they turned round and took their casualties back, over 'roads littered with bricks and plenty of telephone wire to wrap round the wheels'. Inevitably a tyre was punctured, and the crew 'parked the ambulance and started to

he morning after. Citizens of Coventry on their way to work shortly after the bombing

A street still littered with debris. Note the firemen in action in the background. This photograph was taken on Saturday, 16 November

The car in the crater. This picture was taken on Sunday, 17 November

ping down the ruins. Most banks escaped serious damage

ast journey. A burned-out bus in the city centre

A rescue team in action, searching the ruins

Fire fighters in action, on the Saturday after the raid

change the wheel' when 'halfway through a warden arrived to say, "You can't do that here. There's an unexploded bomb – just there"' – 'just there' being about ten yards away. 'We carried on,' this driver comments. 'We couldn't move without a wheel and what was one more bomb anyway?'

Like many others that night, he decided that the busier one was the better.

You were only concerned with your one little corner at the time and only conscious of things to deal with – badly injured patients, bricks and debris to negotiate, holes in roads, closed because of unexploded bombs, falling, blazing premises, etc. . . . . You did what had to be done and if Jerry caught up with you – too bad.

Although at least a few bombs had fallen in almost every part of Coventry and some had been jettisoned, or dropped by mistake, over a wide area within seven or eight miles of the city, it had rapidly become clear that the attack was concentrated within a radius of roughly a mile from Broadgate, the 'Piccadilly Circus' of Coventry, and especially on the narrow, largely medieval streets around the Cathedral, in a rectangle roughly three-quarters of a mile long by half a mile wide.

Close to the very centre of the target bullseye was Little Park Street, where Mr J. B. Shelton, struggling to defend his little community of people and horses, realized around nine o'clock that things were steadily getting worse.

By now flames were everywhere. I went hurriedly to my back door and opened it, only to find that the flames met me. There was no hope of saving anything. I had a tank of three hundred gallons of water, but this I had stored in case the hay shed and stables fired. Opposite my house were stored many gallons of varnish and turpentine used in repair work. This now fired and on the west side everything was burning. Cardboard and plywood floated on the wind and drifted like snowflakes, some pieces as large as the top of a water bucket. . . . Many fell on the stable roofs, but happily the slates were sound. On the north side I found there were thirty or more houses and shops burning with fury and that the fire was advancing towards my corn store; and on the south side two houses were ablaze and a government meat store which joined the wall of my house and contained three hundred tons of meat. . . . The fat caused a big blaze which seemed to reach the sky and so lit the place that it was brighter than daylight. The only pleasing feature was the lovely smell of roasting joints. On the east side a garage, on which incendiaries had fallen, was well alight, with flames from petrol reaching the top of a sixty-foot ash tree standing near. This heat spread to another factory adjoining the other side and the flames ran along my wooden garden fence, which had to be pulled down and the blaze checked with soil. This gap . . . enabled fifty people, who had no other escape, to reach a shelter. They streamed across carrying dogs, cats, canaries, fowl, etc., and the other fence on the opposite side of my garden had to be removed to let them through to St John Street.

Now, after his heroic fight to save them, Mr Shelton was to see the accumulated possessions of a lifetime destroyed in a few minutes.

At last the flames broke through into Mr Shepherd's house and a cupboard and a piano caught fire. We carried a few buckets of water and checked the fire downstairs, but in the roof the flames spread and with care of the horses coming first no more water could be spared and we had to watch the flames burning through his house towards my office and library. When I could spare a moment I rushed into the office and at risk from falling timbers and bricks brought out about forty books and dropped them into two iron washtubs. Turning these upside down I hoped the books would be saved. With sadness I had to leave deeds, photographs, paintings, papers and at least five hundred books in their cupboard to be devoured by the flames. As my house burnt down the fire from surrounding places got worse. The sparks were now much larger and fell more thickly and they dried the ground we were continually damping and burnt holes in our clothing as we walked about; and all the time high explosives kept falling and we would lie on the ground to evade the blast. Towards 11.30 p.m. we saw that it was quite hopeless to save any of the haysheds, cornsheds and stables intact. As I looked up into the hayshed a large piece of blazing plywood came sideways through a crack in the boards and set alight the already overheated trusses. I called to Mr Shepherd, 'Water – hayshed – quick!' and ran up the ladder into the loft, throwing down the trusses not on fire. The tank was opposite the shed, water was soon handed to me, and the immediate danger was over. Meanwhile . . . the flames devouring my library were more fierce than ever and around 1 a.m. my library, office and the dividing wall crashed in, making two large holes in my corn shed which was on the ground floor beneath the hayshed. The terrific heat set alight my three tons of oats, but by sprinkling a few buckets of precious water over the oats we saved the adjoining stables, although unfortunately the heat soon renewed the danger to them.

Most people not in shelter were during this second stage of the raid fully engrossed in similar private struggles, but one of the few men out and about in Coventry that night with a roving commission was Harold Tomley, the Civil Defence Staff Officer of the Central Division, studying his area's problems on the ground. After helping to drag the contents from a blazing shop in Smithford Street, about three hundred yards from Broadgate, as already described, he continued, with his faithful young messenger still in attendance, the strangest tour ever made through the ancient centre of this historic city.

The soldier left us and we continued down Smithford Street, but when we reached the junction with Hill Street high explosive bombs started to drop all around us, and a policeman called to us and said, 'You had better come in here for a bit', so [we went] into the police box at the corner of Holyhead Road where we spent the next ten minutes. . . . The box swayed about with the blast and we expected it to topple over every second but it stayed upright and as soon as I thought it safe we continued our journey. . . . I left the brave young messenger at the large public shelter in Spon Street, turned into Crow Lane and . . . the office. The warden said . . . he had been unable to make contact with any of the Wardens' Posts so I started to pack away my books and papers . . . and one of the phones rang just as I was going to try the Posts myself. It was the manager of the Gaumont Cinema, who was also Head Warden of Post 109. In a shocked voice he told of a bomb which had fallen at the rear of the cinema screen, the blast having passed over the audience and smashed all the glass screen between the auditorium and the foyer, which happened to be full of people having a chat and a smoke. He had some pretty horrible casualties and was unable to make telephone contact with Control Centre or Hospital, could I help?
The phones did not produce anything so I made my way through the completely deserted streets, skirting the bomb craters and picking my way through the debris, to the First Aid Post in King Street.

The first call for a rescue party had come within minutes of the start of the raid. The rescue men were mainly professionals, recruited from the building trades, and called in to tackle the most difficult cases, where it might take not hours but days to locate a missing person. Most of the people trapped that night were dragged out within a few minutes by people on the spot, often firemen or wardens, but sometimes ordinary civilians.
The then Miss Moseley remembers her father offering to go and

help when he heard that an old lady 'was trapped by fallen ceiling beams' in the house opposite their own in Kensington Road, Earlsdon, only to be told, 'There's plenty of us, it's your big saw we want.' Soon, with its help their neighbour was freed, and 'tucked up' in bed in a relative's home.

Rescue work was often, however, even more heartbreaking than other ARP activities. Senior Warden Les Coleman, based on Post 403B close to his home in Dennis Road, Stoke, found that his most tragic task that night was 'trying to rescue a young child'. He and other wardens could 'hear crying in a demolished house' and gradually worked their way 'towards the crying', but 'eventually the cries faded away and we couldn't work in the dark any longer. The baby was found dead next day.'

If there was one section of the Civil Defence services which that night faced a more bitterly frustrating task than any other it was the firemen. Mr George Kyrke had, he remembers, been still at his office when the sirens sounded – he was trying to keep his accountancy practice together – and had hardly reported to the Central Fire Station, to which he was attached as an AFS man, when he was ordered to take his crew to what was soon to become the second most famous fire in Coventry, at Owen Owen.

When we arrived the building was well alight. All doors were locked. An iron grille delayed action by us. By the time we gained entry we realized that it was impossible to save the place from the inside so we played on the fire from a hydrant outside. . . . We had lost all notion of time [but] it must have been about midnight when we saw an object which appeared to be attached to a parachute falling in our direction. Four of my crew ran for shelter into Millets Stores' doorway, so Charles S., my deputy, and I took over the hose and continued to damp down the raging fires. A terrific explosion threw us to the ground and when we recovered ourselves, very dazed but not seriously hurt, we found the rest of the crew had disappeared. Charles and I tore away bricks, stone and rubble and after what seemed an interminable time we managed to free one of the buried crew. He was still alive and asked for a cigarette but before we could light it, he died. We struggled with our pump but could not get it going; it was badly damaged. Then, climbing over the piles of rubble, we found a pump at the bottom of Cross Cheaping unmanned. Using the murky water of the River Sherbourne we managed to get the pump working, only to be foiled by leaking hose. There was nothing we could do so we decided to return to the Central Station – if it was still there.

It had also been a busy night for the industrial ARP services. The night driver at an aircraft works at Baginton remembers volunteering to drive a seven-man detachment, armed with picks and shovels, to the Armstrong Siddeley works at Parkside, to help dig out the victims of a direct hit on a shelter. 'It was getting very warm,' he admits, and the journey along the London Road, around 11 p.m., through 'rubble . . . glass, wood and brick dust' was also enlivened by falling bombs. Back at his base he was puzzled to find no trace of the elderly gatekeeper, but discovered him 'lying flat on the floor under a large bench with his hat and coat on'; he was finally coaxed out by the offer of a hot drink. The driver's adventures were not yet over, for, on his way home to Old Bilton around midnight he narrowly escaped, thanks to the moonlight, running into 'a balloon shot down right across the road at the bottom of Knight-low Hill'.

This was the time 'around 23.45 hours' at which, decided Mr A. W. Staniland, in the Observer Corps Plotting Centre 'the raid reached its height, the plotting table looked like a vast shuttle service of enemy aircraft, with no reports of any being brought down' – though those on duty comforted themselves with the thought that 'no doubt this was happening further afield'.

The dominant memory of those whom duty or choice took outside that night is of loneliness; it was possible to walk the length of a street and not see another soul. The ARP Controller of Courtaulds having reluctantly abandoned his vantage point on the factory clock tower and set off on the three-hundred-yard walk up the Foleshill Road to 'B' Division Police Station, remembers how 'on my short walk I had gone past houses either damaged or on fire, or both, and hadn't seen a soul'. He soon discovered that he might as well have stayed at the factory, for, with 'communications . . . non-existent. . . . the superintendent in charge decided that it was dangerous and useless to send out any more of the personnel and we were invited to occupy the cells which he considered to be relatively safe.' Here he 'fell asleep for several hours', one of the few people who managed to obtain any rest in Coventry that night.

9

JUST WAITING AND PRAYING FOR MORNING TO COME

*'We were all sitting huddled together, just waiting and
praying for morning to come.'*
Coventry woman, then aged ten, recalling the night of
14–15 November 1940

MOST Civil Defence workers were too busy to notice the passage
of time, but for people in the shelters the night seemed interminable.
Among them was the future Mrs Marjorie Whittaker, who had been
forced, as already described, to enter an underground shelter in the
High Street where the only seats were 'some forms and boxes'.

We'd been there about two hours when suddenly there was a terrific
bang and all the lights went out and we were in the dark. . . . So we just
sat there and waited and we could hear the screaming of the bombs. It was
just non-stop. . . . I got in the end that I wished a bomb would drop on
us because it was so terrible waiting and hearing the bombs. . . . We just
didn't feel we could take any more.

One family who lived near the Birmingham Road, a mile from
the centre, also found the raid surpassing their worst imaginings. 'It
was like a nightmare to us all and seemed never-ending. As the
bombs crashed down hour after hour it was like the end of the
world.'

The darkness in most shelters – in Marjorie Whittaker's the only
illumination came when 'somebody lit a cigarette' – occasionally
hid even greater horrors. One woman, then aged ten, remembers a
man squeezing silently in beside her family in the British Thomson-
Houston shelter in Ford Street, half a mile east of the Cathedral,
and it was only when 'morning came that we discovered his head
was covered in blood'. This shelter had been intended for works'
employees and their families, but, as the night wore on, more and
more ordinary citizens pushed their way in until 'we were all sitting
huddled together, just waiting and praying for morning to come . . .

The only consolation in my young mind was that I was with my parents and knew that they would protect me from harm.'

Another schoolgirl, three years older, remembers feeling a similar confidence until one of the groups of refugees passing the entrance to their brick surface shelter in Glendower Avenue, called out '"the Cathedral is on fire" so we came out to look at the glow. Then I *was* frightened and felt that this was something even my father couldn't protect me from.' Another child, aged ten, spending the night in a large underground shelter in Sovereign Place, off The Butts, found consolation in close physical contact with her mother and all night long 'snuggled in her fur coat. She used to stroke the inside of and all round my ear. This had a soothing, lulling effect. . . . Every time she stopped I asked her to start again.'

The Rev. W. B. Sells, also in The Butts that night, discovered 'out in the midst of it all in the street about half a dozen children of all ages up to about ten, cowering down on the street. They were from the slum area and had come out during the lull to look for their parents, who had obviously left them alone at home while they went out to the pub.' The children were 'absolutely terrified' until he escorted them to safety in 'the deep shelter in the Tech. grounds, where they spent the rest of the night'.

Not far away in the same street was the young Civil Servant at the YWCA hostel where, as previously described, she and other girls were forced by a warden to join the rest of the hostel's residents in the cellar. Here she found the raid 'less frightening. . . . We joked and ate chocolate and even played silly games', until 'at midnight a warden came to tell us our house was on fire'.

We picked up our precious cases [their 'emergency bags', kept packed for such an event] and filed out. No panic. Outside it was bright moonlight. The house was burning, there was a glow of other fires all around. Strangely I wasn't nearly so frightened then as I had been under the stairs. It was dramatic and unreal, but we were all in it together. For the time it took to cross the road to the technical college where we spent the rest of the night I was an onlooker seeing in a detached way some weird and wonderful theatrical scene and yet at the time I was at last *in* the war. This feeling didn't last and I admit that as I lay under a blanket on the floor of the corridor I was convinced I would die and resentful because I didn't want to. I prayed, but with no conviction, and thought of the King in *Hamlet*:

> My words fly up, my thoughts remain below:
> Words without thoughts never to heaven go.

I thought of my family and how sad they would be if I died. The bombs whistled down relentlessly, viciously, one came very close and fell in the road outside, but we were not hit and it seemed a miracle, but I had no hope that I would escape.

Many people who endured that night in Coventry now readily admit to having been afraid. 'We were terribly frightened,' says Marjorie Whittaker candidly of her uncomfortable hours in the dark below Anslow's. The then ARP Controller of Courtaulds admits that while watching the raid outside he had 'been more excited than frightened', but when, as described earlier, he set out to walk to the nearby police station, he began 'to experience real fear'. 'I wasn't exactly frightened,' Dr Harry Winter, busy operating at the Coventry and Warwickshire Hospital, has written, 'but the sound of a bomb whistling down from five or six thousand feet above you isn't a comfortable one. I *was* feeling pretty shaky.' Like everyone around him, however, he kept his private anxieties to himself. 'Throughout the packed hospital there was not one cry of fear, not a sign of panic. We didn't have a case of hysteria all night long.'

One woman then aged sixteen, remembers that 'morale was excellent' in her shelter near Crow Lane, and in spite of the frequent arrival of soldiers from the Drill Hall who 'told us of places that had been hit' the occupants still managed to sing 'We're going to get lit up when the lights go up in London', and, perhaps with even more feeling, 'When they sound the last All Clear'. A schoolgirl, three years younger, also felt that 'morale was high' among the civilians surrounding her 'until the soldiers from the smokescreen unit in Whoberley Avenue came in. . . . One of them was crying and very frightened; he was swearing and hysterical and one could feel the hysteria "catching on". My father shook him and told him to pull himself together as he would upset the women and children and eventually his pals took him off.'

Another man whose nerve gave way at the Central Police Station was dealt with even more firmly by that imperturbable police officer Sergeant Groom:

Sometime later in the night . . . a little man came into the charge office . . .

wearing one of those ridiculous type of steel helmets, rather like a cabbage leaf.* 'Sergeant,' he says, 'your men and the wardens are digging out some people who've been trapped and they want some cigarettes and some tea.' I was secretary of the police club at the time and I'd got plenty of cigarettes down below. Twenty Players and a box of Swan matches were handed over to the little warden. . . . . He'd been gone about five or ten minutes, I suppose, when suddenly he dashed into the office. He was like a gibbering lunatic. He said, 'They've all been killed, they've all been killed', and he threw the cigarettes and matches down on the desk. Now as far as I was concerned this sort of conduct in the police station didn't meet with my approval. You could burn down the Cathedral, you could ruin all the buildings round it, but the police station should be a little oasis of calm and quiet. I went round the corner and I said, 'What did you say?' and he was shouting and screaming his head off. I picked him up by his coat and shook him and smacked his face and said, 'Behave yourself. Don't carry on like this. What's happened?' and he said, 'I've just been in Dun Cow Yard and a bomb fell in front of me and it killed all the people who had been rescued. One of your officers has been killed and some of the others have been killed.' So I sent out one of my officers . . . and he confirmed the tragic story.

The reactions of animals were as varied as those of humans. Among the less heroic was undoubtedly Tony, the black and white Persian cat owned by a woman who worked at the Co-op, while her husband was in the RAF, and lived in Queen Isabel's Avenue, Cheylesmore. When the raid started she 'bent over him every time we heard the sound of bombs falling', but finally, distressed by his 'horrible frightening cries', put him outside. 'He slunk away with his stomach touching the ground [and] I spent the following hours worrying about him.' Tony, however, clearly one of nature's survivors, turned up next morning 'sitting in the garden washing his face' and 'lived to a ripe old age'. Chloe, a black kitten, belonging to a woman who worked in Rootes aircraft factory and living in Tennyson Road, Stoke, was made of sterner stuff. 'Looking out from the shelter,' her owner remembers, 'I noticed Chloe in the garden leaping in the air and patting at pieces of charred paper which were floating from the direction of the bombed houses.' Nor did that noisy night discourage Chloe from subsequent 'nocturnal rambles' on one of which she met 'a charming black

*i.e. the high-domed type with a chin strap issued to fire-watchers.

and white tom', an encounter commemorated by four delightful kittens.

Only the largest shelters were equipped with proper lavatories and the wardens were reluctant to allow the occupants to leave any others. A woman living in Daventry Road who ventured out to the bathroom was conscious of a 'rocking sensation' like 'walking along the corridor of a travelling train' and, when she reached her goal, found 'the water in the lavatory pan swaying'.

In one Anderson which by midnight was sheltering fifteen people the shelter door consisted of four separate pieces of timber and 'each had to be lifted before one could crawl out. . . . Each time we had arrived at the last door *bang* went another bomb and down came all the doors.' It was not until around 3 a.m. that all fifteen managed to get outside at last.

One fourteen-year-old who ignored the advice of the Special Constable in charge of his shelter in Villiers Street to 'use a garden or other open ground' rather than enter the nearby house, lived – though only just – to regret it. He had hardly left the shelter when a bomb came down on the nearby houses.

With the aid of wardens a search began for him. His house was on the edge of the crater, which was considerable, and the rear, including the toilet, was completely wrecked. We heard faint calls which we eventually traced as coming from beneath the water tank which had been on the roof of the outside toilet and was now precariously placed at the edge of the crater. After some very delicate manipulation we were able to lift the tank sufficiently to get him out, relatively unharmed.

The cat owner previously quoted, proud of her house's two toilets, 'one upstairs and one outside in the yard only a few yards from our shelter', found her neighbours and herself 'too frightened' to use either, until 'Mr S. very bravely dashed out to fetch a bucket which stood in the yard. We all turned our faces to the wall and whistled tunes when we had to use it.'

The traditional 'bedroom utensil', beloved of comedians (was there one during the war who did not make a joke at some time about 'Poland' or 'Jerry'?) was still common in many homes. One woman living in Coundon remembers how her husband fetched such an object for the use of her two young children but later, when he left the shelter to empty it, 'there was an extra big bang' and 'he returned with only the handle in his hand.'

Another universal desire was for that never-failing panacea, a cup of tea. One of the few shelters where this was achieved was that to which Mr E. A. Cox had returned after his epic dash home from his work at the Food Office. He seized the opportunity while in his house to fetch bedding for his children – who 'curled up on it and were soon fast asleep and slept through the lot' – and to make a hot drink by the moonlight coming through the unblacked-out back window. He was so 'sparing with the tea' that the resulting liquid was 'almost too weak to get out of the jug', but it 'was wet and hot and appreciated by the few people we were able to share it with'.

In the shelter below the canteen of the British Thomson-Houston factory in Ford Street enthusiasm for obtaining tea suddenly waned. Just as one man was going upstairs to obtain some 'there was a big explosion; a bomb had dropped directly on the canteen, wrecking it'. The young mother in Lincroft Crescent, quoted earlier, whose children were fast asleep on cough mixture, recalls as 'the most delicious drink of my life' the tea made by her husband on the dining-room fire, for 'the electric fire had long since gone' and 'there was no gas'. But if tea was essential saving possessions was not; her husband sternly refused to allow her to go back indoors to fetch one particularly cherished 'wedding present, a Westminster chiming clock'. Another man also managed not to go thirsty, for his basement contained his store of home-made wine. A friend, sheltering with him, remembers how as the pounding and shaking they had that night caused first one cork then another to 'pop' he cursed the bombers responsible, remarking that 'Jerry had now even got inside his bottles'.

Concern for something other than one's own immediate safety was a helpful distraction. The seventeen-year-old girl, mentioned earlier, who had taken shelter with her girl-friend and two young airmen for the evening, found that as time passed their boy-friends became worried at the consequences of not being back in camp by 23.59 hours, believing that 'the CO would not believe them and they would be on a charge in the morning'. Once resigned to staying where they were they became gallant companions, for 'it got very cold in the shelter and one of the boys gave me his greatcoat'. The fifteen occupants jammed into one Anderson, previously mentioned, were meanwhile passing the time, as one of them remembers, in nostalgic memories of 'days of plenty' and discussing 'what they would like for Christmas'.

Many people resorted in private to prayer. At Bond's Hospital, a monument to the piety of an earlier age, the matron found in her mind one particularly apt petition:

Visit, oh Lord, this house and drive far from it all the snares of the enemy. May thy holy angels dwell herein to preserve us in peace and may thy blessing rest upon us for evermore.

One normally devout churchgoer in Cheylesmore, however, found her faith ebbing away as the night wore on. 'I found myself cursing instead of praying,' she admits. 'My neighbours were very surprised.' A woman crouched beneath the dining-room table in a house in Daventry Road admired her husband's composure as he steadily read through the newspaper while eating 'a whole box of Cadbury's Milk Tray chocolates', explaining that '"I'll see the so and so's don't kill me before I've finished this lot."'

Most reports of the progress of the raid which reached people in shelters were garbled and misleading. Mr E. A. Cox in his shelter in Spon End remembers how 'every so often a warden would pop his head in and say, "Won't be long now, folks." I wonder where he got his information.' The occupants of the brick surface shelter on the corner of Glendower Avenue received progressively more alarming despatches from the frightened or bombed-out people who from eleven o'clock onwards flowed past it towards the safety of the countryside. 'As each group passed they reported the latest news,' one occupant remembers. 'Someone called out, "The Birmingham Road is blocked. Can't get into town" and later "The Cathedral is on fire."' This last, of course, was true, but not the grim postscript that reached one shelter that the bombs had struck while the choir was at practice and that its members had been wiped out. One of the occupants of the 'old Rudge shelter' in Crow Lane, then a sixteen-year-old, remembers how 'sometimes a warden would come down and say something like "Woolworths has gone" or "West Orchard has had it".'

In most domestic shelters there was little information of any kind and the occupants could only guess at the progress of the raid. One family, huddled into the shelter near St Luke's Church in the Holbrook district, were cheerfully told by other occupants, from a distant street, 'That's *your* house gone for a Burton', after one particularly loud explosion, but 'almost immediately, as if in reply we heard our clock in the kitchen chime the quarter hours'. A housewife who lived in Tennyson Road, Stoke, found herself trying to identify the source of the noises outside. High explosive bombs were easy to distinguish, for 'they brought down on us constant trickles of earth' and the accompanying shock waves 'felt like the approach of an underground train'. The clatter of incendiaries on the concrete surround to the house was by now familiar but a 'hissing noise' was more puzzling until she realized that it came from 'the nosecaps from the hot anti-aircraft shells as they fell in the rainwater tanks'. For one twelve-year-old boy, lying with his brother and sister on a makeshift bed in their coal-hole in Jenner Street, near the Coventry and Warwickshire Hospital, the successive stages of the raid were marked by the failure first of the electric light, then of the gas, and finally by a rush of soot down the chimney 'so that by candlelight one looked at everything through a haze', all accompanied by 'bangs, very loud crashes . . . whistles, shrieks and one noise that I'll never forget like someone dropping a very large tin bath', which he later decided must have been the collapse of the houses opposite. Mr Ken Pittaway, then Chief Electrical Engineer at Courtaulds, remembers how in the brick shelter he had built in his garden in Coundon 'the blast raised and slammed the heavy chequer plate door fixed at 45 degrees angle over the steps to the shelter. I jumped out of my skin each time.'

To one seventeen-year-old, quaking under the stairs of the family home in Stoke the bombs seemed to be 'landing as if being sowed like seeds, row upon row, each row coming closer', but she had time to notice her parents' very different reactions.

Poor mother, terrified, with all the clothes she could get on, several pairs of everything and silver and documents in bags in each hand, anxious to run, if anywhere to run to. Had to hold her back. First time she'd really given way, caused by uprush of air and ear-bursting explosion of anti-aircraft guns nearby. . . . Even dad was unable to sleep through it, as he'd done most nights before. One night a bomb had dropped rather close and woken him. 'Are those damn fools still at it?' he asked and went to sleep again.*

---

*'Dad's' confidence proved justified. He was destined to live for another twenty-three years and die at eighty-nine: 'a calm man with a clear conscience'.

The curious and capricious effects of blast constantly amazed those who observed them and Coventry that night provided many examples. The Holbrook family quoted earlier were not surprised to find the back door off its hinges but were puzzled as to how the front door managed to get up the stairs and right inside a bedroom, although not a pane of glass in their windows had been broken. At Lillington, outside Coventry, hit by two ill-aimed land-mines, the manager of one Coventry firm was astonished to find 'a door key shot out of a lock by the blast and straight through another door opposite', and 'heard of lots of instances where slivers of glass had penetrated wardrobes and doors'. In Cedars Avenue, Coundon, one housewife discovered with incredulity that though there was 'chaos all round' and the fragments of the broken back door had been blown into the front room 'eggs in a rack in the pantry were unbroken'.

Fire, too, had some unforeseen results. One family living in the Copsewood area found the last straw for their ragged nerves was when 'the fire burnt through the wires to the batteries in the loft and the whole time both front and back doorbells were ringing continuously'. In Wainbody Avenue, Green Lane, all the lights in an unoccupied, unblacked-out house suddenly sprang on, until one man from the house next door 'plucked up courage, ran over and managed to turn them off'.

But, however extraordinary the circumstances, law-abiding people found it hard to break the habits of a lifetime. One AFS man, on his way back from vainly attending the fire at Owen Owen, passed a wine shop in Hales Street with the front all smashed, helped himself to a bottle and 'broke the neck and drank part of the contents. . . . I realized that I had committed a very serious offence,' he admits, 'and replaced it in the shop.' The occupants of the shelter in the garden at Judges Court, Mrs Megan Ryan recalls, were longing for hot tea and 'we had only half a pint of milk', but outside the door of a neighbour's flat – she had left the city for the night – were two whole pints. 'I stood and looked at those two bottles of milk,' remembers Mrs Ryan, 'and decided that it would be all right as I could give her the money next day.'

The first great surprise of the night had been the exploding incendiaries. The second was the parachute mines (sometimes called land-mines), huge cylinders of explosive which drifted slowly to earth and exploded on impact. Like the 'doodlebugs' of four years later the blast they produced as they exploded spread damage over a wide area. To have one's house wrecked by one of these out-size monsters carried with it a strange kudos, so that in retrospect every modest-sized bomb tended to become a land-mine. But the reality, fifty, mainly on the central area, was bad enough, though a few failed to explode, producing one story which two 'Specials' in 'B' Division were never allowed to forget: sent to inspect an un-exploded land-mine lying in the street, they took shelter behind it when another bomb was heard whistling down. Many people, seeing parachutes drifting to earth in the moonlight, misinterpreted, understandably, their meaning, among them the young Geoffrey Green and his friends, enjoying a grandstand view of the raid from the organ loft of St Mary Magdalen in Hearsall Lane, Chapel Fields, known locally as 'the church with the blue roof', which was perched on a hill a mile east of Broadgate. 'Suddenly,' Mr Green remembers, 'in the light of the fires we began to see three parachutes drifting down. There were four of us . . . in our teens, and we cheered our heads off, because we thought they were German airmen who had been shot down'.

The same mistake, sometimes with tragic results, was made by other observers. At Lillington one man remembers a neighbour making for a descending parachute armed with an axe, only to realize his mistake halfway. One such incident gave rise to the rumour that certain individuals, variously described as Polish troops, airmen, Home Guards and WVS workers, had waited with outstretched arms to catch the supposed parachutist. The true facts were less sensational, though sad enough. A local woman warden and two Polish airmen, seeing a mine descending near Moseley Avenue, 'mistook it for a person', as another warden remembers, and ran to detain him. 'We found their bodies apparently unharmed,' this eyewitness remembers, 'but the blast had destroyed their lungs.'

A similar mistake was made by some residents of Three Spires Avenue, Coundon. One woman who was then aged sixteen and living at No. 21, remembers how her father returned from one sightseeing trip outside around nine o'clock, to report 'seeing a tablecloth-like thing draped over the tree in the street three doors away and a dark object lying in the road'. Prudently he left it alone,

but some neighbours 'decided to push "the object" out of the way....
It exploded and blew them to pieces.'* The explosion also wreaked
havoc in Three Spires Avenue and killed several people. But, near
miraculously, the family at No. 21 escaped with their lives —
though not their house.

We were protected by the dividing wall of the two houses and window
shutters. The blast blew a large hole in the wall between the two rooms,
all the bricks fell in the dining room. We heard no noise, we were all
suddenly covered in brick-dust and plaster. Shocked and agitated, we
all scrambled out of the house, all of us alive and without a scratch. At No.
19 they were all alive except for Mrs B. who had helped move the mine.
The shelter then was our only retreat. We spent the rest of the night
crouching together in inches of water.

One woman, cowering under the stairs of her house in Canley
Road, Earlsdon, remembers her husband, a Home Guard, running
in to report a parachute mine drifting their way, and a moment
later she heard the greatest noise of shattering glass of the whole
turbulent night: it had landed on some large greenhouses a hundred
yards away 'which had disappeared and left a hole big enough to
put a double decker bus in. . . . It seemed like half an hour before
the stuff stopped falling.' Another mine, ten minutes' walk away,
did even greater damage, leaving 'no trace that there had ever been
a house there', though the occupants, in the reinforced cellar, might
have survived had not the blast 'severed the water main' so that 'man,
wife and two children were all drowned'.

Another unforeseen feature of the raid was that many people found
themselves forced to move their place of shelter not once but twice
or even three times, as each successive refuge became untenable.
The daughter, then aged twelve, of one Jaguar car worker, living
in Ash Grove, a cul-de-sac off Stoney Stanton Road, which runs
north-west from the centre of the city, remembers what happened
while her ten-year-old sister and herself were crouching under the
stairs in their night-clothes, and the house received a direct hit at
the front and caught fire.

We managed to get through the door then into a brick surface shelter
outside the front gate. There we stayed for perhaps two hours while our

*The problem this incident posed for the Registrar of Deaths is described on page
227.

house was gutted by fire. . . . After a while the walls of the shelter became so hot from the burning buildings that we decided to move again to another shelter further along the cul-de-sac. During all this time we had not seen another living soul, as most of our neighbours were trekkers. . . . However, when we moved to another shelter further along, we found a family who lived higher up the 'Grove' and went into their shelter. I can't say that I was very scared, although I remember my mother wept as we watched our home burn. But to us as kids, it was quite an adventure.

Before long this shelter, too, became overheated, and they were forced to move again 'to a public shelter about two hundred yards away'.

I'll remember that run all the rest of my life. Although it was November the air that met us when we emerged from the shelter was hot and acrid. It was brilliant moonlight and with all the fires it was as bright as day and the sky was red, 'just like blood', I remember thinking, and then, suddenly I was deadly frightened. And so we ran, down that road, which reminded me vividly of a film I had seen, *The Last Days of Pompeii*, with the buildings on fire and dropping into the road as we ran. It seemed we ran miles until we got to the public shelter, which was crammed with people, who were packed further in to make room for us. Children were crying and screaming, women weeping, and everybody scared stiff. The air was so foul we could hardly breathe, but there we stayed until morning.

Churches, being solidly built, often with a cellar beneath, made popular shelters but more than one that night became uninhabitable. Those who had taken refuge beneath St Osburg's Church, about a mile and a quarter due west of the Cathedral, were driven from the church into the church hall, then, when that was damaged, 'fled to the church house' only to find it level with the ground and finally 'took refuge in the house cellar' until 'an unexploded bomb slid down the cellar steps so they were forced to abandon it'. The crypt of the Cathedral seemed at first to offer a measure of divine protection, as well as several feet of solid stone above one's head, and one mother who normally spent the night in the cellar of a relation's house, two minutes away, remembers that night that she installed herself and her three-year-old son there. Here, as the bombs came down, one man struck up a 'hymn' never heard in the consecrated precincts above, 'Ten Green Bottles'. Around 11 p.m. the impromptu concert was interrupted when the two members of the Cathedral fire guard decided to move the shelterers elsewhere. Outside, remembers the woman mentioned earlier, 'it was like daytime' from the fires, prompting her small son to remark, 'I don't like this sort of sunshine.'

Escorting people from one shelter to another was a common duty that night. One warden whom the sirens had caught still at work in his office in the city centre and who, being unable to get back to his outpost in Wright Street, volunteered to help locally, found himself ordered 'to get the people who were standing about not knowing where to go, down a shelter under Timothy White's building in Broadgate'. He had hardly done so when 'burning timber started to fall in the entrance filling the shelter with smoke' and the whole contingent had to be transferred 'to another shelter down the hill under the stores of Owen Owen in Trinity Street', which also rapidly became uninhabitable. By now the people 'were frightened to move, but with pushing and dragging . . . we managed to get them all in', though 'some needed first aid, having been cut by flying glass'. Before long 'a water main burst and the shelter began to fill with water', but understandably, the morale of the unfortunate victims was beginning to crack and during their next enforced tramp to a shelter 'in a Corporation Yard a quarter of a mile away . . . owing to panic during the move one adult and three children had to be taken to hospital, injured by falling stones'.

In the minds of those who organized such moves was the fear that the people affected might, after all, have been safer where they were. Senior Warden Les Engleman of Post 403B can still remember his horror at finding that a surface shelter near his home in Dennis Road, Stoke, in which he had placed two bombed-out people, had suffered a direct hit, though he later learned, to his vast relief, that shortly before the bomb fell the new arrivals had moved again to another, more secure-looking, shelter. He could, he reflected, only 'play it by ear', hoping to do what was best at the time.

Tragically, some people moved from safety into danger, like one boy then aged seven whose last memory of his mother is of her carrying his brothers and himself across to their shelter in Silver Street, while his father retreated to his 'local', the Swanswell Cottage. In response to her shouts, as the bombing grew worse, '"Where is your father?" someone went up the road to fetch him. He came to join us all and then the shelter got a direct hit.' When his uncle arrived an hour later the small child, dragged from the ruins, learned that 'my parents and brother Frank were dead and my other brother Patrick had a head wound. . . . If we had stayed in the house we would have been safe.'

Also bereaved that night was a nurse from the Coventry and Warwickshire Hospital who was off-duty at her home in Beanfield Avenue, on the southern fringes of the city. Driven from the house by an unexploded bomb, they had moved in with friends further down the road, whose house

suffered a direct hit by a bomb. My husband and son, who were just outside, were killed by falling debris. The lady who owned the house and myself were in the kitchen and escaped serious injury, though her eye was badly hurt and she subsequently lost it, and my hair was on fire. We went to the bottom of the garden and took refuge under the hedge and stayed there till morning.

What did it feel like to be in a house or shelter that suffered a near-miss? The then schoolgirl daughter of the manager of a Coventry shoe shop, living in Cheylesmore, who was settled with her parents in their usual 'safe place' against the inner wall of the lounge, still retains vivid memories of such an experience:

About three hours after the raid commenced an uncanny silence was followed by a terrific roar, and the house descended on us. The first person to speak was my mother and she called each one of us by name. We replied except for my father, who had been furthest away from the wall and who groaned. My first impression was of being surrounded by bricks and dust and being puzzled as to why I could see the moon so clearly. We climbed carefully over the debris, although it was still falling around us. My father was bleeding from the head and obviously in pain. We made our way to the shelter, which . . . was suffocatingly full. After about a two-hour wait, during which my father tore the shirt from his back to stem the blood from his head, an ambulance arrived to take my father away, but no one could tell us his destination.

The wife of a Daimler worker, living in Highland Road, remembers how, after they had seen King Henry's School and the goods yards of Coventry station blazing in the distance, they took refuge under the stairs, until around ten o'clock their windows were blown in and dust swept into the house from a bomb in Poplar Road behind them. It was, they decided, time to go.

I grabbed the eiderdown off the bed and we all went to the shelter outside.
I had put a deck chair and two boxes in the shelter. I sat on the chair and
the boys (aged thirteen and nineteen) sat on a box each side of me, so
that I could have the eiderdown round all three of us. . . .

We heard one plane that dropped two bombs very near. My husband
(he told me later) was going to say, 'This is for us', but he only got out,
'This . . .' and we got a hit outside the shelter, which brought it down on
us. It seemed as if I was floating on air and when I came to they were just
getting us out. My husband (not protected by the eiderdown) was the
worst injured, his head was cut open and his foot was injured. I had a
terrible black eye and my back was bruised. My sons were all right, just
a few bruises and scars but another lady in the shelter with us lost a leg
and [later] had to be taken to a mental home, where she died.

A fourteen-year-old schoolgirl living a 'mile or so from the city
centre', had settled down under the stairs and, having dozed off,
woke 'with a start to find plaster falling all around' and her 'mouth
filled with dust'.

My father was already outside fire-watching and I well remember my
mother and I making a run for it to the Anderson, with bombs dropping
all round, my mother clutching the large brown handbag containing
birth certificates, insurance policies, bank books, identity cards, money
and last, but not least, our precious ration books. Not loitering to take in
the spectacle my mother and I dived into the shelter. . . . It was the first
time that I had felt very frightened.

The Anderson demonstrated that night in Coventry its remarkable capacity to stand up to punishment. Among those who owed
their lives to it was one junior jig-and-tool draughtsman working
at the Humber factory and living 'in digs' in Walsgrave Road,
Wyken. He had been reluctant to face the discomfort of the damp
Anderson outside but had eventually moved there with a fellow-
lodger, leaving his landlady and her family beneath the dining-
room table. In spite of the bunks provided in the shelter he 'found
it difficult to drop off due to the cold and the noise' and the 'severe
cramp' in the legs, which his 'fellow-boarder periodically rubbed
to lessen the discomfort'.

About 2 a.m. . . . we suddenly heard the whistle of bombs coming down . . .
immediately followed by two or three explosions. The shelter rocked. I
heard debris falling around us and water started to trickle through the
roof. From then on I forgot about my cramp. I jumped out of the bunk

and found that the entrance to the shelter was . . . jammed with bricks and in the dark we could not see what to do. In the meantime water continued to pour in. . . . Through a small clearing in the rubble I could see a glow of light, but could not hear anyone about outside. Everything was deathly quiet. . . . We decided to try the emergency exit but at first we could not find the panel in the dark and after possibly ten minutes we felt the loose panel. By this time the water was all over the shelter floor and it was a muddy mess. However we eventually managed to slide the emergency panel away and, after pushing a few bricks away, scrambled out into the fresh air. When we looked around we saw what had happened. A string of bombs had dropped right across our shelter, obviously not very large ones. One had dropped in the garden next door, the blast turning the water tank on the flat roof of the outhouse onto our shelter. One had fallen on the house next door, partially demolishing ours and others in the street, and houses across the other side. I have no recollection of seeing anybody about until we scrambled through rubble into the street, when an air-raid warden came and told us to take shelter.

10
HAVING IT ALL THEIR OWN WAY

'It soon became obvious there was no defence of any value.'
Factory ARP Controller, recalling midnight,
14 November 1940

AROUND midnight another wave of German bombers swept across Coventry, as they had been doing with complete impunity for the past five hours. By now the new arrivals had little need of *Knickebein* or other navigational aids, for Kampfgruppe 100 had done their pathfinding task well, and the city provided a blazing beacon which even the least experienced crew could hardly miss.

About this time Flight-Sergeant Handorf, piloting Ju 88 'Bruno', found himself approaching Coventry at a height of about 6000 feet:

The aircraft are now over the edge of the city and far away stretch the plants of Coventry's engine and armament industry, a part of it already in bright flames. . . . There lies the target: a large factory block. . . . The giant chimneys stand dark and rigid in the bloody cloud of the neighbourhood; the plant down below stands out as bright as day in the light of the flares, muzzle-flashes show up on a few roofs, but the shells from the flak burst wide. . . . Schmidfeder pulls the bomb lever. . . . The Oberleutnant sees clearly in the last flicker of the dying flare the heavy bombs whistling down as Handorf banks the aircraft on its wing tips and makes a sharp curve. A few seconds later bright flames shoot up from the dark buildings; blazing columns of smoke and flame grow mushroom-like to cover the battered workshops and serpent up almost to the height of the Ju. 88. A faint smell of burning penetrates through the cracks in the thick glass plating of the rear turret. Both bombs have found their mark . . . Handorf has brought the aircraft back over the target in a wide sweep; two heavy bombs still wait in the racks to complete their mission. This time there is no need for the Oberleutnant to drop a flare; the fires make the target area as light as day. The still undamaged buildings stand out dark against the red glare of the fire . . . two giant workshops still remain. A tug at the bomb lever, a sharp turn of the aircraft and the second bomb load whistles earthward. . . . Once more a red fire glows steeply upward;

here is another factory that will do no more war-work for Herr Churchill. . . .

Dense smoke clouds billowing higher and higher above the industrial quarter hide the view of destruction. . . . The flat cloud cover which still lies at about 10000 feet above ground level has now assumed a red background, changing to a reddish colour here, to a greyish red there. . . . Searchlights and the glowing path of tracers still flash almost invisible in the red reflection of the fires. Fresh hits flash in the distance as further waves of attacking aircraft arrive over their objectives. [In front of 'Bruno'] its nose set on course for the coast, the night sky lies dark under the cloud cover which still shimmers faintly red above the aircraft . . . . Handorf sets his machine back on the old course, guiding himself by burning Coventry whose glimmer dies gradually away in the mist behind. . . . Down below lies the dark English countryside only interrupted from time to time by some gleam of fire. Only rarely does the finger of some searchlight flit across the sky. The flak has died down too. The Channel coast must soon be in sight.

On the ground, through the sinister droning and the crackling of the flames, one could, as 14 November came to an end, hear the chimes of the Cathedral clock, for the tower housing it, though blackened by smoke, still stood. People hearing that familiar, reassuring sound, comforted themselves with the thought that the Cathedral must still be undamaged and told themselves that so long as it stood no real harm could befall the city. Happily they could not know that already for an hour or more it had been merely a blazing ruin.

About a quarter to one in the morning of Friday 15 November while Midland Regional headquarters in Birmingham was signalling London 'FIRE SITUATION AT COVENTRY EXTREMELY SERIOUS. CITY ALIGHT' Mr A. W. Staniland managed 'to get five minutes' relief from what had been a very arduous job', in the Observer Corps Report Centre, 'of plotting the graphs of the tracks of each plane for later study'. Emerging into Hertford Street, which ran into Broadgate, he was confronted by

a terrific and satanic sight, fire raging all around us, with the exception of the block which we were in and an adjacent block at the rear. A tobacconist's known as Salmon and Gluckstein on the corner of Broadgate was burning furiously. The Cathedral and Old Palace yard [were] also in flames and everywhere [was] chaos, rubble and destruction.

Some firemen, exhausted by their earlier struggles, their occupation gone with the failure of the water supply, had already made their way back to their stations and fallen asleep on the floor. Other ARP workers at all levels, from the Control Centre outwards, though still wide awake, waited in frustration for a chance to act. The defence of Coventry, like many battles, had broken down into a series of small-scale engagements, fought by local units as best they could, with little direction from above.

A similar fragmentation occurred with time. The night may in retrospect have seemed to form one single sequence of excitement, activity and fear; at the time it was composed of a disconnected series of separate episodes, each with a character of its own. There were moments when the bombs appeared to be coming down all around and the whole weight of the Luftwaffe seemed to be concentrated on your road. Then others when suddenly the sky seemed to be clear and, except for a distant droning and the occasional sound of a falling wall or firebell, all was as peaceful and orderly as on a normal November night.

The wife of an aircraft fitter, living two miles from the city centre, remembers how, after her husband had brewed some tea, people crowded in with them 'until we had all the neighbours around our teapot' and the shelter was filled with chatter and candlelight, until suddenly unprecedented violence burst in upon Lincroft Crescent.

Above our houses were parachutes with marker lights for the bombing runs. Crunch! A blast of devastating force, my husband was blown against the shelter. The bomb . . . exploded about two hundred yards away. My husband and neighbours ran to where they thought the blast came from. This road, Prince of Wales, was a tragic sight, houses blown to bits, surface shelters a hundred yards from the bomb were split to all angles, cries for help came from everywhere. [The neighbours] did what they could to rescue people from surface shelters, comfort them, and then on again to anything that needed help. As they were coming back towards our houses, another stick of bombs came whistling down.

Some people had longed for the new day, like one mother of two small babies who, quaking beneath the table of her house in Wainbody Avenue, Green Lane, had reminded herself that 'if we survived until midnight surely we would live throught this terrible ordeal.' It seemed at first that she had been wrong, for in the early hours of Friday 'the house shook and our lit candles fell to the floor extinguished by the blast. Glass shattered, the roof caved in and ceilings collapsed.' But, by the standards of Coventry that night they *had* been lucky; the whole family groped their way from the ruins unharmed.

For some people that night there was no respite, like Dr Harry Winter at the Coventry and Warwickshire Hospital.

About 1 a.m. the engineer sent up a message that our steam supply had failed. Fortunately, we still had a good supply of steam-sterilized dressings in the drums, and we managed to use a sterile solution for the instruments instead of boiling them. By this time the windows in my operating theatre had been blasted out, and a bitter cold wind was blowing across the room. It was too cold to uncover the patients and too cold to operate, for I was shivering from head to foot. The windows of the second theatre had also been blown out, so we were forced to move into the ground-floor theatre, the windows of which were protected from blast by an outside brick wall. We decided to take turns doing the operations, but since the one theatre could not cope with the large number of cases, we could take only the most urgent ones. When I had a few minutes off between turns, I went along the corridors for a cigarette. It was an amazing scene . . . far worse than the descriptions I've heard of the front-line casualty clearing stations of the First World War. Patients were lying head to toe on every inch of space. The nurses were marvellous. With hurricane lamps and hand torches they moved about among the patients, comforting them and giving them little sips of water. . . . Near the entrance lobby I noticed the hospital superintendent. He was kneeling beside the patients lying on the floor and as I passed along I could hear a few words of their prayer. . . .

Although we have only 440 beds, we had 275 patients in when the raid started and I estimate that at least 300 more were admitted during the night. New patients were put on top of the beds while the old patients sheltered underneath them.

By 4 a.m. I couldn't keep a steady hand any longer. . . . Then our emergency lighting failed just as I was in the middle of an operation. We quickly rigged up an automobile headlamp to a battery set and I finished the job. Bombs were still crashing down, and every few minutes hunks of earth and debris crashed against the brick wall outside the theatre. By this time no one bothered to duck.

When news of the 'chaotic conditions' at the hospital reached the Control Room Dr Alan Ashworth learned that both the Coventry and Warwickshire Hospital and Gulson Road Hospital [now possessed] no water, no sewerage, no electricity, no black-out, no windows. When I managed to contact Regional Control I was able to convince them both hospitals would need to be completely evacuated as soon as possible after the raid was over.

In Little Park Street Mr J. B. Shelton now faced the moment he had long dreaded:

At 1.30 a.m. we decided to move the horses. I had made provision for such an emergency three months before. . . . At the rear of each horse a large chaff bag was kept to blindfold it if necessary and each horse was tied with a cord, with a sharp knife kept in readiness in case a quick exit was required. Now came the critical moment. We paused, wondering what was the best method to coax the horses out. I suddenly remembered that the horses were hungry as they had not been suppered up, and so I fetched an armful of the sweetest clover I could find, went into the stables, coaxed and patted each horse with some reassuring word, and let them smell and taste the clover. This had a calming effect and the hungry horses followed me and were out in the floating fire before they realized it. Four horses were brought out without the bags over their heads, but the fifth, a young horse, required a bag and caused some commotion. . . .

I finally persuaded it to leave the stable. It plunged and reared through the fire but we headed it towards the garden where the flames were not quite so bad. By now the smell and taste of the clover and the knowledge that other horses were near calmed it. We tethered each horse to a fruit tree in the garden and gave them a good feed of clover. Away from the fire the night was cold and clear so we tied large bags on the horses to keep them warm. When they had had their fill it was interesting to see two of the horses lie down and go fast asleep. . . .

Crash after crash followed every few moments. . . . The falling walls, girders, pillars, machinery crashing four storeys, the droning of the planes as they let go their bombs and the rattling of shrapnel on corrugated sheeting was deafening. . . . One had to guess where the noise like thunder came from. I found out afterwards that it must have been the crashing of the pillars of the Cathedral.

Mrs Megan Ryan, barely a stone's throw away in Judges Court, was facing an agonizing decision: what to save from the home into which, as a young bride, she had moved only six weeks before, and now menaced by flames spreading from the adjoining chemical factory.

It is ridiculous the things one grabs in an emergency. My library book that I was reading, some knitting I was doing . . . I opened a drawer . . . there must be something else . . . and there was a wedding present table-cloth on the top and I grabbed that. There was a meat safe which we tore off the wall. The food that was in that meat safe came in very useful next day. We were halfway down the stairs again . . . when the wind veered and we were told that we had now got more time and we started to pile things up. We were pushing things into a suitcase to begin with, but my husband said, 'This is ridiculous, it will take too long', and he took a big armchair and smashed the window. It seemed an awful thing to do. . . . One doesn't smash one's window deliberately. First of all he threw a mattress out, and we began to throw things out of the window on to the mattress. We even tore down the fitted wardrobe that he had only finished making the day before but that was wood, good wood and wood was getting scarce. We threw it all down on to the mattress and then someone called out that the roof was going . . . and we jumped up on the window-sill and so down into the garden.

Later that night her husband seized his first-aider's satchel and hurried off to the factory where he was an apprentice.

Some time, maybe three o'clock in the morning, someone came and told me that I had to be very brave and listen to what he had to say and he told me that my husband was certainly dead because they had found his first-aid equipment at the bottom of the spotter's tower. . . . But I didn't take it in. I was busy dragging an armchair out of a burning flat at the time and that was the only thing that mattered.

Not far away at this moment was Harold Tomley, still indefatig-ably touring the Central Division.

I proceeded along Jordan Well into Earl Street. There was the body of a youth lying on the pavement just underneath the Council House clock; he was dead. Later I heard that he was one of the brave body of police messengers.

A R P General Headquarters was located at the Old Technical College down a short lane right opposite the Council House clock, so I decided to go down and have a few words with the old gentleman who was on duty every night. . . . I returned to the street, but only took a few paces before I gazed upon a sight which would have made anyone feel very sad. One of the gems of ancient Coventry was a half-timbered building of the Elizabethan period where before the war I had attended the occasional chamber concert, Old Palace Yard. Now the flames were devouring it. I quickly retraced my steps and made contact with Control Centre. The officer at the other end of the line groaned, and replied, 'What a tragedy, but we cannot do anything about it, there is no water.' . . .

The Cathedral by that time, after midnight, was inside a huge sea of devouring flame. I stood outside and gazed through the empty window apertures at the huge building completely fire-filled, as if all the air in it had been transformed into flame. . . .

I continued on my way, but stopped under the pillars of the National Provincial Bank at the corner . . . Salmon and Gluckstein's shop on the opposite corner was burning, and I counted eight fires in Broadgate, and a little further on the large Owen Owen store still burning. There were two fire escapes in action, with firemen on the top . . . but the water coming out of their hoses was a mere trickle.

Three-quarters of a mile north of the Cathedral at the Coventry Climax Works in Widdrington Road was Leonard Dacombe:

Several bombs had been dropped on our factory. One had hit the top of a jig boring machine and another had hit the base of a milling machine and had tipped it over. Mr F. [another fire-watcher] was with me in our post when a string of bombs crossed our shop and one landed each side of our post about twenty yards away and we felt them tunnelling under the concrete floors, but they didn't explode. About 2.00 a.m. Mr F. and I were walking across the shop when we were hit by blast. As I was floating through the air, I saw him pass me and crash against the wall. I followed him into the wall. When we picked ourselves up we realized how fortunate we were, as we had been thrown along a gangway between heavy machinery. . . . [A little later] the noise of battle was beginning to die down, so we went to check how things were going and we saw that one of our air-raid shelters, which was under our small canteen, had been blown out of position and was nearly lying on its side. Also, a bomb had hit a girder on the way down, which had broken the fins off it. The bomb had then spun into a stack of camshafts and had broken them up into little pieces. We stood around this bomb and smelt the orange-coloured greasy substance inside it, not realizing that the detonator was still alive. . . .

We went for a walk across the yard to see how the fires were going on and met some of the works firemen watching tracer bullets going up into the sky. . . . It was not long after that a parachute mine landed in the canal. This not only destroyed the test shop, but also most of our machine shop and assembly shop. Blast blew the walls out and the roof off and heavy chunks of clay landed everywhere, breaking up the machinery. At this stage I noticed that the shop was getting flooded, then I found that a large pipe of about twelve-inch diameter had broken. This was the base of a sprinkler stop valve system and water was pouring out everywhere. Luckily there was a large wheel below the break, so I was able to turn it off, but got wet through in the process. It was probably 3.00 a.m. by this time and, returning to my Post rather wet, Mr F. and I heard a loud scream which we thought was another bomb coming down close by. When we realized that it was the sound of a small motor-cycle revving up to go over Cash's Lane Bridge . . . we had to laugh, thinking that we were had that time.

It was still dark; black-out did not end until 7.54 a.m. Long before then, however, the flight from the devastated city had begun. One of the first to see it was Aircraftman Fray, who, on his message-running trips from Bramcote to Baginton early in the night, had 'reported that dozens of women, children, men and dogs were on the roads leading out of Coventry'. Around 10 p.m. he was given a new task, to take out a 'Queen Mary', a long, low-loading transporter used to move aircraft, to collect as many of these refugees as he could.

I did a shuttle service, travelling from Bramcote to the outskirts of Walsgrave Road picking up as many people as possible, women in nightdresses, children and men in pyjamas or just trousers, until I had to turn around in the road with about 150 aboard. I made four trips and we put everyone in an empty hangar on the drome at Bramcote. Other drivers were on this journey also and we must have had over a thousand people in the hangar when a stick of bombs splayed across the drome and hit the next hangar, which had five or six Wellington bombers inside. This caught fire but . . . was very soon put out, although I remember screams coming from the hangar with all the people inside.

One woman in a shelter in the Coundon area, on the north-west side of Coventry, was astonished at the height of the raid to hear a bus going by. The vehicle stopped and the driver identified himself as 'a young man who had taken over an abandoned bus and was bringing people up from the town to the apparent safety of the suburb'.

A little later, around 3 a.m., Leslie Worthington of Owen Owen watched 'a stream of bombed-out people' flowing past his house in Knoll Drive, Styvechale. The more weary accepted his invitation to come inside, until 'we finished up with seventeen of them sheltering with us'.

As it began to get light the noise of battle died away outside. 'After hours of wondering when it would be our turn one felt towards morning too numb to care,' remembers one woman then living in Tennyson Road, Stoke, but spirits revived a little as people realized, almost incredulously, that they had survived the night after all.

By now, too, the last night-fighters were coming in to land, their pilots and observers bitterly conscious that once again the Luftwaffe had escaped them. Fighter Command had, by the night-fighting standards of the time, made an impressive effort, with a total of 135 sorties, of which the largest single number, forty-three, were by Hurricanes, though there had also been thirty-five by Blenheims, thirty by Defiants – an ineffective single-engined two-seater, withdrawn from day use after several near-massacres – a dozen by Beaufighters, the specially designed twin-engined night-fighter just coming into use, and even five (a measure of the defence's desperation) by ancient Gladiator biplanes, slower than the Ju 88s they were trying to intercept. But during the whole night there had been only seven sightings of enemy aircraft and though two Blenheims had opened fire neither had achieved a kill. The Chief of the Air Staff, Sir Charles Portal, was to tell the Cabinet that day that 'a continuous fighter patrol' had been maintained 'over Coventry itself', though he admitted this had led to 'only one inconclusive engagement' but no one in Coventry has any recollection of seeing any British aircraft at all.*

One woman, then aged eighteen, and living on a farm at Honiley near Kenilworth Castle, has etched on her memory the sight of 'enemy planes coming and going unmolested' against the striking background of 'the scarlet glow in the sky like a highly magnified angry sunset such as artists paint but are never seen in reality. Still in broad daylight,' she remembers, 'there were enemy planes around flying blatantly low over our own heads, so low that they could have been hit by a rifle. Bursting with triumph they circled round and round, gloating over their success.' Many echoed this young woman's question: 'Where was our Air Force?' 'It soon became obvious,' remembers the then ARP Controller of the Courtaulds factory at Foleshill Road, 'that there was no defence of any value. . . .

*For full details of these operations, as recorded at the time, which do not necessarily agree in all particulars with the final account compiled after the war, on which I have relied, see paragraphs 8–15 of Note on German Operation 'MOONLIGHT SONATA', in Appendix B, page 267.

We just had to sit it out and wait. . . . The Germans seemed to have it all their own way.'

Portal informed the Cabinet that eighty British aircraft had been sent 'to attack the enemy aerodromes' in France, but the 'fairly good results' he claimed seem to have been mere self-deception, like the suggestion that only 'some 300 enemy bombers' had reached Coventry; the true total was far higher.

The defences had, however, scored at least one success. Anti-aircraft gunners near Loughborough, by superlative skill or amazing good luck, had brought down one bomber on its way to Coventry, while at Birmingham gunners claimed to have seen another break up in the air, though the official history makes no mention of any wreckage being found. Two enemy aircraft shot down out of (we now know) 552 despatched was by any test a resounding defeat. Of these a diversionary force of twenty-one had been briefed to attack London, and another twenty-two assigned to mine-laying and minor operations, but of the 509 given Coventry as their primary target German records suggest that 449 reached it, and all of these returned safely to their bases. The number involved is borne out by the recollections of Observer Corps member A. W. Staniland who had by the time his crew were relieved, about 7 a.m., personally 'recorded the tracks of some 400 enemy aircraft'.

It had also been a frustrating night for the gunners of the 85th H.A.A. Regiment, who had been continuously in action for eleven hours. Many legends were later to gather round their efforts, all of them unfounded. One particularly persistent story was that naval guns had been brought in to defend the city and several people claim to have heard their distinctive roar. 'After some of the minor raids before 14 November,' remembers Colonel Lawrence, Commanding Officer of the regiment, 'people would say, "You put up a good show last night, you had the naval gun in action again." There was no truth in this whatever.' Other families were convinced that 'mobile guns on the railway' ranged up and down engaging the enemy, but these were also phantom artillery. Another widespread belief was that the guns fell silent in the early hours, either because their barrels became red-hot through over-use, a pleasantly colour-ful detail, or, a more mundane explanation, because they had no more shells. There was even, according to one informant, a 'story that a gun was fired until the barrel burst'.

This last rumour had, as will shortly be explained, some slight foundation in fact but the rest were mere myths. No gun barrels were changed during the night because, as Colonel Lawrence points out, there were none in Coventry, and even if there had been 'no one in the regiment had the knowledge to change one'. About seven barrels did have to be replaced next day, but this was done by a detachment of the Royal Army Ordnance Corps sent in from outside. The expenditure of ammunition had indeed been prodigious, and far more than previously contemplated, when a short raid by a maximum of seventy-five aircraft was the worst anyone had foreseen. All told, according to an official Ack-Ack Command account, 'over 6700 rounds were fired . . . an average of ten rounds per minute for the eleven hours. At one gun site of four guns nearly 1300 rounds were fired . . . an average of two shells per minute throughout the night.' The figures recorded by Colonel Lawrence were even more impressive. The working life of a 3.7-inch gun barrel was only 2000 rounds, but on that single night the four-gun site at Binley fired 1391 rounds and the site at Ryton 1319, despite the mishap of a 'premature' when a round blew up in the breech, parts of the barrel being found a quarter of a mile away. The legend of the silent guns arose, the Command's historians believe, because 'one station ran out' and had to 'borrow ammunition' from its neighbour. Colonel Lawrence agrees. 'There was no organized cease fire at any time' although 'the odd gun or even the odd gun site stopped' while further ammunition 'was moved to the gun pits'.

But if the intensity of fire was more than could have been expected accuracy, if equally foreseeable, was disappointing. The Command's public relations men, drawing up the official version for intended publication, put the best face on events they could.*

Gun-stations had to resort to individual fire. Stations with GL [Gun-laying] and Visual Indicator Equipment were able to fire fairly effectively by this means in the early stage of the attack, but as it developed and the noise from shelling and bombing increased many VIEs were unable to function properly and eventually they were firing on purely estimated

---

*This account was written for *Roof over Britain*, the propagandist booklet intended as Anti-Aircraft Command's answer to the R A F's *Battle of Britain*. When published, in 1943, however, the text quoted above was omitted. It finally appeared in General Pile's autobiography, in 1949.

heights. Some gun stations whose communications with GOR [Gun Operations Room] were broken off continued firing either by sound or at concentrations of searchlight beams.

Colonel Lawrence put the matter more succinctly. 'Most of the shooting was wild', he acknowledges, though 'with no communications, my site commanders did a very good job.'

The Gun Operations Room in Radford Road also had its problems.

As the night went on the work in the GOR became extremely difficult. More than fifteen bombs fell within fifty yards . . . close enough to blow the black-out boards from their position. Time after time a certain conscientious NCO cursed but carefully put them back – apparently oblivious of the fact that a nearby timber yard was ablaze.

To no one was the thought that the Germans were roaming about the Midlands at will more repellent than to the Prime Minister and around 10.30 p.m. Colonel Lawrence was called to the telephone to find an irate Winston Churchill on the line. 'He appeared to be very angry, asked who I was, and what was I doing about it all. With bombs dropping all round my Gun Operations Room,' Colonel Lawrence remembers, 'I assured him that all were doing their best.'

Some gunners that night were, to their fury and amazement, actually forbidden to fire on the enemy, among them Gunner 'Henry' Hall (he had been christened Leonard William) who was helping to man a Bofors gun of the 113th Light Anti-Aircraft Battery at the RAF station at Bramcote.

Bramcote was not operational at this time, but Wellington bombers were arriving. I've never seen so many, lined up wing tip to wing tip. Our gun-site was high up on the corner of what was called the stand-by building [which] housed spare electrical generators in case the main power lines were cut. On each gun-site was an officer to stop us from firing at the German bombers. We could have hit them with a stick, they were that low. But we were told that if we opened up the Germans would have seen all the Wellingtons and would have obliterated them. My personal feelings were we *should* have opened up and helped the poor devils who were being murdered.

Among the city's passive defences were a number of smoke-burners, of little value in the moonlight, and fifty-six barrage balloons, thirty-two of which belonged to No. 916 Squadron, based at Baginton.

At 20.30 hours telephone communications broke down completely and squadron headquarters were out of touch with flights and sites. Despatch riders were rapidly brought into service and . . . in some places it was only possible to get through on foot. Then came another catastrophe. All lighting failed. Emergency lighting was brought into use at once.

Service on a balloon site was not customarily considered very dangerous but 916 Squadron had that night its share of excitement. The crew of one site had to abandon inflating a new balloon to 'deal with incendiaries' – a serious matter with so much inflammable gas nearby. The crew of another flight soon faced greater excitement:

All the windows of our headquarters were blown in and several D.A. bombs fell within a few yards. Huts on Sites 18 and 40 were destroyed. The crew of Site 18 evacuated to their dug-out, but a D.A. fell adjacent to the wall of the dug-out and they had to leave that too. When a delayed-action bomb fell about ten yards from the [balloon] bed of Site 8, the men were in their Anderson shelter, but on hearing the balloon cable was falling, they turned out, hauled down the balloon and bedded it.

A similar, but far worse, problem faced the Leading Aircraftman left in charge of No. 33 Balloon Site, by the Leamington Road. In the early part of the evening he caught reassuring glimpses of his charge riding peacefully in the moonlight, but after midnight the cable became slack and was soon 'showing a distinct loop', probably, he decided, because of ice forming on it. 'Sometime between 2 a.m. and 3 a.m. it began to fall', until the heavy cable 'was at an alarming angle' stretching low across the countryside; the balloon supporting it, he guessed, had been 'ripped open by shrapnel from our guns.'

The immediate danger was from our cable falling over the overhead power cables in the next field and across the main London Road, the A.45. . . . The telephones to headquarters were out of action, so I called for someone to go and notify the flight commander what had happened. The chap rode off on the site cycle just as though it was an ordinary day, but he told me later he was really quite scared. . . .
We managed to get the balloon down to treetop height, then it dived

down out of sight. . . . There were showers of sparks from the trees and overhead cables as our cable crossed the live wires. Everyone was warned of the danger of touching the cable. The flight commander arrived and . . . we started to trace the cable and find where the balloon had finally come down. We found it in a farmyard and the cable ran over a haystack on to a Dutch barn, then across the overhead cables, on the branches of some fir trees and back to the winch. No more cable could be hauled in while it was attached to the balloon so the Flight Commander decided we should cut it. We found a ladder on the farm and he and I climbed up on to the haystack with a pair of wire cutters to cut the cable. There was an element of risk in this as the cable was 'live' and could fly in coils when cut and the tension released. The CO did the cutting at the first attempt. As he did, we both dropped flat into the hay. As we thought, the cable flew and there was a shower of sparks from the Dutch barn and the surrounding trees but no one was hurt.

The next thing to do was to haul in the cable, which we did, accompanied by a good show of sparks until we got it off the power lines. The next job was to make sure all the hydrogen was out of the balloon as by now the mixture of gas and air was becoming dangerous. . . . While all this was happening, the raid was still going on over Coventry. . . . Before we had finished clearing up the All Clear sounded.

II

MUMMY, WHERE'S OUR HOUSE GONE?

'The destruction seemed beyond belief.'
Coventry resident recalling the morning of Friday
15 November 1940.

'WHEN dawn broke the following morning it was drizzling.' This opening sentence in an eyewitness account recorded by the BBC a few days later aptly caught the spirit of that muddled, melancholy Friday when the people of Coventry realized that the final Junkers and Heinkels had at last departed. The speaker went on:

There was a mist over the town as men and women began to crawl out of their shelters, look for their friends and survey the ruins of their city. The could hardly recognize it. Remnants of walls with their ragged brickwork stood up like drunken sentinels helplessly guarding a scene of chaos. Hardly a building remained intact. It was impossible to see where the central streets we knew so well had been. Fires were still raging in every direction and from time to time we heard the crash of a fallen roof or wall. Up to that night we were surprised if we heard that this or that building had been hit. That Friday morning we were surprised to hear that a building hadn't. And as we walked round the ruined streets we hardly knew what to do. It seemed so hopeless with our homes and shops and so much of our lovely old city in ruins. You might say we were dazed.

The raid which had begun so dramatically ended in anticlimax. For hours sleepless and fearful citizens had longed for the All Clear, but though the 'Raiders Passed' signal reached Coventry at 6.16 a.m. the sirens, with electricity cables torn apart, were silenced. A few people heard a single, distant siren, echoing eerily across the mist-shrouded fields from outside the town, but most people stayed under cover until wardens and policemen shouted 'It's all over!' into basements and Andersons. One Special Constable remembers being 'repeatedly asked if the All Clear had gone', as he made his way from the Council House about 8.20 a.m. to his parents' house. Dr Alan Ashworth, still on duty at the Control Centre, could hardly believe his eyes as he looked out from the entrance at ground level:

It was a terrifying sight. About fifty yards to the left, the Cathedral was smouldering; pieces of burning wood work were still dropping from charred and burnt beams. Immediately opposite and as far as one could see, the city was a mass of flames. It reminded me of a film I had seen of the great San Francisco earthquake. It was completely out of hand and unchecked and as the morning passed the flames passed up the road, the heat of the flames cracking windows and melting the glass in the Council House itself.

A few yards away Provost Howard was standing in the ruins of the building he had fought so hard to save.

I was surprised to see that the Cathedral, now without pillars or roof, seemed to be far larger than before. The appearance of the ruins was so completely different from the Cathedral before the destruction that it was impossible to think of them as the same building. But the long heaped-up piles of rubble seemed to retain an immense degree of beauty, as though they possessed something living and imperishable within themselves. . . .

A little later the wife of the curate of St Thomas's, Mrs W. B. Sells, also visited the ruins, which were still 'smouldering in the frosty air', and found Provost Howard, who had returned there after going home, 'pacing round in the ruined aisles. To us who knew St Michael's Cathedral well,' she remembers, 'this great ruin was enormously poignant', but as she passed through 'what had been the West Door' Mrs Sells drew comfort from the 'figure of St Michael and the Dragon' still standing 'intact and magnificently indomitable'.

'The whole town looked a write-off.' That was the conclusion of one municipal engineer as he surveyed 'roads impassable with debris, flames licking across the street amid the smoking ruins of distorted and crumbling buildings and bomb craters big enough to swallow a bus'. One woman, travelling into the centre of the city from the Allesley district on the north-west outskirts 'just didn't believe' the evidence of her eyes. 'In Queen Victoria Road and Allesley Old Road there appeared to be no one but us – complete destruction'.

'Utter destruction, which far exceeded any image conjured up by Dante's *Inferno*' – this was also the reaction of architect Mr A. W. Staniland, emerging around seven o'clock from the Observer Corps Plotting Centre in the GPO building. During the night as the building had 'constantly rocked beneath our feet' Mr Staniland had gained 'an inkling of what an earthquake feels like'. Now he saw the aftermath, as he drove home, 'climbing and sliding over the rubble, cutting telephone wires which had fouled front and back axles and wheels' and 'dodging bomb craters'. The two-mile journey, on punctured tyres, took two and a half hours. As he stood contemplating the 'complete shambles' of his garage, the 'oak fence . . . burned by an incendiary' and the 'unexploded parachute mine on the other side of the hedge' his wife arrived from Meriden. A few hours earlier, she had 'lifted the telephone off its cradle' and found herself speaking to the operator at Coventry, who told her before the line went dead, that the GPO building was 'ringed with raging fires and the observers couldn't get out'.

One driver for the Midland Red bus company, based at Dudley, that morning drove in 'a bus load of municipal workmen to help clear up the mess'; they discovered at the first factory they reached a warden 'walking about in a dream, as white as a ghost', the sole survivor from a surface shelter which had collapsed. He had escaped through having left to make tea just before the bomb fell. The bus driver remembers:

While the workmen were getting on with their job I had a walk round . . . along what was a street, all the rubble flattened and still smoking. On top of one pile lay a cat. I stopped to talk to the cat and while I was there a sailor came up to me and asked if I knew where so-and-so street was. I said, 'Laddie, this is it.'

To the professional eye of Civil Defence Staff Officer Harold Tomley, 'the destruction seemed beyond belief' as he made his way home, to find his house in the Radford area so badly damaged that it had later to be demolished. His wife was nowhere to be seen, but he located her, slightly injured – the left side of her face was temporarily paralysed by blast – in the shelter beneath the Rialto Cinema.

For people who had spent the night in shelter the sight of the all-encompassing ruin came as an even greater shock. Marjorie Whittaker, climbing out of the shelter below Anslow's in the High Street, felt that 'all the town was alight. There was debris everywhere', and she found herself picking her way through 'the glass on the steps'. Only a little less surprised were the former residents of the YWCA hostel in The Butts, who stumbled into the fresh air clutching their 'emergency bags' of essentials, to find their recent home burnt to the ground. 'I walked along with my suitcase,' remembers the Civil Servant previously quoted, 'not knowing what to do but so thankful to be alive that nothing else mattered. . . . Everything I owned, except for what I had with me, was gone, but I didn't care . . . I was free of the burden of possessions. Ever since I've been able to understand the peculiar freedom of the tramp.' Her sense of liberation increased on discovering that 'the office . . . had gone too'.

Alderman George Hodgkinson, Vice-Chairman of the corporation's Emergency Committee, rapidly encountered, on emerging with his family from beneath the stairs of his wife's parents' house at 6 a.m., two of the problems with which he would soon be confronted officially. With no water in the house he set off with a jug for the nearest shopping centre in Moseley Avenue, where the AFS were still damping down a fire, but they refused to fill it because their supply was probably contaminated. Further exploration revealed an uncle who still had a storage tank full of water but none to spare for sanitation, and a notice was posted in the toilet: 'Do not pull the chain before leaving'.

The universal sound in Coventry that morning was the crunch of glass underfoot, but even more unforgettable was the smell, or rather the smells, mainly acrid and unpleasant but including the fragrant cigar aroma hanging over a wrecked tobacconist's near the GPO, remembered by a member of the Observer Corps, and the homely smell of roasting meat recalled by one woman, who passed 'a butcher's shop with its windows blown out, a fire still raging and a whole pig hanging in the window cooked to perfection'.

Coventry that morning was full of strange sights and the even greater dangers which some areas had escaped. A sixteen-year-old girl in Hertford Square found herself fascinated by the sight of 'a Coventry Climax pump on the rubble of the Co-op in West Orchard still partly glowing with the heat'. An aircraft worker remembers seeing 'a corporation bus in a thirty-foot bomb crater' and a worker at the A P aircraft factory found the roof damaged by 'the wheels and back axle of a lorry blown on to it, the driver's cab being jammed on the roof of the next building'. Scattered about Coventry, as an early count revealed, were at least twenty unexploded parachute mines. A Special Constable saw one caught in a tree in Coat of Arms Road, while the young Geoffrey Green, making his way home from the St Mary Magdalen's church tower, remembers another 'like a great iron coffin, swinging between the gable ends of two houses'.

To a woman living in Canley Road, Earlsdon, the 'telephone wires . . . hanging all across the buildings and down into the road' made the deepest impression. 'We had to pick our way through them, like going through a jungle.' An airman's wife in Queen Isabel's Avenue, Cheylesmore, stared in amazement at the 'kerb stones from the front path . . . dislodged and sticking up in the air'. Most uncannily, 'you could see straight through the bottom wall' of the terraced house opposite, for though blast had completely carried away the lower part, the upper part was held up, arch-like, by the walls on either side. To one woman who lived in Woodside Avenue, final proof of the violation of the normal domestic privacies was provided by the spectacle of 'an old-fashioned wooden clothes mangle, blown on to a roof at a crazy angle'.

This was the scene in Jenner Street, behind the Coventry and Warwickshire Hospital, as observed by one twelve-year-old boy whose father was gatekeeper in a factory:

The houses opposite had been bombed and were on fire. . . . The street and gardens were full of shrapnel and parts of incendiary bombs, as well as all sorts of rubbish. Our part of Jenner Street was covered in mud from a bomb which landed in the hospital grounds. A very large stone landed on the bed in the house next door. At the top end of Jenner Street was a small food warehouse. This was on fire and as one walked by all the tins were popping due to the heat. My father kept the car in a lock-up garage nearly opposite this warehouse. An incendiary bomb landed on the running board, but someone saved the car. I remember seeing a parachute from our back garden . . . wrapped around a chimney of a house in Howard Street.

One ten-year-old schoolgirl had spent the night in the shelter below the badly bombed British Thomson-Houston works.

At last the All Clear went and we tried to get out of the shelter. That itself was a feat of ingenuity – we had to climb up a straight ladder into the now devastated canteen. Ankle-deep in glass we made our slow way along until we were outside and had our first glimpse of Coventry, absolutely flattened.

At last we reached the top of our road [Oliver Street] only to be told our house had gone. Fortunately it was virtually all right. There was of course no water, electricity or gas.

That never-to-be-forgotten moment of wondering whether or not one's house still stood was also experienced by a girl of thirteen whose family had moved into their brand-new 'semi' in Glendower Avenue only a year before.

We learned of the end from a man walking past just before 7 a.m., shouting, 'It's all over, they've gone.' We were cold and stiff . . . after what seemed like days rather than hours in the shelter. Our house was almost opposite and as we came out and saw the moon shining on the windows, we felt surprised and lucky that it was still there. . . . We opened the little front gate and walked up the path and round the side of the house, to walk into debris. . . . There were incendiaries on the front lawn and all over the place. . . . A lot of roof gone and all the windows at the back, and the kitchen door blown off. My parents started clearing up, I started looking for our tabby. After some minutes I could hear her crying but could not see her. Half an hour later I discovered that she was under the house in the footings, having gone under the stairs and squeezed through a small hole in the floorboards that were cut away round the electricity meters. She would not come out for a long time, but eventually I managed to 'talk' her back by starting from the front door end.

First reactions that morning were blunted by the long hours of bombing which had left all but the most stolid feeling numbed. 'We felt like people who had just completed a long arduous journey and arrived safely at their destination' – that is how one carpenter living in the Holbrook area describes his family's attitude. 'Suddenly one was conscious of *quiet*,' recalls another housewife, then living in Treherne Road, the uncanny silence in the house being due, she decided, to 'the gas and electricity meters in the pantry ceasing to function'. 'I felt the assault on the normal decencies of life of ordinary people,' remembers one man who lived in Coundon, conscious of houses 'with the front blown out and bedroom furniture hanging drunkenly', for all to see. Others consoled themselves with jokes.

'My name should be Ibsen,' observed one man in Leamington Road to his neighbour, pointing to the exposed 'dolls' house' frontage of his home.

The 'first job' of one young mother in Daventry Road, on realizing they were still alive, though without gas, electricity, water or a front door – it had been blown in hours before – 'was to make a fresh bottle of food for the baby, who hadn't stirred for twelve hours. There was a spark of life in the fire. Running up the stairs to fetch her a clean night dress I could see the people passing by from the shelters and I heard one child crying: "Mummy, where *is* our house?"'

Just as it had seemed inconceivable that anything at all could be standing next morning, so, inevitably, people tended to assume that anyone missing from their accustomed spot had been killed. One warden remembers the anticlimax which ended a prolonged rescue attempt in Cambridge Street, where the elderly occupant of one bombed house could not be accounted for. 'We had been digging for about an hour and a half, when a voice from the crowd said, "What are you looking for in my house?" It was the old man who had that night decided to go to a friend's shelter.' An eleven-year-old schoolgirl arrived back with her parents at the ruins of the family home in Ash Grove to find her 'two elder married brothers weeping in what had been the back yard. They knew we always sheltered under the stairs and ... thought we were dead and buried under the debris.' There was an equally happy reunion for Mrs Megan Ryan, who, hours before, had hardly taken in the news of her husband's supposed death.

I was walking across the rubble when he arrived, smoke everywhere, and he called across, 'What's the matter, you look as if you had seen a ghost?' because I grabbed a post. It was a charred post, must have been a doorway, and the words that my friend had said earlier all came rushing back. ....

The girls working at the factory had been ordered to the shelters and there had been a direct hit. He had taken off his first-aid equipment to dig into the shelter to try to get them out, but they were all dead.

'Our feelings on seeing the devastation,' recalls one wartime Special Constable, of the moment he stood beside the ruins of his home in Villiers Street, 'were mostly of relief that we ourselves had come through unscathed. It was a long time afterwards before the realization of what we had lost was borne in upon us.' At that moment the survival of any possessions was a subject for rejoicing, and he remembers being delighted to find 'my daughter's doll, which she still has, and the Teddy Bear which has served both our children and is now the treasured possession of my youngest grandson'.

The experiences of the Mayor of Coventry and his family, as remembered by his daughter, were typical of those of thousands of others that morning.

We came out hardly believing we were still alive. . . . The moon was now shining low in the sky but it was pale against the red glow all over the city. . . . With the crunch of broken glass beneath our feet and stepping over dad's carefully made black-out shutters (blown from kitchen and living room windows) we managed to push the kitchen door open half-way – the blast had jammed it. As we all went in we heard, 'Oh! What a lovely boy! Billy's a lovely boy!' coming over and over again. It was our budgie. Dad exclaimed 'Well! Thank God here's something else alive'.*

The kitchen was reasonably intact . . . but a thick layer of dust covered everything and soot from the chimney plus dead ash from the grate were blown into every corner. Gas was off and soon the water went – the electricity followed. Mum, as ever practical, set about lighting the kitchen fire. . . . We *must* have a cup of tea, mum said . . . and dad insisted on lacing the tea with a drop of whisky, before any further inspection.

Mum began preparations for some sort of breakfast for us all . . . mainly for dad who *always* started his day with porridge. Bombed or not, mum was making sure of that. My sister, dad and I then went through the ground floor of the house, the living room first, front sitting room and hall and then upstairs. Everywhere our feet crunched on broken glass and plaster, a sound to become very familiar. . . .

I said bitterly, 'I'll never, as long as I live, want to own anything I can't pack and carry in a case.' I was well and truly told off by dad. *We* still had a home – others did not, so would I please shut up. He did insist that mum must not see it all immediately but mum too wept when she saw our home . . . and mum was never the 'weepy' type.

The Moseleys' bird was not the only one to survive the night. A woman living in Cedars Avenue, Coundon, was upset to find her budgerigar's cage 'all bent up' when she got back from the shelter, and its occupant gone, but a fortnight later he flew back again,

*This informant adds: 'That budgie lived for quite a while afterwards but the canary was only just alive and died later that day.'

identifying himself by repeating the words his owner had taught him. First-aider Dick Baxendale, returning from night duty at his machine-tool company in Canal Road, found that he also faced the consequences of a similar dash for freedom, for the same bomb that had wrecked his roof and broken his windows had liberated his chickens from their run and they were parading all over the street.

Cats, by contrast, proved loath to leave their accustomed surroundings. One woman living in Queen Isabel's Avenue, Cheylesmore, was, she confesses, 'very much distressed' by the sight of 'cats with singed whiskers sitting among the ruins' of their former homes, though much relieved when her own 'black and white Persian, Tony', who had 'slunk away with his stomach touching the ground' in the middle of the raid, 'turned up as if nothing had happened', showing his contempt for the Germans by using 'the crater across the road as a loo'. Tony had, though he did not know it, survived the raid only to face a greater danger, for his mistress 'couldn't face the thought', she admits, 'of him getting lost in any future raids' and, with a heavy heart, prepared to take him to the RSPCA clinic in Ford Street to be put to sleep. However, 'the long queue of people with dogs and cats' all waiting for the same sad purpose gave her time for second thoughts and the sight of Tony 'sitting in the garden washing his face' proved too much for her resolution. 'My sister looked at me and I looked at her. The cat was reprieved,' she remembers, and he lived to a ripe old age. One woman remembers seeing 'rows of houses in Stoney Stanton Road burnt to a shell' with 'all the cats belonging to them sitting on the windowsill. I walked half a mile to try and get them some milk but nobody would let me have any.'

Probably the prevailing impression on everyone that morning who was not actually bereaved or bombed-out was of the stupendous mess that a heavy air raid caused. Mr Ken Pittaway, then Chief Electrical Engineer at Courtaulds, remembers his first thought on leaving his shelter to return to his home in Coundon was of 'tiles!, tiles!, tiles! – roofs, bare of tiles, the whole Avenue'. Worse was to come:

The house was as though a tornado had given it a great shaking: pictures down, mantel-shelves empty, lumps of plaster, pierced window panes with holes where metal had drilled its way through like a diamond. . . . I lit a coal fire and made breakfast conscious of all the dust right in the food. But the cup of tea was nectar.

Tea was a universal need. 'Never was there a sweeter cuppa anywhere,' believes one woman whose kettle, filled from the rain water butt, boiled on an open fire. Another housewife, in Lincroft Crescent, two miles from the city centre, remembers how an informal tea-party developed as people re-discovered 'the sheer relief of being able to talk without shouting. . . . The chatter of the night's excitement, the thankfulness for our lives being spared, grew, until we had all the neighbours round our teapot.' Providing a cooked breakfast was beyond most people's surviving resources, but some strange meals were served and eaten with zest. One family living in Oliver Street and lacking 'water, electricity or gas' extracted from the store cupboard the most luxurious item it contained, a tin of salmon. A woman living in Queen Isabel's Avenue, Cheylesmore, enjoyed an equally unusual breakfast: 'a tin of stew', heated up by her neighbours, which 'we shared with my cat'.

In the walled garden of Judges Court, which now resembled 'a gigantic rubbish heap', an almost holiday atmosphere prevailed, as Megan Ryan observed.

We propped boards on bricks to lay a communal breakfast table. People produced whatever food and crockery they could find. I was delighted to discover our food-safe still intact in the courtyard though its contents were a trifle dusty. I didn't see who chose treacle tart and cold fish for breakfast, but someone found it acceptable for the plates were emptied.

Mrs Ryan saw, too, a sight which typified the determination of one of her neighbours not to let being bombed-out disrupt his usual habits.

In what had been a ground-floor flat and was now a framework of charred beams a man stood shaving in water which dripped from above into a cracked bowl. 'Nice and warm,' he grinned. 'Must turn up for work looking spruce, even if the office *is* burned down.'

Besides the shared experience of dirt and debris many people have more personal memories of that morning. A 'Special' about to leave his damaged home for his job as a draughtsman at GEC Ltd, on the Foleshill Road, was astonished to find that the wireless set still worked: 'It told me Roy Fox had just played "Nights of Gladness".' In Cox Street a shopkeeper was observed trying to boil

a kettle on a still smouldering incendiary bomb, and the same eye-
witness, a local factory worker, remembers a policeman asking to
borrow a ladder to retrieve 'a pair of field glasses hanging out of a
plum tree'. This man, while helpfully trying, with a workmate, to
prevent people going down a street which contained two unexploded bombs, also encountered at least one citizen who was far
from grateful – a woman who owned a small shop in the street. She
called them 'all the names she could think of' for interfering with
her trade and when the bombs had finally been defused had her
revenge by refusing to serve them.

Among most people, that day, there was a general readiness to
help. One office worker found that her aunt had taken in 'a whole
shelter full of people' who had been soaked by a broken water main.
'When I arrived . . . there she was,' this observer remembers, 'with
a houseful of folk. . . . There was a huge fire in the grate and a
Tilley lamp. . . . There seemed to be kettles and pans everywhere,
and tea or soup was being handed out to all and sundry'.

Those fortunate enough still to have a roof over their heads, or a
tap that worked, readily shared these blessings with complete
strangers. One woman, then a fourteen-year-old schoolgirl,
remembers visiting one such oasis in Hearsall Lane. 'A continual
stream of people armed with buckets trudged through the house to
the kitchen', but 'the lady of the house did not appear to be in the
least perturbed'. An electrician's mate at Morris Motors in Durbar
Avenue, who lived only a hundred yards away, remembers a couple
approaching him and explaining 'they had been bombed out'. With
his wife away in Yorkshire and room to spare he 'offered them
shelter. It was five years before they left.' A woman living with her
father in Woodside Avenue 'invited in anyone who was passing',
until their guests included 'one lady with a parrot and another with
a dog. We made endless cups of tea and sandwiches.' When
supplies began to run short, her father, she remembers, 'said,
"Open that tin of salmon" and I said, "But that's for an emergency."
He replied, "What the devil's this?" – I was told of that for years.'

The night had left many grim and gruesome legacies. Dr Ashworth's wife, emerging from her shelter in Leamington Road, had
a hideous reminder of the perils through which her family had just
passed: the sight of 'a dog running down the road with a child's
arm in its mouth'. A Coundon man, on his way to work a little

later, noticed 'a car with two people in it on the pavement', and, on closer inspection, discovered that though the vehicle 'was not touched', the occupants 'were both dead'. Mr E. A. Cox, returning to his job at the Food Office in Warwick Row, remembers carrying his cycle round the rubble surrounding one crater which contained human remains. 'If I had had any breakfast I would have lost it,' he confesses. 'A woman's head lay on the edge of the rubbish with her eyes wide open. It turned my stomach. . . . A little further on a man's body was lying in the gutter minus his head.'

Alderman George Hodgkinson found that 'the local shopping centre' near his home in Moseley Avenue 'presented an awful sight. There were human torsos badly burned lying around, the victims of a land-mine.' A quarter of a mile away, in the beer cellar of the Motor Hotel, he saw the consequences of a direct hit, for here 'the bodies of women lay piled up one upon the other, a tangled mass of humanity'. One man coming of the night shift at the Armstrong Siddeley factory in the centre of the city had an even more distressing experience: as 'I came into the Much Park Street area . . . I saw a van filled with bodies they had been collecting. I saw two men carrying a stretcher with a body on it and a little girl running after them screaming "Mother!" I shall never forget that all my life.'

The best antidote to brooding on such horrors was activity. Not knowing if her husband (in fact detained at the Control Centre) was alive or dead, but fearing the worst, Dr Eveleen Ashworth set about imposing order upon the chaos in Leamington Road that had been her home.

I hunted among the ruins of my house for some clothes for Winnie [her fifteen-year-old maid] and the girls [her daughters aged three and seven]. I tried to collect what I could out of the house and got some blankets and what clothes I could find that were not full of holes. . . . Something had gone through our wardrobe from one end to the other. I put what I could find in our air-raid shelter. I also looked among the rubble for matches, candles, tins of food, etc., and stored these. I had a standing order for two rabbits a week from a local farmer. He came as usual that morning, so I said 'Leave them', and paid him.

I could see clothes, including my daughter's school hat, high in the trees across the road. On the railway line an engine was wrecked on a huge pile of rubble and was so precariously balanced it rocked in the breeze. . . . A delayed action bomb went off in the open ground near the railway line and further rocked the engine.

Among the last people in the city to learn that he had been bombed out was Dr Alan Ashworth, for only at midday was he able to leave the Control Centre and it was 1.30 p.m. before he reached his home and knew the worst:

The roof had gone: the front of the house over the garage had fallen out on the drive, and the floor of the bedroom over the garage had fallen on to my car, and my motor-cycle, which was in the garage, was crushed completely. The only part of the house which was more or less intact was the rear back corner. . . . There was no sign of my family.

Dr Eveleen Ashworth, after taking her two small children to safety, was in fact in a house in a nearby road, as she remembers:

On hearing in the street outside a voice saying 'Has anybody seen Mrs Ashworth?' I rushed out to greet my husband. None of us had had any food since the day before, so that friendly neighbour boiled an egg for each of us and we had tea; this was the only meal we had that day.

Dr Alan Ashworth takes up the story:

My wife and I returned to the house and tried to assess what might be salvaged. I found myself picking up from the debris personal items, such as battered photo frames, looking at them and throwing them back – the same reaction as I have seen in documentary films of refugees returning to their homes after the war had passed through their villages – and I understood their feeling of the futility of it all. I had a grand piano which appeared to be comparatively undamaged. My wife and I cleared as much of the plaster, etc., as possible from the carpet and placed it over the piano to protect it at least from the rain.

While the Ashworths were salvaging what they could from the ruins of their home the evacuation of the Coventry and Warwickshire Hospital was proceeding. Among those affected was the fourteen-year-old Bedworth girl whose experiences in the woman's surgical ward have already been described.

We were all taken outside on to the grass verges in front of the hospital. It was very, very cold and you could see the frost on the trees and grass, but nobody seemed to feel it. We were all too amazed to see the destruction and to know we were still alive.

As the morning went on the ambulances came and we were put in and after what seemed an endless journey we found ourselves in Stratford on

Avon. . . . We all had to have a good scrub when we got there as we were unrecognizable, hair matted with oil, cuts all dried in blood, all our possessions lost, gas mask, ration books, identity cards and all. The ARP wardens were wonderful and sent a telegram to mum to tell her I was all right but I don't think she ever got it.

The apparently endless stream of ambulances flowing into and out of Coventry helped to spread the belief that the number of injured was enormous, few people realizing that most of those being moved were ordinary hospital patients. In addition to ordinary peacetime ambulances 'ARP ambulances' consisting of vans adapted to carry stretchers on racks and Midland Red coaches with seats removed to accommodate eight to ten 'passengers' lying full length, were used and in Jenner Street an observant ten-year-old boy already noticed how the gate leading into the hospital grounds, usually kept locked, was especially opened that morning, to let the vehicles in. 'All that day,' he remembers, 'there was a line of them waiting to get into the hospital, some civil but also some Army ones. At times the line didn't seem to move.'

While existing patients were being removed as fast as possible, others were still being brought in for treatment. Two of them were transported by the night driver from the aircraft factory at Baginton who, on returning to duty that morning, had been sent with the works ambulance to an incident in Much Park Street.

I inquired where I could put them and a voice shouted up, 'Do the best you can and put them somewhere.' The room was crammed full, a large room, waiting room, corridor, overflowed with the injured. Most of them had tickets on, either round the neck or arm. . . . A big black woman whispered to me as I was coming out. Could I give her a drink of water? She was in a terrible mess. . . . This is where I first felt sick, seeing so many injured. I returned again to the city but while waiting for more victims . . . managed to get a double whisky down me.

Another man who helped to load ambulances at Gulson Road Hospital was a member of a rescue team from Birmingham. 'There were,' he remembers, 'sad scenes as families were split up, parents and children having to be sent to different hospitals.' After an exhausting day this man and his colleagues got back to their depot to find that the storekeeper there at least was unmoved by events at Coventry. 'When we handed in our emergency ration tins . . . all he could say was, "I see you have eaten all the bloody chocolate"!'

12

CLOSED, BUT NOT FOR LONG

*'One of the girls said, "Where is my machine?" It had
just disappeared down a large hole.'*
*Coventry factory worker recalling the morning of 15
November 1940*

WHILE housewives all over Coventry faced a massive task of
clearing up, most people with jobs went to work more or less as
usual, or at least tried to, for the familiar daily routine was something to cling to at a time when all the normal landmarks of life
seemed suddenly removed. Usually, however, they found they
had had a wasted journey. Leonard Dacombe, coming off the
eventful night shift at the Coventry Climax factory, remembers
how the crowd of expectant employees swelled, until 'our managing
director, after a tour of inspection, called us all together in the yard
and told us that although the factory was badly damaged, most of
the machinery was in a reasonable condition, so we had better go
home and report again on Monday morning to start clearing up the
mess'.

Mr Dacombe's next thought was to try to find out what had
happened to his 'young lady' and he set out for her house, carrying
his bicycle over the ubiquitous rubble. The future Mrs Dacombe
had meanwhile been turned away from her workplace, Thomas
Bushill Ltd, for the best of reasons – it had been burned down – and
had then 'called at the Friars Road factory of Coventry Climax' to
inquire after him, only to be 'told that the Widdrington Road
factory had been destroyed'. They finally had a joyful reunion at
her home, and Mr Dacombe then faced an equally emotional meeting with his landlady who 'burst into tears when I came in', having,
'as I was so late', assumed the worst.

One woman, who looked after her widower father at their home
to the west side of the city, was also determined to get to work that

day, though they agreed that 'whatever happened' they would both 'get home by seven in the evening'. The journey to the factory where she held a managerial position took two and a half hours. Finally, she arrived to find 'hundreds of people' standing outside the factory gates, inside which were delayed action bombs, and 'we were told to go home and report on the following Monday. I was offered a lift home and we covered thirty-two miles, to avoid craters, ruins, etc.'

The morning proved equally frustrating for the young trainee draughtsman from the Humber Works whose escape from a wreckage-blocked Anderson outside his 'digs' in Wyken has previously been described, for after the usual roundabout journey, 'when I arrived at the Humber Road gates I was told by the gateman that unless I was a maintenance man or electrician I would not be allowed in', as the works were 'extensively damaged'.

In most firms Friday was pay day, but with records in disarray and banks temporarily inaccessible, employees who did manage to get to work were usually given a payment on account. Some, however, 'terrified at the prospect of being in the city another night' or 'eager to return home to Ireland', demanded every penny owing to them, as one punch card supervisor in the accounts department of the Daimler No. 2 Engine Works at Brown's Lane, Allesley, three miles from the city centre, observed. She saw the chief wages clerk and accountant return 'visibly shaken' from an encounter with a group who had formed in the late afternoon 'demanding pay in full. There had obviously been ugly scenes', only averted by the payment of 'subs' (i.e. advances) of £10 a head, drawn from the safe.*

For people from outside Coventry the journey to work provided spectacular evidence of the severity of the riad. One woman living at Bedworth and working at the Courtaulds factory in the Foleshill Road while her husband was away in the Army, remembers that the driver of her coach shrewdly predicted that they would need him again in half an hour. Only the shell of the main works was still standing and half of her own 'shop', the warping shed, lay in ruins. 'One of the girls,' she recalls, 'said, "Where is my machine?" It had just disappeared into a large hole. We looked down and there was her pinafore still on the end.' Here, too, the workers were sent

---

*£10 was a private's pay for more than fourteen weeks. A soldier or sailor could not, however, ask to go home on the ground that he did not like being shot at.

home again and 'just after we had gone a delayed action bomb went off and killed a foreman who happened to be in the yard'.

One millwright, who faced a ten-mile journey from Warwick to his factory in Pool Meadow, found that no train services were running to the main station but finally reached Tile Hill station in a cattle truck, took a bus to Hearsall Common, and from there walked the remaining mile through the heart of old Coventry.

The sight [in Spon Street] was awful. There were shops and houses still burning and people had stacked their furniture in the middle of the street and small children sat on top of it, with their mothers crying. There were also sides of beef, whole pigs and sheep from butchers' shops all over the place. Finally, reaching the factory the managing director . . . met me and said, 'Come on, millwright, we're all in the front line now, get the machines off the roof and let's get the shop going.'

The Birmingham tinsmith who had enjoyed a particularly easy run home the night before faced this morning a very different journey back. One of his regular passengers, who had been on all-night AFS duty, refused to turn out, on the grounds that 'our factory was probably flattened by now', while the wife of another had refused even to wake him as he had only got to bed an hour before. The driver set off alone:

I had no sooner reached the Swan at Yardley, to turn on to the Coventry Road, when I began to doubt whether I should reach Coventry that day for it seemed as if every Army vehicle had had orders to report at Coventry and were all using the main road from Birmingham. . . . It was a lousy morning, a very damp mist, very cold, and though it was now about 7 a.m. it was very dark. I took my place in the lane behind an Army lorry full of soldiers and I could see the glistening of a cap badge, or the glowing tip of a cigarette . . . in the darkness of the interior. I noticed . . . how serious and grave everyone was. There was no chatter, no shouted witticisms, . . . no jokes were bandied back and forth . . . From what I could see in the dim light, everyone seemed tense and expectant.

An hour and a half later this man, still 'about seven or eight miles from Coventry' was stopped by a police inspector.

He asked me where I was going . . . if I could prove I worked in Coventry . . . and what petrol I was using, 'supplementary' or 'basic'*. . . . When I

*It was legal to use the 'basic' petrol ration (later abolished) as one wished. Additional 'supplementary' petrol could only be used for the purpose for which it had been issued.

had satisfied him . . . he let me through. . . . I think it was my steel helmet marked 'Warden' and my service respirator on the back seat which finally swayed him. He told me that he was turning back 95 per cent of private cars because their occupants were only intent on seeing the extent of the damage. He said he had no time for those sort of people and a few that he had turned back this morning would be prosecuted for misuse of petrol. . . . So he let me through. . . . It was well turned 10 a.m. by now and . . . drizzling, a really awful morning. I noticed it was beginning to get darker again and an unpleasant smell seemed in the air. I was still more than seven miles away from Coventry. I began to wonder why it was so murky . . . and suddenly the almost unbelievable truth burst upon me. The murk was smoke from the fires of Coventry unable to get away because of low lying cloud and the smell, which I was now able to recognize, was that of burning. . . .

Finally when stopped for the third time, this driver decided 'to call it a day', and, following police instructions, turned off down a side road and made his way home.

A Birmingham man drove into Coventry that day with his father with whom he ran a family plumbing business and was reassured to see the traditional 'three spires' still pointing skywards in the distance.

A few minutes later I stopped. We were in what looked like a brick and rubble field. 'Where the hell are we?' my father asked. I replied, 'At the moment we are in the middle of the Alvis car factory.' As far as one could see it was rubble and timber. I drove on for half a mile. I stopped again and this time *I* did not know where I was. Everything was flattened. . . . We had had enough. We returned to Birmingham.

The devastation around the Alvis factory, clearly a legitimate military objective, also impressed the driver who had that morning brought in a bus-load of workmen from Dudley. 'The whole row of houses' opposite the works, he noticed, 'had had the effects of blast', leaving '90 per cent with all the tiles off and all the fronts of the houses missing'. Each successive stage of the journey provided further evidence of the efficiency of the German attack. It was, he felt, 'as if Jerry had drawn a ring around Coventry before the raid and after it was all over not many bombs had fallen outside that ring. That's how accurate the bombing was.'

To enter Coventry that morning with a civilian vehicle was far from easy. Mr A. Swaby, a future director of the old-established family building firm of Garlicks, remembers waiting in its yard in Far Gosford Street congratulating himself on having instructed the firm's drivers, some of whom lived as far afield as Warwick, Kenilworth and Corley, to take their lorries home with them, both as a protection against bombing, and to ensure transport for 'any workmen who happened to live near'. Instead of the expected fleet of vehicles, 'from 9.30 a.m. I had drivers walking in saying, "Can't believe it. The b——s wouldn't let my lorry pass."' The situation was only resolved by Mr Swaby walking to St Mary's Street Police Station to get postcards signed as impromptu passes, armed with which his drivers tried again. 'I had them all in by 11 a.m.,' Mr Swaby remembers, 'plenty of punctures, too', though none rivalled his own score of eleven that day as he drove from factory to factory, plus two collected in his car on his way to work.

Some people who managed to get into Coventry did so on foot like a farmer's wife who lived beyond Kenilworth, but was determined to deliver, as promised, orders of swedes, live cockerels, and dressed chickens to various customers in the city.

We got as far as Standard Motors, about two miles from where we wished to go, when we were stopped by a policeman. No cars were allowed further, only ambulances, so we left the swedes in the car, put the cockerels in the sack making it easier for carrying, and I took the basket of dressed chickens, and we set off to walk with our loads. As we walked we saw a lot of City of Birmingham ambulances going to the city. We walked over the common and opposite the shop we saw a huge crater bang in the middle of the road, a burnt-out garage on the right with a wrecked and twisted bus nearby . . . we went down a side street . . . and . . . at last we reached the shop . . . and delivered the produce. We then proceeded towards Spon Street [where] a dreadful sight met our eyes. Nearly all the shops on one side were still smoking and some well alight . . . we saw nothing but destruction on every side. We saw one house on a corner which was cut in two lengthwise, and up in the bedroom I saw a neat row of coats and dresses on coat hangers, in a wardrobe, but the wardrobe was gone. There were several Union Jacks put out above the ruins, but everyone we saw was very quiet and busy trying to deal with their own private upset. . . . We stood looking up Smithford Street – a narrow street with many shops. It looked just like a picture we had of the ruins of Ypres in the 1914–18 war. On the other side of the road there was the only baker's shop . . . able to function. . . . We joined a queue and were thrilled to get four buns. . . . Threading our way through the broken glass, bricks and rubble we reached our last shop where we found the shopkeeper dreadfully distressed at losing her house, so we told her if she could get transport later on we would willingly put her up. . . . When we reached Hearsall Common, tired out and very upset, we were . . . thrilled to find a Birmingham corporation bus which took us to where the car was parked.

For some other tradesmen that morning it was also business as usual. One Special Constable, on the way from his badly damaged house in St Paul's Road, Foleshill, to his parents' (which turned out to have been 'bombed at the back' and to be 'alight at the front'), was 'more than surprised to meet a milkman determined to go on his round and serve his customers'. A woman working for a news-agent in Jordan Well recalls that the business opened as usual. 'People came in for their Woodbines and we heard the whole story,' she remembers, though 'for a while we carried on business with half a shop, windows boarded up and no stock.'

The destruction of some familiar store could seem almost as great a blow as the loss of one's home. A farmer's wife found it hard to believe that the Singer shop had been wrecked; she had bought her own much used sewing machine there. A girl living in Glendower Avenue, Whoberly, could not take in the report of her father that 'the new Owen Owen store which we had watched being built for so long' was now 'just a mess of tangled metal'. After all, she reflected, 'I had just had a new dress from it.'

Owen Owen was already the second most famous ruin in Coventry. Its general manager, Leslie Worthington, when he arrived to see what was left of the premises 'gutted from roof to sub-basement', found his way 'barred by a sign attached to a rope saying "Keep Out, Unexploded Bomb"' but he eventually reached the premises, to find 'a naval officer putting in the boot of his small car the deton-ator-fuse he had just removed from a land-mine. I made a rough sign,' remembers Mr Worthington, 'which read CLOSED – BUT NOT FOR LONG and stood it at the front of the building. In a matter of moments the manager of Lyons asked if he could put up a temporary stand on the forecourt and sell refreshments.'

Another shop whose destruction made an enormous impact was the central branch of the Co-op. One woman who worked there, the wife of an airman, remembers leaving her home in Queen Isabel's Avenue, Cheylesmore, that Friday morning, despite her eleven hours in the Anderson, preoccupied with an errand entrusted to her the night before by the manager, who had asked her to call at another branch on the way to work to exchange some tobacco for a different brand.

I swept up the broken glass, put the front door in position . . . exchanged my little parcel and proceeded to find my way to the central premises. It took me three hours [but] I eventually arrived in West Orchard to find the whole central premises destroyed [and] the manager, Mr B., and several of the staff . . . standing viewing the damage with dismay. I walked up to Mr B., and handed him the parcel of tobacco. He couldn't believe I could be so conscientious after such a night . . . I never knew what happened to the tobacco.

The central Coventry branches of the great national banks had, it soon turned out, got off comparatively lightly. Anxious citizens soon discovered that their strongrooms were still intact, though one manager had to organize a financial rescue squad to tunnel through the debris to reach his now urgently needed reserves of cash. The staffs of all the banks turned up in force that morning, 'eager to get on with the work', according to the local newspaper, and though many people wanted to draw money out, to get away, the first customer that Friday at the Coventry Savings Bank arrived soon after it opened to deposit some.

Offices had suffered as severely as shops, including the Central Division A R P headquarters. 'I made my way to the office,' remembers Harold Tomley, 'wondering what I should find; what I did find was a huge pile of bricks; the furniture in the top storey' – salvaged from houses bombed in earlier raids – 'had provided a wonderful start for the blaze. Somewhere underneath the pile were the steel safes with all my records if they were not burnt to ashes.' Mr Tomley sought out the corporation's A R P officer who readily 'approved my suggestion of temporarily working in Warden Post 107, which was located in a classroom of the Technical College at The Butts.' By nightfall he was back in business.

Miss Lucy Moseley duly set out for her work at the Coventry Registrar's office at the usual time.

I made my way gradually towards the town, having to detour at various spots, appalled at the destruction. Looking 'up the town' from Greyfriars Green the whole city centre appeared to be a still burning and smoking ruin. The old Market Hall with its big clock tower had gone. . . . Never again we would go to Glenn's sweet stall to buy large quantities of their boiled sweets to pack in a box and send off to my aunt in the USA. (She said she could never buy such sweets and they always reminded her of home.) One of my tasks each week pre-war was to call for cheese at the stall kept by the Galsworthy Brothers who, in spotless white aprons, always asked one to taste a small piece before purchasing.

Never again would we pass the Market Square on a summer Sunday evening and hear the Salvation Army Band – and a regular 'Speakers' Corner'. . . . Now and again I met people I knew returning home after having tried to report for work. I'm afraid we were all a bit emotional. The greeting was usually 'Thank God you're safe! How are you all?' and it was heartfelt and warm. Eventually I did reach Little Park Street about 10.15 a.m. where our Superintendent Registrar . . . was standing on the doorstep. Such a smile he gave as he saw me and said, 'Here's another one at last!' For a few moments we were all discussing our various experiences. We and our families had all survived. Around us Coventry burned! The cardboard box factory of Thomas Bushill and Sons, not a stone's throw off, was a wreck, flames and smoke still pouring from it. The corner of Little Park Street and Earl Street opposite the Council House was well alight and the fire was spreading fast. In sight was one lone fireman with a hose – but the water supply went suddenly. We watched as a gents' outfitters gradually went down in flames. . . . I remember discussing in the cold gloom with a colleague what the numbers of dead would be – we felt it could be thousands.

Another organization for which there could be no respite was the Ministry of Food, and its caretaker, Mr E. A. Cox, returned next morning to find the building, like every other in central Coventry, with no electricity. This left him with a new and distinctly unwelcome duty, attending fifty paraffin lamps, badly needed on that dismal November day.

The lamps had pumps attached which needed using fairly often to maintain a good light. . . . Those lamps nearly drove me insane. All day long there were repeated calls for Mr Cox to attend to the flaming lamps. I got so I hated my own name. All fifty had to be filled twice a day but the main trouble came from the front office where there was a lot of draught from the doors continually opening and shutting. . . . If I had dared, and I was very much tempted to, I would have loved to kick those lamps one by one through the back door and use a heavy hammer on the lot.

Everyone out and about in Coventry that morning noted the loss of familiar landmarks. The Queen's Hotel in Hertford Street, the regular meeting-place of local businessmen, had been badly damaged, the whole front of the building having been brought down, though a bar was soon open among the ruins. Even worse hit was a link with the old Coventry, the King's Head, on the site of an old inn from which the mail coaches had set off to London and Liverpool. But there was one distinguished survivor. The wooden effigy of 'Peeping Tom', kept in a glass case in the hotel – he had formerly for more than a century looked down on the traffic in Broadgate – had, it was learned, been given a 'fireman's lift' from the building by a Coventry headmaster then serving in the A F S and dumped outside a nearby bank, in whose vaults, unseen but safe, he spent the rest of the war.*

Coventry's trams were a familiar feature of the city's life and the sight of twisted tracks sticking yards into the air impressed many people that morning. For the Permanent Way Foreman of the Coventry Tramways Department, however, they represented something more than a bizarre spectacle.

I made a tour of the roads to see what damage had been done to the track. The power cables had been ripped out during the raid and left trams standing where they were . . . some . . . in twos and threes . . . in Stoney Stanton Road, Binley Road, Stoke Road, Bell Green Road and Broadgate. All had to be towed back to the depot. . . . Making my way over the tracks, I found tram lines ripped up, craters everywhere. Where a bomb had been dropped in the track . . . in places the rails were standing up twenty to thirty feet in the air. To get the trams back to the depot they had been taken up side streets where there were no rails to run on. Walking up Stoke Road, a lady came to me . . . and said, 'There is part of a tram line on our back lawn.' I went to find out what it was . . . a complete crossing complete with sets. With the cement, the sets, the parts of line attached to it, the whole thing would weigh about fifteen cwt. . . . Where the crossing should have been was twenty yards from the house. It had blown over a three-storey house on to the back lawn and it took five men to move it up the garden path and on to the street.

Further along the road an old lady came to me and asked me if I was looking for pieces of tram line. She said, 'There is a piece of tram line on my son's bed.' I found a piece of tram rail about twelve feet long. . . . It had gone through the roof and landed across the bed. It had to be dragged down the stairs. I sent the cart out to pick up things belonging to us and

*'Peeping Tom' is now in a glass case in the Hotel Leofric.

the men were told that sets and pieces of rail were lying in back yards, etc. A caretaker from a school asked us to clear his school yard. We had a load of sets and rails from there, yet it was a good quarter mile from the nearest track.

For the self-employed the destruction of their business could mean near-ruin and a tragic end to a lifetime's effort. One seventeen-year-old girl, living with her family in the Stoke area, witnessed that night just such a tragedy. After a night under the stairs her father and brother set out that morning to see if the family still had a livelihood from the signwriting and lampshade-making business they had built up.

They had to clamber over piles of hot bricks and ashes and as they approached could smell a lovely smell of cooked soups, ham and tongue, the cooked remains of half of the canteen supplies, tins lying around with all their lids popped*. . . . The cast iron presses and blocks for cutting out price tickets and the black-out lampshades . . . all welded into solid blocks. Ashes from the card and paper store room knee deep in ash flakes, like grey and black snow. They managed to locate the yard outside the building and the old disused well cover, under which father had suspended the business books, wrapped in oiled silk, every night for several weeks, much to the amusement of all his business friends in the same yard. 'There goes old J. burying his books again!' The books were safe and dry. Father was the only businessman to get all his bills paid and dues collected, with the exception of the cost of one poster which had been delivered the night before the raid, being a Thursday. The shop had been closed and my brother had the key to fit the poster while the shop was closed. This he'd done but no one had seen the poster so no one could be expected to pay for it.†

Some unfortunates that morning found both home and livelihood gone, like Mrs Megan Ryan, whose hairdressing business had been knocked out by a heavy paving stone which had come through the roof, and was paralysed by the lack of gas, electricity and water, while her first married home had gone up in flames before her eyes. 'We'd married two months before,' reflected Mrs Ryan that morning. 'Then we had a home, the salon with its financial security and I

*As a precaution, amply vindicated by events, this man had kept the other half of the supplies for his factory canteen at home.

†This was the end of this business. 'My brother worked at the Food Office issuing ration books and I got a job at an estate office,' this informant reports.' Father having lost everything it was now up to us.'

was fit. Now the home had gone, the salon was closed and I was ailing' – in fact in the early weeks of pregnancy – 'and we were down to an income of only eighteen shillings a week', her husband's wage as an apprentice.

We began to search for our belongings, piling them together. My wedding dress, worn less than two months before, improbably lay unharmed. Books were still stacked safely in our book-table, though its top was burned to charcoal. Our wedding present china lay unbroken on the torn mattress. From men working amongst the smouldering ruins of the next door factory Peter borrowed a small hand-cart. . . . We had decided to go to my father's house on the outskirts of the city.

Pushing, pulling, lifting, we manoeuvred the laden hand-cart around bomb craters, over debris and the snaking useless fire-hoses, until we came to the outer suburbs. As we pushed on the desolation lessened, until we came to whole streets which had escaped destruction . . . where children played and housewives went about their daily chores.

13
A GOOD NIGHT'S SLEEP

*'A certain number of people left Coventry and police took
steps to deal with them in the surrounding districts.'*
Ministry of Home Security Weekly Appreciation Report,
22 November 1940

'PEOPLE were pouring out of Coventry on anything they could
find, even hand-carts and horses and carts.' This memory of one
War Reserve policeman of the morning of Friday, 15 November,
while he was himself removing his own family, is one that thousands of other people share, though it found no place in the news-
reels of the time.

Before the war the government had believed that a cordon of
police or troops might be needed to prevent panic-stricken hordes
of civilians, their nerve irretrievably gone, pouring out of bombed
cities into the surrounding countryside, spreading terror wherever
they went, and though this never happened what occurred in
Coventry in November 1940 was not impossibly far removed from
this recurrent nightmare.

The authorities later boasted that when, on Saturday 16 November, transport was provided for the 10000 people expected to want
to leave, only 300 turned up. This tiny response meant nothing.
Thousands of people had gone already, and many children were
waiting to leave with their schools. Some – perhaps most – of the
evacuees had left in a planned and orderly way to find temporary
accommodation of their own, often with friends and relatives. But
a sizable minority, as every account makes plain, had simply fled,
abandoning jobs and homes with as little deliberation or thought
of the consequences as a soldier flinging away his rifle and running
in panic from the field of a lost battle.

The exodus had begun long before midnight, while the raid was
still at its height. In the early hours of the morning the numbers
leaving grew. One Special Constable, making his way home to St

Paul's Road, watched the crowds of adults walking towards Bed-worth, some with children but many merely 'with their pets and cases of belongings' and all seemed 'dazed'. Within an hour or so the flow of refugees had increased to 'a steady stream making their way into the country, some carrying 'canaries and other birds in their cages'. At RAF Bramcote, where some of the first refugees had been taken, 'every man on the station gave up his breakfast' and Aircraftman Rex Fray recalls seeing 'over a thousand in a queue with blankets round them all filing into the cookhouse'.

This was the experience of the tinsmith who was trying to drive into Coventry from Birmingham at about 8 a.m.:

In the faintly improving light I could now make out the figures of people walking. Small groups of people, all on foot, and all walking in the same direction, towards Birmingham, some carrying bundles; now and again I could see a group pushing a piled-up pram. I saw a boy of about ten or eleven years old, pushing a bicycle, and suddenly, like a flash of lightning, the reason burst upon me. These poor unfortunate people had been made homeless in the raid... and were now trying to reach a place of comparative safety. . . . Never before or since have I seen such a pitiful sight. These poor, miserable, homeless, bewildered souls, walking as if in a dream, anywhere to get away from the horror of the last fifteen hours. . . . This was not a film taken in a foreign land, these were our own people in England. It was unbelievable that such a thing could happen. . . . In my imagination I could see myself and my family, shambling along, going God knows where, anywhere, carrying with us our few precious things we had managed to salvage, our backs turned to our stricken city, obscured by evil-smelling black smoke.

A similar reaction affected the veteran journalist Hilde Marchant whose press pass had carried her through the military cordon:

It was a familiar sight – one I had seen in Spain and Finland. Yet this was worse. . . . These people moved against a background of suburban villas, had English faces, used the English tongue, wore English clothes. They were our own kind. . . . As we came nearer the city both sides of the road filled with lorries, cars, hand-carts and perambulators. . . . The lorries were packed with women and children sitting on suitcases or bundles of bedding. On the pavement the women rested their heavy suitcases or looked down the road to see if there was a corner in the over-burdened lorries. . . . The children were trying to sleep on their mothers' shoulders as the lorries rocked them over the bricks and tiles that carpeted the road. The luggage racks of the baby cars that wriggled through were stacked with baggage and perhaps a baby's high chair, or cot, or a rocking horse. But the most pathetic of all were those who just leaned against the railings at the roadside, too exhausted to move, their luggage in heaps around them and a fretful tired child crying without temper or anger. There was just bewilderment and frustration in their faces. They did not understand that they had survived.

The wife of the Rev. W. B. Sells, travelling in by car from Leamington around 7 a.m., was struck by the dejected appearance of the 'hundreds of homeless refugees, prams and bicycles laden with their possessions, streaming out of the city along the Coventry to Kenilworth Road. As they moved slowly along, their whole attitude was one of blank despair.'

One of those making her way to Leamington on foot was the seventeen-year-old girl caught in Coventry overnight after her intended date with a girl-friend and two airmen, as described earlier. 'The scene as we walked down the Birmingham Road was like something from a film,' she agrees, as 'people with cases, blankets, parcels, prams and children trudged wearily away from this devastated city', and she still remembers 'a lovely hot cup of tea from the mobile canteen' manned by the Salvation Army. (Her reception when she got home was less welcoming. 'My sister,' she remembers wryly, 'told me off for staying out all night.')

Leamington, a dignified Spa whose mere name suggested security, was a popular destination that morning. One woman living in Highland Road, Coventry, who had found herself bombed out set off with her husband and two sons for relations there, along 'roads full up with people moving their goods on prams, trucks, and any old things they could push'. Once arrived at her destination she became embarrassed, she confesses, at the thought of displaying the black eye she had received during the raid, though her son consoled her by pointing to the long cut – it had required eight stitches –·on his father's head. 'Come on, mum,' he told her, 'they will think you had your own back and hit him with the frying pan.'

The arrival of refugees in towns and villages for miles around Coventry spread the news of its ordeal all over the Midlands. Warwick, Stratford-on-Avon and Rugby all witnessed the arrival of evacuated hospital patients, bombed-out people, or ordinary residents of Coventry who had had enough. The wife of one inspector at Nuneaton railway station entertained two of them as unexpected guests for breakfast, brought home by her husband from among the crowd 'trying to get trains to relatives in various parts of the country. I gave them breakfast and they had a wash, then went back to the station to catch a train for London.' Nearer Coventry not merely hotel-keepers but ordinary householders were soon sadly turning away applicants eager for any sort of roof over their head, as one farmer's wife remembers on returning from a visit to Coventry.

Eventually we reached home and almost at once a car-load of people arrived asking for shelter . . . so shocked that all they asked was a roof over their heads and a chair. We fixed them up on mattresses on the floor of one room and they sat round a fire and had tea and tried to talk. We did the milking in the dark and just then another car-load of people came who had lost everything except the clothes they were wearing. Altogether we had seventeen people sleeping in our house that night.

Not merely spare rooms but living-rooms were pressed into service. One woman working at the Daimler aero-engine factory, living at Meriden, remembers that 'we had three or four additional people sleeping on the lounge floor' and 'everyone with beds "doubled-up". I shared my single bed with the accountant's secretary.'

Few of those who left that Friday did so with much regret. One woman, whose house off the Birmingham Road had been badly damaged, still feels grateful to the neighbour and his wife who 'drove us to relatives in the country', although 'there were five of us in the Austin Seven, complete with dog, blankets, food and hot-water bottles'. A young mother from Daventry Road, taking her baby to stay with her husband's parents at South Littleton, experienced, she now recalls, 'an immense feeling of relief when passing through the shattered streets of Coventry, knowing that whatever might be going to happen in a few hours' time I should not be in it'. Another housewife, in flight from her 'blasted' home in Treherne Road, was struck by the contrast between the devastation they had left behind and the tranquil countryside. 'It didn't seem possible that the place was normal as always,' she felt, as she and her husband cycled up the long main street of Little Harrowden, *en route* to her mother's home in Kettering.

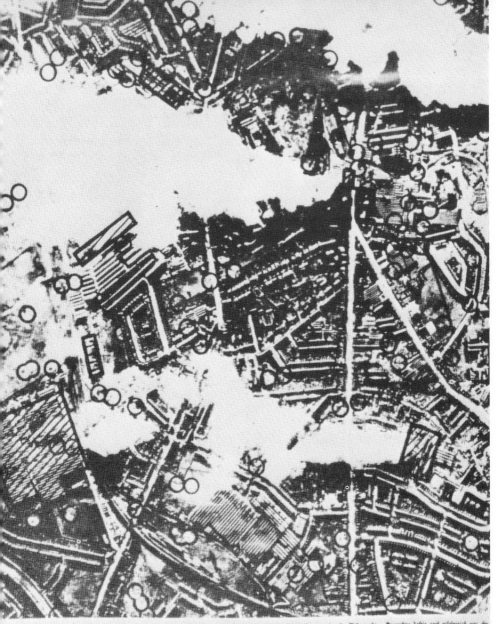

entry — coventriert

Am 15. November meldet der Bericht des Oberkommandos der Wehrmacht: „Besonders heftig und erfolgreich war der
reifende Angriff starker Kampfverbände der Generalfeldmarschälle Kesselring und Sperrle auf Coventry, wo zahlreiche
Motorenfabriken und große Anlagen der Flugzeugzubehörindustrie sowie andere kriegswichtige Einrichtungen mit Bomben
schweren und schwersten Kalibers belegt wurden, die grundlegs Verwüstungen anrichteten. Ungeheuere Feuersbrünste, die von
großen Rohstofflagern genährt wurden und bis zur Kenntlichkeit sichtbar waren, vollendeten das Vernichtungswerk . . . Nach
diesem Großangriff der deutschen Luftwaffe, der die Vergeltung für einen britischen Angriff auf München darstellte, erfanden
die Engländer ein neues Verbum „to coventry", coventrieren. Mit diesem Wort, das man mit „restlos zerstören" übersetzen
könnte, gaben sie den Erfolg des deutschen Angriffs zu, dessen Wirkung das von einem deutschen Aufklärungsflugzeug auf-
genommene Bild deutlich zeigt. Die Vierecke umschließen zerstörte Fabrikanlagen, die Kreise die schlimmen Bombentrichter.

entrated. This was a German reconnaissance photograph, issued shortly after the raid.
propagandist caption, which blames the British, not the Germans, for coining the verb
coventrate', reads: 'On 15 November 1940 the German High Command issued this
muniqué: "The non-stop attack of strong formations under the command of Field Marshal
selring was particularly successful. Numerous factories making aircraft and other factories
ortant to the war effort were bombed with bombs of every calibre. The utmost
astation was caused. After this large-scale attack which was an answer to the British bombing
Munich the English invented a new word 'to coventrate'. With this word, which could be
slated as 'complete destruction', the success of the German attack was admitted."'

Above left: Demolition. For days after the raid dangerous buildings were being pulled down or blown up

Above right: U X B. Soldiers digging for an unexploded bomb

Below: On guard in the ruins. This solitary soldier was photographed in the High Street on 20 November, nearly a week after the raid, when a road had been cleared through the debris

Army to the rescue. The presence of troops, apart from the practical help they gave, helped
ise morale. Note in the background the burned-out shell of Owen Owen's store, which
also hit by H.E.

rmation. A Ministry of Information loudspeaker van giving instructions on where to
in food and shelter. This picture was taken on Saturday, 16 November

Water. Fetching water in buckets from a standpipe, or a street still with a supply

Food. Citizens enjoying sandwiches and tea from a WVS mobile canteen

One member of the night shift at Armstrong Siddeley, who set out to walk to Nuneaton and at Walsgrave village caught a Nuneaton bus which had been turned back there, even managed breakfast of a kind. 'I had still got my mashing [i.e. tea and sugar] and sandwiches that I had rescued before I came out of work' and 'the conductor asked a lady in a nearby cottage to mash the tea and we all shared it before we started back to Nuneaton'.

Few of those whose adventures in Coventry during the great raid have already been described were still there on the following night. The Rev. W. B. Sells, after finding 'the church, hall and vicarage' of St Thomas's little harmed, apart from 'thick coats of dust over everything', had spent the morning touring 'the slums and Butts area' on the fringes of his parish. 'I called on many people,' he remembers, 'especially the old, and found them mostly dazed but defiant.' After being up all night he was not sorry when 'after a morning of stunned, rather dreamy wandering the vicar ordered me off to Leamington with my brother-in-law' – who had arrived by car – 'to have a good night's sleep'.

Escaping from the same area was the young woman Civil Servant bombed out of her hostel who had taken refuge in a house set aside by the YWCA for the purpose. 'Somehow my boy-friend found me, after he'd sustained the initial shock of finding the hostel burned down,' she remembers. 'I was determined not to spend another night in Coventry and together we started to walk to Chesford Grange, near Kenilworth, where I had friends.'

Leonard Dacombe found that his 'young lady' readily accepted when, having exchanged his push-bike for his motor-cycle, he 'called about 4 p.m. and asked her if she would like to go over to Northampton to get some rest'. Despite being constantly stopped by police and asked for their identity cards, Mr Dacombe and his passenger reached Northampton safely and, as it was too far for most of the Coventry refugees, secured rooms in a commercial hotel, the prelude to a much-needed 'quiet weekend'.

The trainee draughtsman at Humber's, bombed out of his digs and turned away from his factory, had a more fatiguing and solitary journey. Having carried his cycle over the rubble to Pool Meadow in search of a bus, or at least food, and finding neither, 'I decided the only thing to do was to cycle to my aunt's, five miles north of Leicester'. His cycle's 'inner tyre was split beyond repair but . . .

after an extensive tour of the neighbourhood I found a garage who sold me an inner tube . . . tied my suitcase to my cycle . . . set off . . . and arrived very weary indeed'.

The bicycle, Coventry's first great contribution to private mobility, really came into its own that day, even when merely pushed. The daughter of a British Thomson-Houston employee, then aged ten, vividly remembers her family's flight from their bomb-damaged home in Oliver Street 'to my grandfather's house in Blackheath, Staffordshire'.

We queued in the road for a drop of water from a water cart and then . . . my father put me on his bicycle and off we started. All the way we were joined by hundreds of others with the same thought in mind – to get out of Coventry – many having lost their homes and all their belongings.

As we were on the outskirts of Coventry an unexploded bomb went off, just as we were passing the spot, and I can still remember the feeling of fright as we ran. My father threw himself on top of my mother and myself as we flung ourselves to the ground, and we just lay there waiting for the debris to settle, and praying hard that we would be spared.

We walked on for many miles and finally managed to get a lift into Birmingham by some kind lorry driver.

While most people were trying to get out of Coventry a few – apart from the firemen, troops and rescue parties already thronging the roads – were trying to get into it. One family living in Glendower Avenue never forgot the kindness and persistence of an aunt who set out from Wellington in Shropshire, fifty miles away, laden with a cooked chicken, milk and tea, walking the final stages of the journey. The brother-in-law of a woman who lived in Harris Road travelled from Doncaster to see her and, when stopped by troops after being turned off the train at Berkswell, pleaded with them so persuasively that they allowed him to march, a solitary civilian, in the middle of the platoon so that he got past other check points unchallenged. Another man, finding his house demolished, walked ten miles to Leamington, praying that his pregnant wife had, unknown to him, already been admitted to the nursing home where she had booked a bed. Here was one story which ended happily: he found himself on arrival not merely still a husband but also a father. An AFS man, then living in St Patrick's Road, came off duty eager to let his family know that he was still alive. He set out 'to walk to Kenilworth, five miles away' to 'borrow a friend's car. I arrived at Fenny Compton [where his family lived] black from head to foot, hardly recognizable, but what a happy reunion it was.'

There were many similar incidents that day in Coventry as well as outside it. One woman, bombed out of her home in Queen Isabel's Avenue, remembers how her sister opened the front door of her home in Wyken to her and we 'looked at one another and burst into tears'. During the raid they had 'felt too furious to cry'. The house was already full of bombed-out friends and she recalls how 'my brother-in-law still jokes about the night he slept with his wife and sister-in-law'. (Propriety, of a sort, was still preserved: 'my sister slept in the middle'.)

Although official evacuation did not begin until the following day there was one exception: children in residential nurseries, and others for whom their mothers could no longer care. That Friday Mrs Elsie Beaufoy, responsible for organizing WVS (Women's Voluntary Service) Rest Centres in Shirley, about thirteen miles from Coventry, found herself required, at two hours' notice, to provide beds and food for a large contingent.

We were not expecting such a large-scale bombing and hadn't got enough food, etc., in. Anyhow I got my helpers together, as all the shops were closed . . . and told my helpers to go round all their friends and collect blankets, rugs, mattresses, bread, fruit and anything they could possibly get that we might need. . . . Then we had a big boiler which we filled with water and concentrated soup. It was a treat to see these poor children tucking in to hot soup and bread, fruit, biscuits and anything we could get hold of. The next day we had dozens of people asking if they could take them into their homes. We also got a lot of toys and books. . . . When bedtime came we laid them in rows on mattresses or blankets, etc., like sardines, and about half a dozen of us stayed up all night watching them with very dim lights on. They were wonderful and . . . very brave, especially the little ones.

There was also an influx of evacuated infants at Birmingham, coped with very differently, as one woman from Sutton Coldfield discovered on visiting the 1st General Canadian Military Hospital at Marston Green.

There were approximately sixty proud faces turned in my direction as I entered this long ward. I see them now, with their peaceful, mellow, smiling quietness, each of the Canadian wounded lying against his pillows with two babes, one in each arm, sleeping peacefully.

For the Moseley family there could be no question of moving far from Coventry; the Mayor's place was clearly as much in Coventry as the King's, according to a popular song of the time, was in London, but after attempting to squeeze all the bedding into the one bedroom with a roof over it they finally decided to retreat to a relative's home at Milverton. 'By dusk,' Lucy Moseley remembers, 'we were on our way to my aunty's. . . . She and my uncle had a bed downstairs so we had the use of her two bedrooms' where the visitors were able to enjoy 'the sheer bliss of undressing and preparing to sleep in a bed for a whole night'.

By the evening of Friday, 15 November, Coventry contained fewer occupants than for any time for half a century past. No one knows precisely how many people had simply moved out, but a special inquiry a year later produced estimates of from 50000 to 100000, i.e. a quarter to half of those then on the Coventry Food Office 'ration strength'. 'As one man said,' the researchers recorded, '"people were frightened and they just went".' This reaction had affected all classes. It was the poorest, streaming along the roads with their pathetic bundles, who were the most visible, and the most numerous, but, reported the investigators, 'we were told that well over half the population of the district round Cannon Hill, a very well-to-do residential area, left their homes after the November raids in spite of the fact that this district is about two miles from the centre of the city'.

Humbler citizens, with no transport and no spare cash, spent the night in rest centres, which, though really intended for the bombed-out, sheltered that night a far higher proportion of 'refugees', who had left their homes from choice. Of 6900 sleeping in county of Warwickshire rest centres, at least 90 per cent (an inquiry revealed) were not genuinely homeless.

When the rest centres were full the refugees turned to any building available. One War Reserve policeman was relieved to find his family a place to sleep on the floor of the village school at Brinklow. A member of the St John Ambulance Brigade who, around 5 p.m., called in at Corley church, five miles from Coventry after cycling round the area to gather news of relations before joining his own wife and children at Buxton, found 'the church . . . full of people, and more kept coming, having walked from Coventry'. The heroic calm which Ministry of Information bulletins regularly attributed to the inhabitants of bombed cities was not much in evidence here. 'I dealt with one or two people suffering from shock,' this man remembers, and 'one lady in particular started screaming as soon as the sirens went'.

Those still in Coventry as darkness fell had more reason for feeling apprehensive. Few people were about and the occasional journalist or policeman who passed along the empty streets found his feet crunching on the universal glass – 'so thick,' remembers one reporter, 'that looking up the street it was as if it was covered with ice' – or sinking uncannily into 'a road . . . as muddy and soft as a country lane' from the earth flung up by the bombs. Everyone in the city now knew what the Luftwaffe could do and the expectation was universal that the bombers would be back to finish the task. In the Technical College classroom in The Butts, where he had set up the ARP Central Division headquarters, Harold Tomley prepared for another night in action, putting up a bed in his office, while his wife and daughter went off to patrol the areas where they were wardens. Here was one family that emphatically had not 'quit'. Also returning to duty was Dr Alan Ashworth, who 'expected another raid to really finish the city off' and was only too well aware there would be 'no difficulty' in locating the target. 'It could be seen fifty miles away.' He acknowledges 'a somewhat emotional parting' with his wife. 'Although nothing was said, neither of us really expected to see the other again. I expected that I would be buried under the rubble of the Council House by morning.' Mrs Ashworth remembers how 'I went with him as far as I could and . . . went back to spend the night alone in the air-raid shelter'. Happily her husband's forebodings proved ill-founded:

The Control Room was lit by a paraffin storm lantern in each section. The emergency battery lighting, which had been used during the previous night, was exhausted and there was no way of charging the batteries. Most of the staff present were very subdued and it was obvious that we all expected the worst. The sirens went about 7.30 p.m. and planes could be heard passing over . . . but by 9.30 p.m. nothing had happened as I put my head on the bench and fell asleep.

14
THE BALANCE SHEET

'Machines damaged. All work stopped.'
Ministry of Home Security inspector's report on Coventry
factory, 16 November 1940

BOTH because of its immediate importance to the war effort, and because the raid had provided a unique test of the effects of bombing, Coventry was soon being subjected to a closer scrutiny than any other blitzed city. The raid of November 1940 became regarded as an experiment on a grand scale on the effects of aerial bombardment and the citizens as its guinea pigs. Detailed studies of what had happened in Coventry continued for years, as Allied planners sought information on how to do the utmost possible damage to German industry. When, in March 1943, a supposedly definitive *Narrative of the Major Features of the Coventry Blitz*, was drawn up from Home Office documents, it had to be amended by *Additional Notes* seven months later and there remained much detailed information scattered about the files of Whitehall and the City Council which did not appear in either document. The facts which follow are those finally agreed after later cross-checking and analysis, not those accepted at the time.

First, then, setting aside the colourful, but subjective and possibly inaccurate impressions of those who lived through the raid, what was the actual weight of the attack? Here there is little dispute. The figures accepted soon afterwards, and confirmed by the official British historian after the war, was 503 tons of high explosive, delivered by 1200–1600 bombs of weights varying from about 100 lb (50 kg) to about half a ton (500 kg). Included in this total were fifty parachute (or land-) mines, each weighing 1000 kg (2200 lb) and containing 700 kg (1560 lb) of high explosive, and in addition the Germans had dropped about 30000 incendiaries, some

'loose', but most in 881 canisters. The vast majority of the incendiaries were of the standard 0·9 kg (nearly 2 lb) magnesium type
but there were also a few oil-bombs and a larger number of explosive
incendiaries. Estimates for these ranged from 17 per cent to 50 per
cent. The police, impartial witnesses, put the figure at around 20
per cent, though even this is probably too high.

Second, what had the raid achieved in terms of its intended
objectives: to destroy the centre of Coventry and knock out the
armaments factories in and around it? The first official account
came from a Ministry of Home Security inspector who arrived in
Coventry at 10 a.m. on the Saturday and left the following day. His
report, dictated on the Monday, provided for his fellow-officials in
Whitehall this picture of the results of the raid:

The principal damage occurred in the medieval centre of the city, about
three-quarters of a mile by half a mile. Of this at least one-third is completely destroyed, mainly by fire, and probably another third will require
extensive rebuilding. . . . The remainder of the city was extensively
plastered with bombs of all types diminishing towards the outer suburbs.
Within the inner ring of suburbs the majority of buildings, mainly
houses, received at least damage to glass and roof coverings. Several
blocks of houses were burnt out and most streets had one or more buildings demolished by high explosives. On the London Road I noticed the
first crater about one mile from the Cathedral and on the Lutterworth
Road to the east, about one and a quarter miles. I understood, however,
that a few bombs were jettisoned beyond that distance, mostly in fields. . . .
     An inspection on foot was made of the commercial and shopping area
round Broadgate. . . . As far as I could judge, an area of about 600 × 400
feet had been completely destroyed. . . . The principal buildings in the
three street blocks in this area were Market Hall, Fish Market and cinema
and Lion Iron Foundry. . . . All these buildings were entirely destroyed. . . .
Lloyds Bank and the National Provincial Bank were extensively damaged
by fire . . . Barclay's Bank . . . had a direct hit with a 250 kg bomb at the
back of the banking hall, but were doing business on Saturday. In Hertford Street, the Empire Theatre, two hotels and the Central Post Office
were either destroyed or seriously damaged. The department store of
Messrs Owen and Owen, a new four-storey and basement steel framed
building, had received a direct hit from a large bomb and had also been
gutted by fire.

The inspector singled out for mention the area around Little
Park Street.

Another area devastated by fire was between Little Park Street, Earl Street and Much Park Street. This is about 600 × 400 feet and consisted almost entirely of old, closely packed domestic and factory premises of poor construction ... Bushill's Printing and Paper Works in Little Park Street, an old multi-storey building, was gutted by fire. . . The fire had spread to numerous adjacent houses.

The visitor went on to report on what concerned the government most, the interference with production:

Coventry contains factories of all sizes, from very large, both new and old, down to quite small factories mainly in back streets . . . employing a few dozen workmen. At a very rough estimate one-third of the factories in the city have been either completely demolished or so damaged as to be out of commission for some months. One-third have sustained considerable damage which will hinder production for some weeks and about one-third have been only slightly damaged. A few escaped altogether.

Later research confirmed this preliminary assessment, except that most major factories were back in production earlier than anyone had dared hope and almost all – excluding those totally destroyed – within six or seven weeks. Apart from two very large new shadow factories on the outskirts of the city, the same inspector reported, referring to 'shadow' factories whose existence had apparently taken the Germans by surprise, almost every large establishment had been damaged to some extent. Eventually detailed reports of damage were submitted on 111 of the 180 'principal factories'. The City Council, by contrast, recorded seventy-five factories as having been totally destroyed, but this total must have included many small ones.

The detailed reports compiled on the factories which were hit – forming, as has been seen, the vast majority of those in Coventry – make clear beyond question that, contrary to all the tales of indiscriminate bombing soon being put about, the Germans were remarkably successful in hitting their intended targets and hardly a single famous name in local industry escaped.

The Humber Hillman works, for example, producing Rolls-Royce engine components had 'been hit by an H.E. bomb and a delayed action bomb', which 'concealed by debris, exploded fifty hours later, killing several salvage workers. . . . One three-storey building with wooden floors, used as a store, was completely gutted by fire. . . . A steel-framed single-storey factory building received a direct hit by a large bomb.' Hardly less important was the four-storey GEC factory in White Friars Street, where 'an oil-bomb, falling into a lift shaft, started a fire which gutted the building, burning out all floors . . . rendering entry dangerous and salvage of machinery fastened to the steelwork of the upper floors almost impossible'. In Dale Street, the ruins of the Triumph Engineering plant revealed 'evidence of at least three large bombs' and the 'numerous extensions of varied types of construction around the original small building' – a layout typical of many companies in Coventry – were 'still too hot, some fourteen days after the incident to permit detailed inspection', though 'a large number of machine tools were . . . successfully salvaged'.

These items were already assuming in the 'Battle for Production' something of the importance of machine-guns in the First World War, and the damage caused to the country's main machine-tool works, Sir Alfred Herbert Ltd, was therefore all the more serious. 'This key factory, covering some thirty to forty acres, about a mile and three-quarters from the city centre' had been hit 'by eight H.E. bombs and a number of incendiaries'. The Daimler Company factory at Radford had attracted even more. 'These works,' reported the inspector, 'were struck by twenty-two H.E. bombs and three parachute mines which wrecked an entire section of machine shops and half of the foundry'.

The Morris Works in Gosford Street, by contrast, got off comparatively lightly, with two direct hits, by a 250 kg and a smaller 50 kg bomb, 'each of which penetrated the concrete roof and top floor and detonated in the fourth storey'. The Alvis, in Holyhead Road, another of the vehicle factories which had made Coventry's reputation, provided a textbook example of an efficient air attack. 'It was first hit by incendiaries and later by H.E. bombs, causing casualties among the works firemen, which, combined with a shortage of water, hampered control of the resultant fire, until a parachute mine struck and almost completely demolished the building.'

Apart from these world-famous establishments, nine other important aircraft factories had been hit, among them the Rover Co. Ltd ('one shop completely wrecked'), the Daimler No. 2 Factory, in Brown's Lane, Allesley, with 'thirty machine tools destroyed', and British Thomson-Houston Ltd in Alma Street, where two shops had been gutted. Armstrong Siddeley in Parkside, Singer Motors in Canterbury Street, Rootes Securities at Stoke, Standard Motors Ltd at Canley, Riley (Coventry) Ltd in Durbar Avenue and SS Cars Ltd in Swallow Lane, had all suffered in varying degrees.

Three other aircraft factories further out – Standard Motors at Fletchamstead and the two Armstrong-Whitworth plants at Baginton and Whitley – had barely been touched, but 'had temporarily to suspend production owing to dislocation of utility services'. Six other factories were also classed as 'unproductive until utility services restored' and nine more as being affected in varying degrees, from Pattison and Hobourn Ltd in Cash Lane, which 'ceased production for four days owing to presence of an unexploded bomb' to the 'Dunlop Rim and Wheel Co.', which had 'suffered considerable damage to building and stock'. The report on Maudslay Motors Ltd in Parkside was brief and pointed: 'Machines damaged, all work stopped', and that on Clarke, Cluley and Co.'s Globe Works hardly less so: 'Main distribution centre completely wrecked; material store gutted by oil-bomb.' Also regarded as important enough to be mentioned by name were Smith's Stamping Works Ltd in Ribble Road, Mechanization and Aero Ltd in Gosford Street, Reynolds and Coventry Chain Co. Ltd, Spon End, and Sterling Metal Ltd, Foleshill, where the 'pattern shop and stores' had been destroyed and the 'foundry and other departments heavily damaged'. This last, like the destruction of a foundry 'in the city centre . . . which contains stock of very great value' was a particularly heavy blow, for the loss of castings and the moulds from which they were made had, like an interruption in the supply of machine tools, a far more widely felt and longer-lasting effect that the knocking-out of a single workshop or assembly plant.

Perhaps the best index of the scale of the destruction was the reduction in rateable value of property of all kinds which, it was later calculated, had been cut overnight to a third of the pre-war figure. Out of some 75 000 buildings, 60000 had been destroyed or damaged, including 600 shops – among them three out of every four in the centre of the city – 28 hotels, 80 commercial garages and 121 office blocks or individual offices. The largest single category were houses or flats. Of 5800 council-owned houses only 100 had been 'completely demolished' but 4200 had been damaged in varying degrees and, including privately owned residential property, more than three-quarters had been affected, as the final balance sheet compiled three years later showed:

Demolished or rendered permanently unsafe	2306	(3·5%)
So damaged as to necessitate evacuation	530	(9·0%)
Suffered some damage	41500	(64·0%)
Total damaged in varying degrees	4936	(76·5%)

The Germans had also largely put the public utility services out of action. The official report prepared in Whitehall on the Monday morning told the whole story in a few terse sentences.

By dawn most of the water supply of the city had been cut off. . . . Almost the whole of the city was without light or power. . . . The city was entirely without gas . . . I understood also there was considerable damage to sewers. On Saturday 16 November the railways appeared to be completely at a standstill.

Of the immediate shortages the most serious from the point of view of the ordinary civilian was that of water. The reservoirs serving Coventry had been full when the raid began, with their normal 21·3 million gallons, and were not seriously affected by bombs, but the trunk mains carrying water into the city and the network of smaller bore pipes leading off them had suffered an enormous number of breakages. Everywhere desperately needed water was flowing to waste, while the hydrants to cut off the supply lay wrecked in flooded craters or were buried beneath the rubble. Both the 18-inch and 14-inch mains bringing water down from Coundon reservoir into the city had been broken in Barkers Butts Lane; there were two fractures in the 14-inch main from Spon End, in Smithford Street, two more in the 14-inch main from Whitley, in the London Road and Earl Street and others in the 10-inch main leading off from this in Daventry Road, depriving the whole Cheylesmore estate of water. Eventually it was decided that 244 separate sections of water main needed replacing – involving the laying of considerably more than a mile of new pipes – an enormous task complicated by the loss of special tools and equipment during a fire at the Spon End Waterworks, the 'washing out' of its ARP headquarters, and the destruction in the Old Technical College of the Water Department's laboratory, drawing office and records.

About half the city was without water the morning after the raid and on the Sunday the whole system was cut off for a time to enable essential repairs to begin.

Gas mains were even more vulnerable to bombs than water mains and here too it was the distribution system which had suffered most. All Coventry's gas was produced locally at what was known as the 'new gas works' situated on the Coventry–Nuneaton railway about a mile and a quarter north of the city centre. From here gas reached the customer via the chief artery of the Coventry gas supply system, a 24-inch cast-iron main which ran into the city to the 'old gas works', where gas was no longer produced, but merely stored and distributed. Four areas were fed direct from this main. The remaining six areas were supplied through the system based on the old gas works, which were also linked to a 15-inch diameter high pressure 'ring main', which encircled much of the west and south of the city, and also took gas from two other gas holders outside the city boundary. There were therefore two particularly vulnerable points in the whole system, the new gas works where gas was made, and the old gas works, which formed the centre of the distribution system.

The first of these, amazingly, escaped. The giant water-sealed gas holders of the new gas works, each of which held one and three-quarter million cubic feet, though showered with incendiaries, remained intact, also surviving the impact of four high-explosive bombs within a hundred yards. The old gas works were less fortunate. Here, an official report explained, 'the offices and governor houses [containing the main distribution machinery] were set on fire . . . the governors, all maps, plans and records were destroyed and the valves and connections to trunk mains seriously damaged.' Also destroyed was the main gas holder on the site, which held three-quarters of a million cubic feet. The Chairman of the Council's Gas Committee had not long before attended an impressive demonstration in which blazing gas had been extinguished by the use of wet clay, but on the night of 14 November the old gas works would have needed more than wet clay to save it, and he later recalled 'the awesome sight of the municipal gas holder going up like a huge firework'.

Even more serious in their effects were the breakages in the mains. There were five in the chief supply main – the 'driving main' as the engineers graphically called it; five more in the 15-inch steel ring main; no fewer than 300 in the larger distribution mains, ranging in bore down to 4 inches, and 2000 in the 'service connections' linking the factory furnace or family gas stove with the street outside. The day before the raid the Gas Department had produced nearly ten million cubic feet of gas and supplied 75 000 consumers, about half the output going to factories. On the day after consumption was down to one-fortieth of normal and, apart from a small part of the outlying area to the north, the whole city was without a supply.

Although Coventry's electricity now came from outside, via the national grid, its supply system was not wholly dissimilar from that of the gas undertaking. Here, too, the former producing plant, in this case the old generating station site at Sandy Lane, suffered heavy damage, but like the old gas works this was now a distribution centre, where the high voltage supply received from the Central Electricity Board was transformed to lower voltages and passed on to the main supply system. Only two small 50 kg bombs hit the transformer site but they did appalling damage. The first, according to a subsequent report,

demolished one of a pair of 6000 33/6·6 kv [kilovolt] transformers standing in the open: the adjacent transformer caught fire and the conflagration spread to the adjoining 6·6 kv switch house, gutting it and destroying the bank of 250 kva [kilovolt amp] switchgear which it housed. The other bomb penetrated the slate covered roof of the adjoining 33 kv single-storey switch house and apparently burst in mid-air at a point about seven or eight feet above the quarry tiled floor, irreparably damaging two 2 kv switches.

From the main transformer station electricity reached the consumer via local sub-stations, which housed lower-capacity transformers and switchgear, and much of this plant seemed to have borne a charmed life. At the Daimler works the equipment survived the collapse of the building upon it, and in a corporation sub-station in Orchard Crescent, when the dust from a direct hit had settled, the 'ground floor and front first storey wall' had all 'collapsed completely' but 'no damage was sustained by the three transformers and switchgear housed on the ground floor'. Inevitably, too, the distribution cables in many streets had been twisted or broken by blast or falling buildings so that on the morning after the raid few houses and almost no factories had a supply.

The difficulty in getting about, due to blocked roads, impressed everyone directly after the raid, but this, too, was a by-product of the attack rather than a deliberate aim. The commonest causes of obstruction were unexploded bombs and rubble from demolished buildings, but there were also many craters. A first count revealed two hundred within a mile of the Council House and another two hundred further out though the main roads suffered less than the local service roads, and in most places, the official chronicler reported, 'diversions were found easy to arrange', for 'no road bridges on the main routes were damaged'.

Public transport was at first at a standstill. Trams not in the depot were imprisoned where they stood by craters and torn-up track, as well as by lack of power, so that the author of the previously quoted report explained, removing them 'presented great difficulties as the trams had to be dragged over the streets and jacked up round the corners'. The trams were in fact never to run again; the whole system was simply abandoned. But if against the Coventry Tramways Department Göring's Luftwaffe could chalk up a total victory, against the buses the Germans could claim only a partial success: six of the fleet of 181 had been wrecked and 77 more had been damaged, but many of these were soon running again.

The railways presented a larger target and had suffered accordingly. Coventry station was out of action and the LMS (London, Midland and Scottish Railway) produced the impressive total of seventy-seven incidents damaging railway property, mainly boundary fences and embankments, though nineteen bombs had hit the permanent way, eight had fallen on station buildings or goods yards, seven had damaged bridges and one had hit an important retaining wall. The main line to Birmingham and London had drawn seven bombs, including one, which failed to explode, in the station booking hall, and the Coventry–Nuneaton–Rugby line had been hit by twenty-two. The 'Coventry-avoiding goods line', which left the main line a mile east of Coventry station and ran north to join the Nuneaton line, had come off even worse, with forty-five bombs and a parachute mine descending on or close to it.

For practical purposes on the morning of 15 November the telephone system was out of action. Coventry had at that time only

6500 telephone subscribers, but more than 5000 lines – 77 per cent –
were dead and a detailed count later revealed nearly 21 500 faults on
subscribers' lines and apparatus and nearly 1800 on trunk and junction lines – equal to the normal maintenance programme for three
years, though by good fortune the telephone exchange itself had
been saved. The postal sorting office had also survived, but the
occasional postman seen gallantly clambering over the rubble gave
a false impression, for the Post Office had been knocked out as
effectively as all the other public services in Coventry.

The Head Office could not be opened for a week as it was in the demolition area and all approaches to it were closed by the military authorities.

Collections had to be made and taken away to other towns for sorting,
etc.; and deliveries had to be effected from other towns. Such work as
could be done in Coventry itself had to be confined to daylight hours,
owing to the lack of black-out facilities. . . . More than half of the postal
staff consisted of temporary officers, about two-thirds being women and
after the raid many of these failed to return to duty. . . . These factors,
together with the difficulties of the railways and transport generally, made
it impossible to give anything like a normal postal service.

That in spite of such wholesale devastation the death roll had not
been even higher was due to the extent to which people in Coventry
had taken cover. Many of the statistics (including those showing
how the Anderson stood up to bombardment) were lost in a later
raid, but a good deal of information about public shelters has
survived. Fifty five of the seventy-five cellars for which the corporation had provided steel props were inspected and though two
were 'beneath buildings which received direct hits', they had taken
'considerable debris loads without collapse'. Of seventy-nine
public shelters, accommodating nearly 33 000 people (forty-two in
trenches, thirty-one in basements and six on the surface), very few
had been destroyed, though several had become uninhabitable due
to fires nearby. One trench shelter, below the Humber Hillman
works, had received a direct hit, but 'none of the six occupants was
killed and two escaped with only a shaking'. Basements did even
better. The 'strutted basement under Messrs Whitfield's shop in
Broadgate', the Home Office inspector reported, 'stood up well
under debris load caused by fire' while 'none of the several hundred
occupants' of the 'basement under Messrs Owen and Owen's four-
storey steel-framed store, strutted with combined steel and timber'

was hurt, even when 'a large bomb pierced the roof and upper floors, exploding on a heavy steel joist on the ground floor'. All told, fourteen shelters, with room for about 5500 people, were damaged in some way, eleven of them so badly that they were simply abandoned, and it was here no doubt that the fatalities mentioned earlier occurred.

With so many casualties still entombed beneath bombed buildings one could on the morning of 15 November only guess at the number killed and injured. The first estimate given to the Home Office at 6 a.m. was 'about 600' but during the day the expected total was raised to 1000 and on Saturday to 'over 300 killed and 800 injured'. A week later, on 23 November, with most bodies now recovered, it was believed that there were '502 killed' and 'over 800' injured, but these totals were still too low. The actual casualties agreed much later, after further checking, were 568 killed, 863 seriously injured and 393 lightly injured. The total casualty figure was therefore 1824, or 1431 if the 'lightly injured', i.e. those able to go home after treatment, were excluded. In a population of 238400 about one person in every 166 had been killed or badly hurt and one in 130 had been a casualty of some kind, though as so many people had moved out following earlier raids or had spent the night outside the city the risk for those actually in Coventry during the raid was at least double these proportions. The corresponding ratio for deaths or serious injuries for the whole civilian population of the United Kingdom for the whole war was one in 272, i.e. a civilian had a 60 per cent greater chance of being killed or seriously wounded during that one night in Coventry than during the whole six years of the war elsewhere.

15
GO ROUND THE BACK, YOUR MAJESTY

'By the morning of the Saturday [16 November] the worst was over.'
Admiralty Weekly Intelligence Report, on bombing of Coventry, 24 November 1940

RESPONSIBILITY for getting Coventry back on its feet after the overwhelming blow it had suffered rested primarily upon the City Council, assisted by the Regional Commissioner's office in Birmingham and the Ministry of Home Security in London. It had been obvious within an hour of the start of the raid that assistance would be needed from outside, and in the early hours of the morning a Regional Officer was sent from Birmingham to deploy the reinforcements coming in at a Rendezvous Post on the city outskirts, where the by-pass joined the Birmingham Road. The first to arrive were the firemen, followed by fifty-two rescue parties, fifty-five ambulances and specialist teams of from twenty-four to sixty workmen, whose job it was to restore the gas, electricity and water services. With local police officers as guides, they began at dawn to move into the city to the incidents assigned to them.

With the local police tied up with such duties many Coventry people that day found that the policeman in their road was more likely to ask them the way than the reverse, for that morning a hundred police were also sent from Birmingham and fifty more from both Shropshire and Worcestershire, with another hundred held in readiness in Staffordshire. Even more numerous than the police, who had mainly arrived by midday, were the soldiers. The decision to call them in had been taken at 3 a.m. when the Chief Constable, as ARP Controller, had appealed for troops for 'control and the repair of damage'. Six hundred were immediately ordered to Coventry and by 10.40 the Chief Constable was able to report that the first three hundred were already there and 'assisting in the maintenance of law and order', largely by forming 'a series of cordons round the city to divert all through traffic and to prevent the entry of unauthorized traffic'. Meanwhile 'a party of Royal Engineers' had also been 'called in to work in co-ordination with the fire brigade for the purpose of demolishing . . . buildings, if necessary, to prevent the spread of fire'.

The Services were also responsible, as in every bombed city, for clearing unexploded bombs and mines, of which several hundred lay about in Coventry that morning, many causing far more disruption than if they had blown up, as roads were sealed off and whole streets cleared while they awaited attention. Potentially the most destructive were the mines, clearing which was the Navy's job. The thought that 'the Navy's here' may have comforted civilians, but they might have been less cheerful had they known that, of the seven officers in the party, only three – the officer-in-charge, Lieutenant Miller, and his two sub-lieutenants – had had any practical experience. Although a solitary naval officer had been at work at Owen Owen earlier the main party did not arrive until 2.30 p.m., to confront the depressing scene described by Lieutenant Miller:

Working conditions were exceedingly bad. . . . Our eyes smarted and ran in the heavy smoke. . . . Most of the streets, in a wide ring round the ruined centre of the city, were blocked with craters or fallen buildings. It was clear there was going to be grave difficulty in the mere finding of our mines.

We had been informed that the mines were painted putty colour, with white parachutes. This indicated a new departure, so I decided the first afternoon to go out in advance of the others, with [sub-lieutenants] Woolley and Cummins, to inspect two of the most urgent cases, and come to an agreed conclusion whether we would be capable of tackling these mines without further instructions and whether, if so, we could with reasonable safety allow the 'learners' to operate upon them. Mines had been dropped all over the town, so we took two at opposite ends as a sample. Both appeared to be perfectly ordinary 'C' types; so we decided to get on with the job without further ado first thing the following morning.

By the time we had found the local Control it was too late to do more than have a list made out of the mines so far reported, secure a map of the town, fix up a programme and retire for the night to Leamington Spa to establish our headquarters . . . in the Borough ARP Office.

Finding accommodation proved far from easy. The officers, their commanding officer reported to his superiors, only escaped having to sit up all night thanks to 'the strong line taken by the Admiralty and the Ministry of Home Security', who, through the Town Clerk, in 'desperation secured billets for the officers in the houses of well-to-do residents'. The other ranks fared even worse:

The Army authorities undertook to put up the drivers and ratings. Unfortunately, we discovered next day that they had shoved the men into some sort of room in the grandstand on Warwick race-course, with wire mattresses, but no fire, one blanket only and no black-out, so that the fellows could not even strike a match to sling their hammocks by. Rather than that, they went into another room and slept on a concrete floor. . . . No food was provided that night, and though breakfast of a sort was forthcoming in the morning, they had to eat it with their fingers, as no utensils were available. We made such a row about this that the next night the men were accommodated in billets similar to our own.

Undeterred by their treatment Lieutenant Miller and his men returned to Coventry the following morning (Saturday) and spent a busy and profitable weekend, as he later reported to the Admiralty in his breezy nautical fashion.

The city was littered with unexploded bombs. Sub-Lieutenant Woolley, for one, observed an unexploded bomb buried within ten yards of his first mine and reported to the centre. I . . . drove out at once to the spot only to find the job completed. Woolley explained that he had merely wished the Royal Engineers to know that the bomb existed and would require their attention in due course.

The score for the day was nine. Cummins had the misfortune to set off his mine at the first touch to the bomb fuse, but though a good deal of damage was done, both Cummins and his sailor escaped; the former got into an underground shelter about fifty yards away, the latter ran at first in the wrong direction, but escaped at much the same distance, with shock and a couple of abrasions. Conditions on the second day [Sunday] were equally bad, but by the evening the list was clear.

By 9.15 p.m. on the Sunday evening Regional headquarters was able to inform the Ministry of Home Security that all fourteen parachute mines so far discovered had been 'satisfactorily dealt with'. The unexploded bombs, being far more numerous, were more troublesome, though 'by the later afternoon of [Sunday] 16 November', reported a Ministry of Home Security official, 'Captain

Biggs had found nothing new in the way of bombs and no evidence of Italian bombs. . . . The majority of the bombs used appeared to have been 250 kg [i.e. 500 lb], with a good many 500 kg and a comparatively small proportion of 50 kg'. By that evening solid progress had been made. Whitehall was told that forty 'have already been removed from KPs [Key Points], road junctions and railways' with only one fatal incident, at the Humber Works, which had killed 'three men of . . . the bomb disposal section and one employee'. Overall the problem had been reduced to the comfortingly familiar proportions of a military *pro forma*:

U X B Return

Brought forward	163
Reported during preceding 24 hours	48
Dealt with	27
Disproved	nil
Self detonating	3
Remaining for disposal	181

In anticipation of the need for prompt decisions the Council had set up before the war a National Emergency Committee – also known as the War Emergency Committee – consisting of five men, its chairman being the formidable Alderman William Halliwell, described by a local historian as a 'vigorous and uncompromising personality' and 'the strongest man on the City Council . . . dictatorial by instinct and inclined to be a bully'.

Halliwell's deputy, and soon his successor, was Alderman George Hodgkinson, the son of a machine-minder in a lace factory. He had left school at the age of eleven, and later worked as an engineering craftsman and pioneer shop steward before becoming full-time agent of the Coventry Labour Party and later leader of the Labour Group on the City Council. 'In my view,' George Hodgkinson has since written, 'the central authorities did not fully appraise the nature of the problems which would arise in such a calamitous situation'. Now the consequences were his responsibility, for that morning only these two members of the Emergency Committee – both, as Hodgkinson wryly recalled, had been conscientious objectors in the First World War – even reached the Council House.

Herbert Morrison, Home Secretary and Minister of Home

Security, and Lord Dudley, Civil Defence Commissioner for the Midland Region, had, as mentioned earlier, spent the night at the latter's country home in Worcestershire and that morning drove first to the Commissioner's headquarters at Birmingham. They then travelled on to Coventry, where they joined the Minister of Health, Ernest Brown, whose portfolio also covered housing, and the Minister of Aircraft Production, Lord Beaverbrook.

The meeting with the civic authorities which followed was disastrous. According to the compiler of the Ministry of Home Security's Weekly Appreciation Report, written a few days later, the presence of the two senior Ministers 'had a most invigorating effect' leading to a 'valuable' conference, but this is, at best, a highly selective view of the truth. The occasion began badly with the Mayor offering Morrison neat whisky, explaining, as if to rub in the failure of the public services, that no water was to be had, while the Chief Fire Officer provided a striking demonstration of the A R P services' ordeal, appearing grimy and unshaven and then falling asleep at the table. He was probably the happiest person present, for the confrontation which followed was, Morrison's biographers admit, 'very difficult'. The Minister found himself blamed because 'there had been no fighter or anti-aircraft defences and . . . the German planes had been allowed to fly over the city for hour after hour while they systematically destroyed it'. He was also bombarded with suggestions that 'Civil Defence should be made compulsory and even constitute an exemption from military service'. Morrison, who had spent his whole life in local government, listened patiently but privately detected 'an almost total lack of will or desire to get the town moving again', deciding that Coventry, never conspicuously enthusiastic about the war, was now 'pervaded by an air of defeatism'. His first response was to threaten to put the area under martial law, a drastic step not taken in any other blitzed city, and not without irony, since he too had been a pacifist in the First World War. Finally he agreed to leave control in the hands of the all-civilian Emergency Committee, but also tried to provide some of the initiative he felt was lacking, by 'telling the Army G O C to bring in the Pioneer Corps to clear the damage, activating Brown on health problems, [and] instructing the staff of the Regional Commission how to reorganize the town'.

Morrison's goodwill was obvious, but Beaverbrook's intervention merely made bad worse. 'The roots of the Air Force,' Beaverbrook told an harassed official that day, 'are planted in Coventry. If Coventry's output is destroyed the tree will languish. But if the city rises from the ashes then the tree will continue to burgeon, putting forth fresh leaves and branches.' Such high-flown metaphors might perhaps do for Beaverbrook's Civil Servants in London, who had to endure them in silence, but they cut no ice at all that day, as the Mayor's daughter learned that evening:

It was not a very happy occasion, emotions being high and tempers frayed by worry and exhaustion. [I was told that] the 'great man' [Beaverbrook] shed tears and was told sharply that tears were of no use. He'd asked Coventry's workers for an all-out effort and what had they got for it?

Once back in London, Beaverbrook telephoned Lord Dudley to urge him to take over all the City Council's powers but the Regional Commissioner refused, and it was finally decided, though not without many misgivings, to leave the Council to carry on, though Dudley did agree to the setting up of a joint government and local Coventry Reconstruction Committee.

The most urgent necessity of all that Friday was drinking water; as the day wore on water tankers, more commonly used for street cleaning and road repair work, began to arrive, as well as lorries laden with cans, which were deposited at street corners, while Ministry of Information loudspeaker vans toured the surrounding streets calling on the inhabitants to bring their saucepans and buckets. The largest water-lorry was a 1400-gallon milk tanker, loaned, complete with driver, by the Co-operative Creamery, Congleton which might perhaps have been the subject of jokes at any other time, but one volunteer ambulance driver from Birmingham, a teetotaller, remembers being 'unable to get a drink other than beer'.

By Sunday evening a low-pressure flow of water was available in some parts of the city, creating fears of a possible epidemic of typhoid, caused by leakages from broken sewers into the fractured water mains. Immediately after the raid chlorine had been added to water flowing through the pumping stations and hastily printed notices proclaiming BOIL ALL DRINKING WATER were posted throughout the city, but the threat of typhoid remained and Dr Ashworth and his immediate superior, the Medical Officer of

Health, Dr Massey, advised mass inoculation. 'Unfortunately,' Dr Ashworth remembers, 'the posters offering immunization spelt "inoculation" with two "n's". The Medical Officer of Health wouldn't let them go as they were, nor would he have one of the "n's" crossed out – so we had to have a new set. However, we gave about 30000 injections over the next few days.' A woman who worked in the office at the Daimler aero-engine factory at Allesley recalls how during the mass line-ups, when a hundred people were injected in turn, 'it was a source of amusement to watch others, especially the men, turn green and pass out'.

If depression was the prevailing mood on the Friday the dominant emotion on the morning of Saturday 16 November was strikingly different. Spirits had been raised by an undisturbed night's sleep, for the Germans had sent their main bomber force to London. Only six or seven aircraft had reached Coventry and the total bomb load dropped over the whole area (seven tons of high explosive and thirty-two canisters of incendiaries) was so trivial compared to the previous night's that few people were even aware of it. Equally important in restoring morale was the evidence on all sides that the authorities, who had seemed as crushed as everyone else directly after the raid, were now beginning to regain control of the situation.

The sheet-metal worker from Birmingham who had tried and failed to get to work on the previous day, found that morning 'a vastly clearer road. . . . Although there was plenty of traffic . . . it was mainly military and moving fairly steadily. The police . . . had made interrogation lay-bys, where they could wave a car in for questioning without interrupting the flow of traffic.' Forced to park at Allesley, a mile and a half from his destination, he was able, thanks partly to his warden's steel helmet, to get into the city on foot, though the road had become 'a brick and rubble strewn passage, bounded on both sides by smoking ruins', and was soon at work in his factory at Much Park Street, clearing his bench of 'broken glass and a great pile of dirt and rubbish from the roof'.

During the day the number of soldiers in Coventry was raised to 1130 and at a meeting held at the Council House in the afternoon it was agreed to bring in a general reconstruction company of Royal Engineers and a line reconstruction section of the Royal Corps of Signals. All the troops were placed under the command of the

Commandant, 3rd Corps Royal Engineers, who set up his headquarters at 1000 hours on Sunday, 17 November.

While infantry cordoned off the worst affected areas to keep out
sightseers and looters, gangs of Pioneers, the Army's labourers,
were clearing debris and filling in craters. The sight of these khaki-
clad figures encouraged everyone who saw them and an official
report six days later singled out the 'excellent moral effect of the
arrival of troops' as one of the lessons learned at Coventry.

At 11.25 that Saturday morning there was still five major fires
raging, but during the day it proved possible to relieve the 250
exhausted firemen from other parts of the Midlands who had reached
Coventry during and directly after the raid, by others from Manchester and Leeds. By Sunday evening only four fires of any kind
were still smouldering, 'in Cox Street, Whitefriars Street, Jenner
Street and Bishop Street' and even these were now 'without glare',
thus offering no beacon to further bombers. The situation con-
cerning trapped people had been controlled even earlier. At 11.25
on the 16th there remained only 'four outstanding incidents where
people are believed trapped', and that morning fresh rescue parties
arrived from Manchester to help bring them out.

One of the most enduring impressions most observers have of
the aftermath of the raid is of seeing grim, shocked little groups of
frightened people standing about uncertain where to go – not
surprisingly perhaps, for of the 'thirteen relief or shelter stations'
in Coventry 'seven were out of action', according to the Chief
Constable's report. Here too the situation was in hand by Saturday,
as the Rev. W. B. Sells discovered on returning to St Thomas's on
Saturday morning. Outside his church he found long queues of
would-be evacuees waiting for buses, while the church hall and
adjoining school were even busier, being turned into a rest centre:

While we were talking a lorry arrived carrying a complete field kitchen
which the workmen set up in the school. Soon after . . . more lorries came
with two hundred double-tier bunks and mattresses and paraffin lanterns
. . . and in no time they had set them up . . . . Our meals were forgotten as
we set to and helped. . . .

More Civil Defence people came and showed me how to book each
person in: who they were, where they had come from, and where they
hoped to go. Most of them . . . just had what they stood up in and what
they had in their suitcases. They were a sorry sight, especially the chil-

dren, many of whom had come back to their homes from evacuation. . . .
A man and woman arrived to cook and keep the field kitchen going, so I
got them to boil up gallons of water so that people could wash and clean
themselves up a bit. This took a long time, as there were only a few
bowls, but at last it was over and a meal being cooked. . . . After I had
booked them all in, I found that there were 180 men, women and children,
most of them from very poor homes. . . . After a scratch supper of sandwiches, I got them all bedded down at last. . . .

About midnight a girl of about twenty came in and said she had been
sent to help me as a volunteer, so we divided the night up into watches . . .
and, in the middle of the night, while I was dozing, she put her head
down and went to sleep on a mattress. On waking I found her hair literally crawling with livestock. She went crying out of the place and I never
saw her again.

Around lunchtime on the Friday it was announced that food
rationing had been suspended and one woman who had been sent
home from work remembers spreading the glad news to her neighbours, though at this stage, with nearly all the food shops in the
city demolished or closed, it was more helpful to their spirits than
their stomachs. The real need was for mobile canteens. One of the
first to arrive came from Oldbury in Worcestershire, twenty-five
miles away, and the daughter of one of the crew recalls being told
how the canteen staff made soup 'from bones and vegetables
begged from local traders' while 'the Co-operative Dairies supplied
dozens of gallons of milk . . . in large churns, used in soups, cocoa
and other hot drinks. . . . When the water supply finally dried up,
milk even had to be used for washing up.'

Mrs Vera Rose, the WVS Centre Organizer for Oldbury, well
remembers being roused at 6 a.m. that morning to arrange for
relief staff and reserve stocks of food to be sent to Coventry. After
constant diversions *en route* she found the Oldbury canteen at
about 8 a.m., parked near St Mary's Hall in the very centre of the
city.

After treading over many fire-hoses and rubble we went to an underground place where we found one small tap which was still working.
The firemen and everyone who had been working through the night
were so grateful to have a hot drink. We managed to serve hot drinks all
day and through the night, when a doctor from Oldbury came to take us
back and bring a new lot of helpers.

Away from the centre canteens were few. The 'rescue squad of five men' sent to help the Ashworth family in Leamington Road had, Dr Eveleen Ashworth discovered on Sunday morning, 'left Manchester on Friday morning with their sandwiches for the day' but 'could get no food' on Saturday.

In my meat safe under the store in the pantry, which was the corner of the house least damaged, I had some kippers. I had a loaf, stale by now of course, in the bread bin next to the safe. So I cooked the kippers on an open fire for these men. I then put on the rabbits which had been left and dug carrots from the garden. They had this at midday, with potatoes, and were extremely grateful.

Even as late as the following Wednesday some ARP units were grateful for similar gifts. One AFS man who had recently arrived from London remembers how the owners of a house where they answered an appeal to help extinguish 'the six tons of coal . . . burning in the cellar' rewarded them with 'a pot of tea and sandwiches of stale bread and blackcurrant jam', explaining apologetically that it was 'all we've eaten ourselves for two days.'

By now there were a considerable number of mobile canteens in operation, mainly dispensing 'tea and very thick corned beef sandwiches'. The same AFS man saw one weary mother trying to feed 'her very young and puny infant' this same fare, and realized as he 'watched the child's first attempt to stuff the huge sandwich into its mouth' that 'it could have had no other food that day'. The helpers at the Oldbury canteen were particularly impressed by three customers. One was a small boy of about four, whom one of them had found 'wandering in the street', hungry and bewildered; he turned out to be the sole survivor of his family and was passed on to the welfare authorities to be taken into care. The other two consisted of a man who arrived on the Monday after the raid 'near to starvation and with hardly any flesh left on his fingers' with his 'bedraggled small terrier . . . and begged a drink for the dog. . . . His own needs were of secondary importance.' The dog's owner, a master plumber, explained that he had gone back into his house 'to fetch his treasured tools, his dog had followed him and . . . he had dug himself out of the debris with his bare hands'.

By Saturday, as a Home Office historian later wrote, 'the situation had much improved. Sixteen field kitchens had been established to feed the homeless and destitute and more were arriving from military sources.' During Sunday further reinforcements arrived, until by Sunday evening there were twelve 'relief stations' providing both food and shelter, while another seventeen buildings had been taken over as emergency feeding centres, supplying meals, but no accommodation, with the help of Army field kitchens. People in the streets, including rescue workers and firemen, were being fed from seventeen mobile canteens, and six more were on their way from Nottingham and Bristol.

The Coventry raid provided the first major test for the 'Queen's Messengers', mobile catering columns set up by the WVS with the help of specially equipped vehicles provided by the Americans. Among those summoned to Coventry was a twenty-year-old Sutton Coldfield girl who in peacetime had run a school of dancing. A month before she had taken a training course in field cookery, encouraged by a visit from the Minister of Food, Lord Woolton, who 'came and told us we were to learn to cook as we might be needed at any moment'. For her the moment proved to be the afternoon of Friday 15 November, when she received a telephone call to report 'warmly dressed, in WVS uniform, to Jennings Garage, Boldmere Road, at 5 a.m. tomorrow'.

Half awake I cycled down to the garage and there were two smart cream and blue vans waiting for us. Full of excitement at being asked to 'do' something at last, but not knowing what was coming to us, we piled into the vans chattering hard. . . . Dawn was breaking slowly as we shivered and shook on the journey. No one seemed to know what we were going to do but we all made wild guesses and felt very important. Slowly as time passed we realized it wasn't a joke at all. First it was the sight of a few people walking towards Sutton Coldfield, then pram-loads and bus-loads all with sad, sad faces, children, crying, grown-ups too.

We arrived at last at a coach park in the centre of Coventry, at least part of a coach park, for there seemed to be a lot of broken bricks and rubble about. Someone told us to get out and cut up sandwiches. . . . We looked about for a while then someone spotted some old oil cans stacked in a corner, so without more ado they were placed in the centre of the park and an old garage door was placed on top – that was to serve as a table for several days. Sandwiches by the thousand were cut up . . . corned-beef. . . . We cut and buttered for ages and ages.

This WVS member has no recollection of sleeping at all in

between leaving Sutton Coldfield with twelve other Queen's
Messengers on the Saturday morning and their return journey
'tired and sad' three days later, but she does remember an encounter
with one legendary Coventry figure, Councillor, later Alderman
and Lord Mayor, Mrs Pearl Hyde, the portly blonde daughter of a
publican, then in her mid-thirties, and said to be the only working-
class head of a large WVS branch in the country.

When Councillor Pearlie Hyde and I and others were down in the crypt
of the Cathedral she looked at me and said, 'Nancie, your hair is in a mess,
come here and let me tie it up.' With that she untied some files and deprived them of their pink ribbons and tied up my hair in bunches. I felt
a million dollars – and back to work.

King George VI heard details of the raid during the afternoon of
Friday 15 November and instantly decided to visit Coventry. No
public announcement was made, but among the few let into the
secret were the family of the Mayor, who were preparing to move
for the night to an aunt's home at Milverton near Leamington.

As we all worked sorting out extra blankets, etc., to take with us, dad
came upstairs calling out, 'Up early in the morning. Best bib and tucker.
We have to meet the King out on the London Road by 9 a.m.' My sister
and I were speechless. Mum sat down wearily . . . and . . . for the second
time in one day she was in tears. All we could hear went something like
'Oh dear! Doesn't he understand we're in too much of a mess and have
so much to do without him coming?'

The news also caused consternation to the city authorities, but a
telephone call to Buckingham Palace warning that they could not
entertain the King in the normal manner was met with a reassuring
answer: His Majesty would bring his own sandwiches.* In the event
the visit proved an enormous success, the total unexpectedness of
the King's appearance making its impact all the greater so that the
tour rapidly turned into a triumph. When the King visited a rest
centre, in St George's Church, Barkers Butts Lane, where homeless
old people were sprawled listlessly on their bunks, the apathetic
atmosphere was transformed and the occupants scrambled to their

---

*The recollection of the Mayor's daughter, who was not, however, present, is that
Lord Dudley arranged for his butler and staff to bring over a cold lunch from Himley
Hall. 'I doubt if it consisted of sandwiches,' she adds. Possibly the King did bring
sandwiches but they were not needed.

feet and quaveringly sang the National Anthem. In another gloomy street the cry was raised: 'Are we down-hearted?' – a question it would certainly not have been safe to ask the previous day – and the King himself, it was reported, joined in the answering cry of 'No!'

A woman warden then serving with the Oldbury mobile canteen still remembers how the King suddenly appeared there and 'full up with emotion, almost to the point of tears . . . thanked each one personally and shook hands with them all in turn'. One customer, 'a little old lady of about seventy, who had nothing left but what she stood up in went up to His Majesty, reached out as if to embrace him and cried, "God bless you, lad, you've got more pluck than that Hitler bloke."'

Like every important visitor to Coventry the King also visited the Cathedral. 'The King's arrival,' remembers Provost Howard, 'took me completely by surprise. To the sound of cheering he entered the south-west door. I went forward to be presented to him and he shook hands with me. I stood with him watching the ruins. His whole attitude was one of intense sympathy and grief.' The point where the King had stood was later marked by 'a pillar made of pieces of carved stone from the rubble surmounted with a stone inscribed "G.R. 16th November 1940"', until this was replaced 'by a tall pinnacle fallen from the walls, called the "King's Pinnacle"'.

During the tour there was a striking demonstration of the excellence of the royal memory. 'At one point,' remembers the Mayor's daughter, 'His Majesty thought he recognized a man near to him. It was a Welshman, now living in Coventry, who had been one of the workmen building and erecting the little house presented by the people of Wales to the Princesses Elizabeth and Margaret, years previously.' A number of people, by contrast, mistook the slim figure in field marshal's uniform for some visiting 'brass hat', among them the Birmingham tinsmith quoted earlier, who had wandered out into Much Park Street after helping to clear his workbench.

No one was in the street excepting myself. I sat down on the kerb, wearing my steel helmet . . . my face . . . grubby from the smoke and dust . . . still floating about. As I sat down I saw . . . a group of men, coming down the street, walking in the middle of the roadway, because . . . on both sides . . . were mounds of rubble. . . . I was very occupied with my thoughts, so

I just glanced and turned away. . . . Before I could get up from the kerb where I sat the leader of the little group said, 'Good morning', and nodded. The small group had passed me before I realized that he was the King. I was so taken aback, flabbergasted, amazed, overwhelmed that I couldn't even answer him. . . . As he walked away, with his small group of aides, they must have thought that I was the dirtiest and most ignorant of his subjects.

Not everyone, however, was totally overcome by patriotic emotion. The wife of one A F S man, then living in Cedars Avenue, Coundon, had with her sister-in-law, ventured into the city centre 'trying to get some bread. As we went up the Burges towards Broadgate we happened to look at someone important who was being shown round. It was the King. That was nice to see – but, better still, we got some bread.' And at least one famous citizen who was offered the opportunity of being presented to His Majesty declined the honour. 'In the first place,' Councillor Pearl Hyde told the Chief Constable, 'I am too busy. Secondly, I'm too dirty and, thirdly, I'm wearing a pair of your trousers.'

The King duly ate his cold meal in the Mayor's parlour, a windowless room lighted by candles stuck in bottles and as His Majesty came down the steps of the Council House, one observer remembers, 'the crowd went wild and long and joyful cheering broke out. The King was deeply moved and took a while to compose himself.' The young Geoffrey Green, covering the visit for the *Coventry Standard*, which had failed to come out that Thursday but was to reappear the following week, had ten minutes' warning of the King's arrival, and was in time to witness the 'shattering' effect on a dejected group nearby:

I was in Hay Lane, by the corner of Anslow's and there was a queue of people waiting to try and find some news of relatives who were either dead or had disappeared in one way or another when, without warning, the King suddenly appeared in Army uniform. He was walking with a group of people and I always remember a bus conductor who climbed a gas standard and clung on it and waved his hat in the air shouting, 'Three cheers for King George.' It was quite marvellous.

The Mayor's wife had, as instructed, duly turned out 'in best bib and tucker' to meet the royal visitor on his arrival, but had then returned home, and the story later spread that, preoccupied with household chores, she had, when a royal knock came on the front door, called out, 'Go round the back' – an incident now a Coventry legend. The true facts were rather different.

His Majesty asked dad as they proceeded how we had fared and at once asked the Chief Constable to direct his driver to our address. They could not enter at the front door. Dad was all for calling mum to come out but His Majesty just said, 'Well, we'll go in the other way then.' So they made their way by a side passage. . . . Joe Parker had just come up the road bearing a precious roll of roofing felt on his cycle. . . . He called out cheerfully, 'I'll be all right with my roof now, Jack!' Only as he turned into his garden gate did he realize dad was not alone. So down into the garden went the cycle and roll of felt and he rushed into his house to tell his wife. . . .

Indoors mum, my sister and a very good friend of our family had just been resting from their labours. . . . The black-out shutter had been replaced over the living room window (to keep out some of the cold), making it dark, and candles were lit though they guttered in the strong draughts. My sister . . . was perched on the end of the kitchen table chatting to the other two sitting by the range when she suddenly caught sight of dad's bowler hat – followed by a khaki flat cap – passing the window, and in a split second dad pushed the door half open and announced, 'His Majesty the King!'* First shocks over and introductions made, King George went round the house with mum. . . . He was very friendly, natural and kind. He said that one thing that had particularly impressed him so that he marvelled at it was the sheer dogged determination of the housewives everywhere to carry on somehow [although] the task seemed almost impossible.

By the time the party left the news had spread. . . . People stood on the piles of debris removed from houses and leaned out from windowless bedrooms. . . . If the women had nothing else to wave they waved their aprons. I don't think . . . all had dry eyes as the road rang with cheers.

Of the usefulness of this visit, the forerunner of many to other blitzed cities, there can be no question. 'What seemed to impress,' felt one woman then living in Coventry, 'was . . . that he had come to see us at once, battered and shabby as the city was. It did more for morale than any prepared government talk.' 'His visit has had a wonderful effect and it fired the imagination and determination of

*My informant adds: 'When I sat with dad in the hospital the week before he died in 1946 he spoke of that morning and remarked with a little chuckle, "Oh – I'd have given . . . anything . . . for a photograph of your mum's face at that moment!"'

the people to an unbelievable extent,' wrote Lord Dudley to the King's private secretary. 'It was certainly very moving to see their faces light up as they recognized him.' The Chief Constable and ARP Controller, Captain S. A. Hector, one of the few people in authority honest enough to admit to anxiety about the citizens' morale, was equally enthusiastic. 'The visit of H.M. the King to the city on the 16th . . . completely set aside any doubt I had as to the attitude of the inhabitants,' he reported to the Home Office. 'The visit . . . completely sealed the steadiness of the citizens.'

King George himself was well aware of the value of his tour of Coventry. 'I think,' he confided to his diary that Saturday evening, 'they liked my coming to see them in their adversity.'

And so the most eventful week in Coventry's history came to its unlamented end, as the dreary, persistent Midland rain descended, adding to the misery of patrolling police, wardens and ordinary citizens 'sticking it out' in roofless and windowless houses, forming pools in the bottoms of the unfilled craters, covering the ruined buildings with a grimy dark-red paste of sodden brick-dust, washing away the bloodstains on walls and pavements not yet scrubbed clean.

The weather which seemed unkind was in fact merciful. With low cloud blotting out the Midlands, the Germans stayed away for a second night, but, Dr Alan Ashworth remembers, 'at dusk most of the people working in the city had only one idea – to get out of the place', even though driving remained hazardous.

A hundred yards from my house in Leamington Road was a bomb crater in the middle of the road, with nothing to indicate its existence, no barricades, no red lights. . . . A small Morris Minor van came speeding down the road. His front wheels went into the crater, the van did a complete somersault, the front wheels landing on the road followed by the back wheels, and the van came to a halt some fifty yards down the road. We rushed to the van, expecting to find casualties but found a somewhat dazed driver who just couldn't believe what had happened. His passenger must have been concussed but soon recovered and they started off again towards Leamington.

Dr Ashworth himself remained in Coventry and, like many others, spent the weekend trying to restore a semblance of normality to his life.

In my garage I had a motor-cycle, which was wrecked, and my motor car, which was supporting the floor of the bedroom above. On Sunday the 17th I obtained the help of a rescue squad (brought down from Manchester) who cleared the drive up to the garage of the brickwork and debris and started to lever the bedroom floor off my car [which] had had the windows blown in and . . . sundry dents on the roof and the rear. . . . Whilst the rescue men lifted the bedroom floor off the car, using levers, I managed to get into the driver's seat, started the engine, which fired immediately and very smartly backed it out on to the drive. When I came to drive it to the garage, it came to a halt fifty yards down the road – I was out of petrol. The blast had holed the tank in several places. We managed to seal [it] with chewing gum, which permitted me to get to the garage, where the tank was soldered up – and I was mobile once again.

16

A MOST DEPRESSING BROADCAST

'Well, workers, it's hard luck on Coventry.'
German radio station, Workers' Challenge, *16 November 1940*

WHILE refugees from Coventry spread the news of what had happened all over the surrounding countryside the public as a whole remained unaware that the Blitz had taken a new and more serious turn. The first public reference to the attack came in the 8 a.m. Home Service news, but it was given little prominence. 'A heavy attack on Berlin was among last night's RAF successes against German objectives', the precise voice of Frederick Allen told listeners. The bulletin went on:

Last night's enemy air attacks were mainly directed against the Midlands where a very heavy attack was made on one town in particular. It is feared the casualties were heavy. News agency messages say that the attack began soon after dusk and that for some hours German aircraft came over in waves to drop high explosives and incendiary bombs. One of the raiders was reported to have crashed at Loughborough during the attack.

The one o'clock news also began with a minor and anodyne item – 'Two more ships of the *Jervis Bay* convoy are now known to be safe' – but then came what was, by any test, the major story of the day:

The city of Coventry was heavily attacked last night, the scale of the raid being comparable with those of the largest night attacks on London. The enemy was heavily engaged by intensive anti-aircraft fire, which kept them at a great height and hindered accurate bombing of industrial targets, but the city itself suffered very seriously. Preliminary reports indicate that the number of casualties may be of the order of a thousand. The attack was begun by the scattering of incendiary bombs over a wide area. Fires broke out at many points and an indiscriminate bombardment of the whole city followed. It is feared that extensive damage was done and many buildings destroyed, including the Cathedral. The people of Coventry bore their ordeal with great courage. It is known that at least two enemy aircraft were shot down during the attack.

Gradually the news of the broadcast spread through Coventry, and with it a melancholy pride, for never before had the identity of a bombed provincial city been revealed in this way. An even more explicit bulletin followed at 6 p.m., describing the raid as 'very severe' and 'particularly vicious' and declaring – untruthfully – that 'the raiders dropped their bombs indiscriminately on churches, hospitals and the homes of the people'.

The premises of the local weekly, the *Coventry Standard*, were undamaged, but its young reporter, Geoffrey Green, soon learned that 'there was no power at all and it was quite obvious that we weren't going to be able to publish for some time'. The Coventry evening newspaper, the *Midland Daily Telegraph*, was more fortunate and managed that afternoon to bring out a four-page emergency edition, headlined: 'Coventry bombed: Casualties 1000'. The *Birmingham Gazette* next morning devoted its leading article to the attack. 'After the Battle of London, the Battle of Coventry and the Midlands!' it began. 'The indiscriminate character of the dive-bombing raid which has desolated civilian Coventry, but still left it brave and enduring, staggers humanity like the first havoc in East End London.' The leader writer concluded optimistically that 'there is the usual reason to doubt the German version of the destruction of war plants'. Clearly not to be outdone in patriotism, the *Midland Daily Telegraph* in a follow-up story that day, datelined 'Coventry, Friday', declared that, 'The raiders, met by intensive A A fire, sought safety in extreme height, unlike the R A F pilots, who make certain that they are over their target by flying low, with complete disregard of the enemy's ground defences' – an assertion that must have been read with incredulous amusement in many Bomber Command messes. The paper's report, headlined HUNDREDS KILLED IN BIG COVENTRY NIGHT RAID, beneath an impressive aerial view of the Cathedral and city centre, splashed across four columns, also made stirring reading.

Sheer height, however, did not save the Nazis altogether for two of their number were brought down. Unable to pick out legitimate targets such as armaments factories they loosed a stream of destruction on the streets. . . . From dusk to dawn there was seldom a period of more than two minutes when a bomb could not be heard falling. . . . A hail of fire bombs began a series of fires which lit up the district and bomber formations plastered the floodlit areas. In a livid glow from fires, the raiders seeking safety from the A A barrage five miles or more above the city, sprayed their bomb loads over the huddled streets and far beyond. While calcium flares rivalled the raking searchlights for brightness, the whine of diving bombers intermingled with the deep boom of replying A A fire and the sharp rat-ta-ta-tat of pompom and machine-gun bullets aimed at the slowly descending flares. . . .

As the red glare of fires gave way to dawn and the streets took shape under a heavy pall of smoke Coventry organized its emergency services. Rest centres and food kitchens sprang into instant life. Local agents of the Food Ministry cut through red tape and standing instructions to provide homeless people with food and warmth. . . . Splintered and battered as they were, shops and offices opened at the usual time. *Al fresco* shopping and roadside trading continued during the morning while fire brigades, demolition units and rescue squads worked heroically, quelling fires and extricating people trapped beneath the debris.

Whether people who had actually experienced the raid and its chaotic aftermath would have recognized what had happened from this description seems doubtful, but the legend of 'gallant little Coventry' was soon too strongly established to be dispelled. In fact, though many people, especially in the Civil Defence services, *had* been brave, most ordinary citizens who could leave had gone from the city before the raid began, while many of the remainder escaped on the following morning. As for the resumption of normal life, even the *Birmingham Gazette* admitted that 'few shops were open', and the evidence is overwhelming, from the Home Secretary downwards, that spirits generally, on the morning after the raid, were at rock bottom, and that the relief services had hardly started to function satisfactorily. A writer from the London *Evening Standard* who visited Coventry that day – though his account only appeared, in a book, several years later – found 'everyone in the city clamouring for food', and was struck by the sight of 'shivering refugees . . . wandering aimlessly through the ruins', some of whom 'looked completely stunned'.

Another experienced and sympathetic observer, the journalist Hilde Marchant, although highly impressed by the police, 'who that day provided the big shoulder for the public to rest on', also discovered less reassuring signs. 'The people stood around listening to the voice' (from the Ministry of Information van), she noted, 'occasionally asking when bread was coming into the city. There was no clamour. Just sullen resentment at the inconvenience. They had patience because they were too weary to be angry.' Waiting at a door of the Council House she saw 'a long queue of people – men without collars and still in their carpet slippers. Women in woollen dressing gowns and slippers, just as they had come out of the shelter . . . asking for clothes, food and money.' The sound of an aircraft overhead produced 'a wild scramble as some women grabbed their children and ran into the shelters. The plane banked and we saw the R A F markings, but it was some time before the people came out again.' In one shelter, apparently empty, the light of Miss Marchant's torch picked up 'four faces, greenish faces, so still that they looked dead', belonging to an adult couple and two children of about ten and fourteen, sitting in the dark and afraid to leave even to get a meal, for fear of not securing 'a good seat tonight'.

Probably few people who were in Coventry that morning would deny the miasma of depression that hung, with the rain clouds, over the town. 'Everyone seemed to have a whipped feeling,' agrees one senior warden. 'People were despondent. They were very quiet. They seemed to walk around in a bit of a daze.' King George had reached a similar conclusion. 'Poor Coventry is in a very sorry state,' he wrote to his mother just after his visit. 'The people were all dazed from the shock of it.' Even the youngest citizens had that day a pessimistic view of the immediate future. One bus driver from Dudley, mentioned earlier, who invited a group of boys into his bus to recount their experiences, found they were 'soon vying with each other' to see who could claim the most incendiaries extinguished but when at the end of the day he shouted, '"Well, cheerio, lads, see you all tomorrow!" the reply I got was, "Yes, if we are still here!"'

While Herbert Morrison, as described in the previous chapter, was facing the indignant burghers of Coventry, the man he had replaced, Sir John Anderson, who had been 'kicked upstairs' from the Home Office to become Lord President of the Council and unofficial 'overlord' of the Home Front, was reporting to the Cabinet. 'The raid,' he told his colleagues, 'had been the heaviest yet on a munitions centre; the damage had been very heavy and the casualties, killed and wounded, were already believed to be around 600. Communications had been badly interrupted and water, gas and electricity supplies had failed.'

The bombing of Coventry presented the government with a formidable problem, for by any realistic test the raid had been an overwhelming German victory. Instead of playing down the raid the Ministry of Information shrewdly decided to make the most of it and when the Germans claimed, in the words of the *Birmingham Gazette*, to have made 'the biggest attack in the history of air warfare', this was made to seem the boast of a bully who had brutally attacked someone smaller than himself. The burning down of the Cathedral made it easy to present an outstandingly successful operation of war as the ruthless devastation of the homes and holy places of a peaceful little community. The *Birmingham Gazette*'s story on 16 November must have delighted those responsible for British propaganda. 'The proud spire of Coventry Cathedral,' it began, 'yesterday stood as a sentinel over the grim scene of destruction below', while its headline proclaimed uncompromisingly, in a phrase much quoted: 'COVENTRY – OUR GUERNICA'.

The neutral press eagerly followed this lead. Everywhere in the United States, *The Times* correspondent reported, one could hear people talking of 'the butchery of Coventry' and the American newspapers could hardly have been more indignant had the outrage been perpetrated upon Detroit. 'The gaunt ruins of St Michael's Cathedral, Coventry, stare from the photographs,' declared the *New York Herald Tribune*, 'the voiceless symbol of the insane, the unfathomable barbarity, which had been released on Western civilization. No means of defense which the United States can place in British hands should be withheld.' 'The inevitable loss in aircraft production at Coventry,' agreed the *New York Times*, 'will have to be made good in American factories.'

The German public learned of the raid from a jubilant communiqué put out by the Deutschlandsender transmitter, at 14.00 hours on 15 November. According to the BBC Monitoring Service the Germans claimed to have 'inflicted an extraordinarily heavy blow on the enemy. . . . The attack was stated to have wrought havoc and immense fires . . . were visible as far as the Channel coast.' The claim that Coventry had been 'completely wiped out' was supported on 9 December by the publication in the German press of the first reconnaissance photographs.

According to the Civil Servant concerned the German commentators had 'ransacked the dictionary for adjectives to describe the devastation wrought', but it was a word newly coined for the occasion which really captured the public imagination – *koventrieren*, 'to coventrate', soon defined as meaning to lay waste a city by air attack. Far from striking terror into British hearts this addition to the wartime vocabulary was received with gratification, especially in Coventry itself, where people were beginning to feel proud at having been singled out for the enemy's special attention.

At this stage of the war the Germans seem genuinely to have believed – just as the British government did – that the enemy population only had to have their eyes opened to the folly of their leaders to clamour for peace and this was the particular aim of the 'black' station, Workers' Challenge, which purported to be operated illegally by dissident Englishmen. Workers' Challenge tried to demonstrate its proletarian *bona fides* by the use of slang (usually somewhat outdated) and the occasional swear-word, and at 9.10 p.m. on Saturday 16 November delivered this remarkable essay in phoney sympathy, designed to make its listeners' flesh creep:

Well, workers, it's hard luck on Coventry and, of course, it's hard luck on the workers and we're going to tell you something you may have cause to remember. It's this. Coventry is the first place to be attacked in this way, outside of London and Liverpool, but we are bloody sure it's not going to be the last. . . . Most people thought it wouldn't be too easy to smash up one of the biggest production bases in the country but it was and the main question now is 'What's the next on the list?' . . . It's impossible to describe what happened in Coventry. If we began you would switch off. . . . But even if we don't go into details we have got to give you some facts. The BBC says that military objectives weren't hit. That's just bloody bunk and everybody knows it. All attempts to hush the thing up broke down because from the industrial point of view there is none of Coventry left. There has never been such a bombardment before, either in this country or anywhere in the world, relative, that is, to the size of the town. All night long the bombs fell and there was no pause between them. The blaze could have been seen for miles, practically all over the Midlands, and the loss of life is just appalling. Nobody knows how many casualties there were, because there were so many bodies under the ruins.

But one thing is certain: every single death that occurred must be laid at Churchill's door.

The BBC's first coverage of the raid, as has been described, was based closely on the official communiqués, but, perhaps as a result of the Ministry of Information's 'playing up' policy, it was decided to place an eye-witness account in the peak listening time after the nine o'clock news on Saturday 16 November. As speaker the BBC chose Tom Harrisson, the twenty-nine-year-old founder of Mass-Observation, a pioneer opinion-measuring organization, which had achieved fame before the war for its studies of the daily life and attitudes of ordinary people. By good fortune much information had already been compiled about Coventry by a six-man team who had spent several weeks there doing research into war savings and on the night of the raid Tom Harrisson himself was nearby, at Birmingham. Next morning he drove straight to Coventry and spent the night uncomfortably in his car.

That evening three full-time Mass-Observation experts arrived to prepare a detailed report, and next day Tom Harrisson returned to Birmingham to deliver his BBC talk.

I have spent a good deal of life listening to other people talk, but I've never heard people talk less than in Coventry yesterday. Many walked through the city rather blankly looking at the mess, and the commonest remark was simply: 'Poor old Coventry.' The commonest sound was the scraping of shovels and the shifting of rubble. . . . I've been chasing air raids in this country ever since they began: often I've heard awful stories of the damage and arrived to find them grossly exaggerated. But about Coventry there hasn't been much exaggeration: in fact the centre of the town reminded me more than anything of the photos of Ypres in the last war. . . .

As soon as darkness fell, the streets were silent. The people of Coventry had gone to shelter. For more than an hour I was picking my way through craters and glass, and during the whole time I saw no other private car. I think this is one of the weirdest experiences in my whole life, driving in a lonely silent desolation and drizzling rain in that great industrial town. Then I met a gang of young men looking for a drink. I went with them because I wanted one too. We must have visited half the pubs in Coventry before we found one. . . .

I see some reporters stressing the fact that Coventry is clamouring for reprisals. That wasn't borne out by my own observations; for, after all this was a reprisal, according to the Germans, and it only makes Coventry realize that this sort of thing doesn't end the war and only makes it more bitter.

Although the talk finished with a conventional tribute to the 'wonderful' ARP services and an optimistic assurance that 'the work of reconstruction' was already starting, it was its earlier section which caught the government's ear, and caused the programme to be discussed at the next meeting of the War Cabinet on Monday 18 November.

The Secretary of State for War said that he had listened on Saturday night to a special account of the effects of the air raid, given by the BBC. This had been a most depressing broadcast, and would have a deplorable effect on Warwickshire units. Other Ministers confirmed this view.

The Prime Minister said that he did not suggest that the decision to give prominence to the Coventry raid was wrong. The effect had been considerable both in the United States and, from a different point of view, in Germany. The enemy seemed to be alarmed at the publicity given to this raid and to have taken the unusual course of announcing that they had lost 223 dead in our raid on Hamburg on the following night. Unless the publicity in the press had had a bad effect on our morale, he doubted if it had done any harm. Nevertheless, he wished to be assured that the decision as to the degree of publicity given to raids of this character was entrusted to an officer of high standing. He would be glad if the Ministers concerned would consider the present procedure from this point of view.

Behind the discreet wording of the final sentence lay the greatest threat to the independence of the BBC of the whole war, for the Coventry report brought to a head the hostility which several members of the government, and particularly Churchill himself, had long felt towards the Corporation. It had infuriated Lord Beaverbrook who was already campaigning for overriding priority to be given to the strategic bombing offensive against Germany, and who claimed the British public was clamouring for reprisals against Germany. Tom Harrisson had all unwittingly stirred up a political and strategic hornets' nest, as Minute 4 of that day's Cabinet proceedings recorded:

In connection with the previous Minute, in which the account given by the BBC of the position in Coventry was strongly criticized, the War Cabinet 'Invited the Chancellor of the Exchequer, the Home Secretary and the Minister of Information to examine and report to the War Cabinet what changes, if any, were necessary in the constitution and management of the BBC in order to ensure its effective control by His Majesty's Government.'

That Tom Harrisson's assessment of opinion in Coventry directly after the raid was correct there can be little question. Few people were more representative of attitudes there than Councillor Pearl Hyde and her answer to 'reporters from outside the city . . . asking if we were thirsting for reprisals', was, one Special Constable remembers, emphatic: '"At the moment we jump three feet in the air if anyone slams a door. All we want is a quiet night tonight."' The visiting WVS organizer from Oldbury, already quoted, who arrived only an hour or two after the All Clear, also found no eagerness for revenge among the civilian population, though 'two airmen on leave . . . showed us a brick on which they had written BERLIN which they were going to drop next time they were over Germany'. If there was satisfaction at later raids by the RAF it was, one local factory owner admits, tempered by the reflection, 'It'll be our turn tonight.'

The report that Mass-Observation submitted soon afterwards poured a cold douche of realism upon the stories of Coventry cheerfully 'taking it', as well as upon the alleged demand for reprisals. The investigators began by pointing out the special factors which made Coventry different from all previous blitzed cities, notably its small size, so that 'the damage was . . . extremely concentrated', seeming to 'dominate the whole scene', and 'exaggeration and rumour spread much faster than in a big city'. The observers commented:

Nearly everybody knew somebody who had been killed or was missing and plenty of people who had been rendered . . . homeless. . . . These subjects occupied literally 90 per cent of all conversation heard throughout Friday afternoon and evening. Even in Stepney at the beginning of the Blitz there was not nearly the same obsession with damage and disaster. . . .

The small size of the place makes people feel that the only thing they can do is *get out of it altogether*. The dislocation is so total in the town that people feel that *the town itself is killed*. 'Coventry is finished' and 'Coventry is dead' were the key phrases of Friday's talk. Every pub and practically every shop . . . shut . . . even though a considerable number were still intact and might well have continued operating with great benefit to the morale of the community.

The Mass-Observation team distinguished, however, as Herbert Morrison had failed to do, between actual defeatism and a mere absence of militant patriotism.

It should be stressed that *no sign whatever* was found of anti-war feeling, that there were very few grumbles. People were full of admiration for the ARP and AFS services. ... Similarly, there was great admiration for the AA defences, though nearly everybody regarded them as inadequate. ... The tremendous attack which took the civilian unawares was so unexpected by him that he felt it was reasonable that it should have caught everybody else unprepared as well. And the first effect of violent and sudden raids is always to increase people's interest in the personal and local aspects; they seem unable to associate such instances with the war as a whole or with external events. There was, however, considerable feeling of vague futility and very little feeling in favour of reprisals.

Against this absence of recrimination, however, had to be set the feeling of 'impotence' which Herbert Morrison had sensed during his far briefer visit the day after the raid.

In consequence of the above conditions, and the severity of the attack, the investigators found an unprecedented dislocation and depression in Coventry, on Friday. There were more open signs of hysteria, terror, neurosis, observed in one evening than during the whole of the past two months together in all areas. Women were seen to cry, to scream, to tremble all over, to faint in the street, to attack a fireman. ... The overwhelmingly dominant feeling on Friday was . . . utter *helplessness*. The tremendous impact of the previous night had left people practically speechless in many cases. . . . On Friday evening, there were several signs of suppressed panic as darkness approached. In two cases people were seen fighting to get on to cars which they thought would take them out into the country though in fact, as the drivers insisted, the cars were going just up the road to the garage.*

The Mass-Observation findings were not, of course, published (indeed they have remained in the files until now) but someone in the Ministry of Home Security must have realized their value, for the organization was later commissioned to prepare even more

*A short extract from the Coventry report appeared in Tom Harrisson's *Living through the Blitz*, published posthumously by Collins in July 1976, while the present book was in the press. Overall, however, *Living through the Blitz* devotes only 10 pages, of some 330, to the Coventry raid, though the chapter on it does include some interesting eye-witness accounts of post-Blitz conditions.

detailed reports on other blitzed cities. (Tom Harrisson himself, tiring of the Whitehall battles, was later parachuted into Borneo and had a distinguished war leading bands of jungle head-hunters against the Japanese.)

The BBC, having inadvertently offended the government, had meanwhile made amends, on Sunday 24 November, with a thirty-minute programme in the morale-boosting series *They Went To It*, an embarrassing title derived from Herbert Morrison's slogan, then plastered all over the hoardings, GO TO IT! Although the twelve interviews in the thirty-minute programme did not shirk the darker side of the story, so that a casual listener might have felt that *They Went Through It* would have been an apter title, the programme had what would now be called an upbeat approach. Children being evacuated were heard singing 'We'll be jolly friends for ever more', and a building worker, busily hammering away at housing repairs, predicted that 'Coventry will rise as it always has done in the past.'

This programme was not discussed by the Cabinet but at the end of the year the 'three wise men' who had been asked to consider how the BBC could be more strictly controlled produced their proposals, which were accepted by the government and passed to the BBC on 31 December. Lord Reith, who was not consulted, considered the plans 'extraordinary . . . muddled in themselves, humiliating to the BBC', for it was proposed that the Ministry of Information should appoint two advisers to the BBC, one on foreign affairs, one on home affairs, to whose suggestions the Corporation was expected to listen; if it did not, the advisers could appeal to the minister to support them. In the event the foreign adviser proved a highly civilized diplomat, and the home affairs adviser was recruited from the BBC's own management, though technically seconded to the Ministry of Information. The BBC's independence in handling the news remained untrammelled – though not unchallenged – for the rest of the war.

Whatever its effect on the government the BBC's coverage of the raid and the simultaneous reports in the press had a marked effect on public opinion and the city's mere name, like that of Russia a year or so later, was soon a signal for cheers and loosened purse-strings. Among the early beneficiaries of this attitude were a group of AFS volunteers, travelling up from London on the following Tuesday in a relief convoy of hose-laying lorries and heavy pumping units, who, when they stopped overnight at Rugby, found themselves treated as near-heroes. The manager of the dance hall they attended insisted on 'leading us', one fireman later wrote, 'across the black road into a saloon bar where he called for drinks, seeming hurt because we wished to pay for them', and later, following what was clearly a put-up job, it was a fireman and his partner who won the 'spot prize' of chocolates and cigarettes.

Although between mid-November and Christmas there were major attacks, involving more than a hundred tons of high explosive, on a series of other cities, including Southampton, Birmingham, Bristol, Plymouth, Liverpool, Sheffield, Manchester, and, inevitably, London, it was Coventry which continued to attract most public attention. The announcement of a number of awards for gallantry on the night of 14 November renewed interest in the raid. Most notable was the first George Cross ever awarded to a policeman, a thirty-year-old fitter at the Armstrong Siddeley works, Brandon Moss, who, while on patrol as a Special Constable, had worked all night to rescue eight trapped people (four were eventually brought out alive) in spite of a delayed-action bomb nearby and the risk that every fresh explosion would bury him beneath the rubble. Almost as courageous, and newsworthy, were a nineteen-year-old girl warden, a clerk by day, who had helped to dig out seven people from a buried Anderson, though ordered to stay in shelter, and a thirty-two-year-old doctor attached to the Barkers Butts School First Aid Post, who, 'while fires were raging and bombs falling, coolly continued to go . . . on foot and . . . by bicycle from one incident to another administering morphia . . . and applying first aid'. Both received the George Medal and there were other honours equally well deserved, for ambulance drivers, rescue workers and stretcher bearers.

The arrival of goodwill messages from all over the world also provided interesting 'copy' for the newspapers. The town of Coventry, Rhode Island, USA, cabled its 'greatest sympathy in your hour of trial'. The officers and men of HMS *Coventry* made a signal assuring the citizens that they would 'endeavour to repay'. Four hundred people, among them numerous bishops, sent messages of condolence to the Provost on the loss of the Cathedral, and there were innumerable gifts of bedding, clothing and food, the 'shoe town' of Leicester alone sending four lorry-loads of footwear.

The Mayor's Air Raid Victims' Distress Fund had been inaugurated in October and a deluge of donations now descended upon it. The sack-loads of mail which arrived at the Council House, 'first from Great Britain, then in a flood from many parts of the world', as the Mayor's daughter remembers, represented another, though welcome, burden for the Moseley family.

Words are useless to express how we felt for we'd never realized how kind and generous unknown people could be, from so many countries and so many walks of life. . . . Many parcels contained letters, scores and scores of such sympathetic and friendly messages. I saw quite a number of them. All were officially acknowledged by the staff of the Mayor's secretary, but mum sent dozens and dozens of personal letters in addition.

Three weeks after the raid the Mayor's Fund already stood at £35 000; by March 1941 there was a balance of £46000, though £6000 had so far been disbursed. By July 1944 the fund had £67174 still in hand, although 3566 grants had been made, totalling £47056 – an average of no more than £13 each. Years after the war the remaining money, by now something of an embarrassment, was got rid of by distributing it to the victims of foreign earthquakes and other natural disasters – worthy causes enough, but having no connection whatever with the people for whom it had been intended.*

In the weeks after the raid Coventry also received a flood of distinguished visitors. The Duke of Kent arrived to tour a factory; the Secretary of State for War came, a little late in the day perhaps, to inspect the anti-aircraft defences; the Minister without Portfolio, Arthur Greenwood, toured the city and declared its spirit 'unbeatable'; the American Military Attaché came to inspect the ruins and was impressed to learn that drunkenness among the working population had declined. Coventry also continued to attract journalists, among them Hilde Marchant, who paid it a second visit a week after the raid. In the centre of the city she noted that 'squads of demolition workers had carved out the roads again, heaped the bricks in neat squares, and cleared the broken foundations', but

*In 1963 the Charity Commissioners gave permission for the remaining £13 906 to form the basis of the Coventry Charity for Special Relief, intended for any local person in need.

to her 'it seemed as if they had done no more than lay the corpse out in state'. Further out, however, the mood was different:

On the fringe of this dead, depressing area the modest pleasures of the living had flowered again. A theatre was giving matinees, the warm smell of the bakery breathed out into the street every time the boarded door was swung open, the little hat shop on the corner was showing styles on the heads of rather chipped models. . . . The Ministry of Information . . . had issued white posters with two Union Jacks in the corners, and a great blank space for the shopkeepers to scribble any piece of personal abuse they felt for Hitler. . . . The people were anything but gay but they had taken on the stage of widowhood when the will has been read and the estate proved to be rather more than they expected.

The raid left a substantial literary legacy. The city produced a retrospective illustrated guide-book, *The City We Loved*; the vicar of Holy Trinity modestly described how he had saved his church in *Coventry Under Fire*; Mr J. B. Shelton wrote a vivid, and equally modest, account of *A Night in Little Park Street*. 'A Blind Citizen' contributed his *Impressions*, and an anonymous author wrote an embarrassingly sentimental pamphlet, *One of His Own Trees*, the life story of a 'straight, strong young oak' from the days 'long centuries ago, when the Forest of Arden spread over Warwickshire', until the 'night of horror and destruction . . . when the fierce fury of the flames burned into his heart' in the Cathedral roof.

The raid also inspired a large crop of poems, more notable for their patriotism than their literary quality. A rare exception, however, is this one, which, after describing the devastation of the city, ended:

> So the garden will prosper and flourish,
> And the life, love and laughter go on,
> When the smouldering ruins are finished,
> And the twisted girders are gone.

17
A GRIM TASK

*'Joan Alice Tipson. Died November 14th 1940. Aged
13 years.'*
Obituary in Barrs Hill School Magazine, July 1941

LIKE any private individual who had suffered a bereavement,
Coventry could not begin to look to the future until its dead had
been buried. The two great public funerals in the week after the
raid marked a watershed between the sense of shock and grief
following the raid and the realization that life must somehow go on.

The Ministry of Home Security, with remarkably accurate foresight, had instructed Coventry to provide for 800 dead, a need
originally met by requisitioning the swimming baths, but before
they could be used the building was itself hit and an inconspicuous
shed-like structure near the old gas works in Gas Street became
the temporary mortuary. First-aider Dick Baxendale, in charge of
a First Aid Post in Canal Road, came to know the route to it
well. 'You couldn't get your vehicles through very easily . . .' he
remembers. 'You had to pull up at the bomb crater, take your
casualty out, carry it over the bomb crater, and then let the
ambulance wobble over as best it could.' Dr Alan Ashworth also
remembers this building:

Dr Massey had made provision for a mortuary for 500 bodies (to the
quiet amusement of several colleagues, who thought he was overdoing it).
It was in a building adjoining the gasometer of the gas works and had a
corrugated-iron roof. Racks had been erected with runners, which took
an ambulance stretcher and was in fact several layers deep, the upper
layers being quite high to load. The routine practice for ambulance and
stretcher party personnel on removal of a body was to tie a luggage label
on to the body, stating where it had been found, whether the identity of
the body was known, and the number of the ambulance which had taken

the body to the mortuary. These particulars were written with an indelible lead pencil.

It was a sound and sensible system but chance and the weather were to rob even death of its dignity.

During the raid a bomb hit the gasometer, which exploded and completely unroofed the mortuary. Two nights later, it . . . poured with rain, soaking the bodies, softening the labels, in which the writing was largely washed off, making identification most difficult. It was necessary for all bodies to be identified before a burial certificate could be issued, so we arranged for relatives to inspect the bodies. . . . It was soon recognized that it was an impossible routine. We had as many as three or four persons identifying the same body as a different person, particularly the bodies which had suffered the full effect of bomb blast. It was quickly realized that some other method should be adopted and, finally, each body was stripped and all belongings, clothing, etc., were put into a sandbag; each body was put into a coffin, supplied by Regional Control, and both given the same number and entered into a register. It was gruesome work, which was done by the stretcher party personnel. A bottle of brandy was very useful at the outset. . . . Subsequently the bodies were identified by their clothes jewellery, etc., and . . . there were very few who were not finally identified.*

These difficulties were, very understandably, not made public. Instead, on instructions from the Emergency Committee, a tactfully phrased, crudely hand-printed notice outside informed callers:

IT IS GREATLY REGRETTED THAT THE PRESSURE AT THE MORTUARY IS SUCH THAT IT IS NOT POSSIBLE FOR RELATIVES TO VIEW ANY OF THE BODIES.

According to a secret report, submitted by Midland Region to the Ministry of Home Security a month later, this decision 'was accepted' and it must have come as a great relief to the staff of the mortuary, where 'at one time . . . as many as sixty bodies' were 'being received in one hour' with '40–50 per cent unidentifiable owing to mutilation' – 'unidentifiable' here meaning 'unrecognizable'.

Along with the ban on viewing of the bodies went another, distinctly more contentious, on private burials, except for people whose homes were outside Coventry. In every bombed city so far

*A very similar system was adopted after the Allied raid on Dresden in 1945.

private burial had remained the rule, but no place of Coventry's size had suffered anything like the same losses and the Emergency Committee bravely decided that a mass funeral would be far more fitting and less painful than a long drawn-out series of individual ceremonies. (It also unobtrusively overcame the difficulty of identification and Dr Ashworth still suspects that 'some bodies scheduled for the first mass burial were in fact in the second mass burial and vice versa'.) Alderman Hodgkinson, Vice-Chairman of the Emergency Committee, decided after visiting Gas Street 'to try and persuade the people who were clamouring to go into the mortuary and take the bodies away that it was ... a shocking thing to do ... that they ought to remember their friends and relations as they knew them in life'. They were instead 'persuaded to accept a civic funeral and that the bodies should be interred in a communal grave'.

The Home Office report admits, however, that 'the decision to prohibit private burials except for those living outside the city was not ... well received' and even for those families who were exempt from it a time limit eventually had to be imposed, as a later notice made clear:

AIR RAID DEATHS
RELATIVES ARE NOTIFIED THAT THE COUNCIL WILL BE UNABLE
TO ARRANGE FOR BODIES TO BE CLAIMED FOR PRIVATE
BURIAL OUTSIDE THE CITY AFTER 12 NOON ON FRIDAY 22ND
NOVEMBER 1940

No other bombed city had previously held a mass funeral but the idea was eventually accepted without too much resentment and there were strong inducements to agree, for in such cases the Council handled all the formalities. To secure a body for private burial, on the other hand, meant obtaining 'a certificate that death was due to war operations' and a 'Burial Authority' from the Town Clerk's Department and then taking these to the Registrar of Deaths, as well as the customary negotiations with an undertaker. For an ordinary family, too, cost must have been a factor, for the Council (which reclaimed the cost from the government) arranged, and paid for, the public funerals. The grant of £7 10s, payable for the private burial of an air-raid victim, only applied where such burials were officially permitted – which in Coventry meant only for those who had lived outside the city – and was even then restricted to Civil Defence workers, children under fifteen and those 'gainfully employed', which excluded, for example, full-time housewives and pensioners.

Before the first funeral could take place there were some last-minute anxieties behind the scenes. A Home Office report later revealed that there had been 'some apprehension as to the availability of timber' for the coffins, made of rough and unpolished oak, but 'for 400 coffins only ten standards of timber were necessary' and this amount was found by Midland Region at Birmingham. The use of the government's cardboard coffins, kept secretly in store since the start of the war, proved unnecessary. Preparing the dead for burial placed another burden on the members of the Ambulance Service, one of whom recalls being sent to the 'local ironmongers to commandeer his complete stock of nails to seal the coffins'. A Birmingham bus driver who had visited Coventry as an ARP ambulance driver the day after the raid found himself returning a few days later with a bus-load of grave-diggers, brought in to help the Army prepare the communal graves.

The first civic funeral, on Wednesday 20 November, was a great national as well as local event, though *The Times* warned that morning that 'bodies are still being recovered as the work of clearing the debris . . . proceeds' and it was already clear that a second such ceremony would be required. For months a section of the new cemetery had quietly been set aside for air-raid casualties and while other troops laboured more visibly in the streets a small team had been busy with a mechanical excavator, producing 'two deep and long trenches' in which the coffins had been laid in rows under cover of darkness, with Union Jacks draped over them at intervals. The day was a grey and dismal one, suiting the melancholy business to be conducted, and one woman who had found 'the place crowded with people on the same sad errand' when going to report her mother's death at the Council House a few days before, thought this occasion, despite the crowds, 'very sad and moving'. Its atmosphere was well rendered by this account written by one of the officiating clergy:

In the background stood the mechanical trench-digger and groups of soldiers and labourers who had been working throughout the night at the grim task of carrying the coffins. . . . The Bishop of Coventry and the clergy and ministers, the Mayor and civic officials, and the Regional Commissioner all stood about in groups . . . strained and tired. . . .

When all was ready we moved in order towards the gate to meet the crowd of mourners, who were led up the road through the cemetery by a contingent of police, firemen and wardens. Then at the top of the rise the bishop and clergy, followed by the civic officials, took the lead to the graveside. It was a quiet and solemn procession. The soft beat of the rubber boots of the firemen, the measured tread of the police and wardens, marching in step across the gravel path seemed to accentuate the silence. . . .

At the graveside it was possible to turn and look back over the long line of mourners still approaching. It was a pathetic sight; women carrying wreaths; here and there a child with a bunch of flowers; the black suits and dresses relieved occasionally by a splash of colour of the uniform of a husband, a son or a brother on compassionate leave. It seemed as if there were no end to this long dark line, which moved slowly across the grass. At last the great crowd was gathered around the graves.

The Roman Catholic priest stepped forward and, hardly lifting his eyes from the book, read the service. Men and women in the crowd knelt on the grass or clay and crossed themselves. . . . Then the Bishop stepped forward . . . and a simple but dignified service followed. The Free Church ministers offered 'free' prayer expressing the thoughts and moods of those sorrowing folk. . . .

The service concluded with one or two beautifully phrased prayers of the English Prayer Book and the Blessing. . . . The Mayor, carrying a wreath, led the mourners up and down the long gravesides, and as they followed they laid their wreaths and dropped their posies and sprays into the graves. Some peered anxiously at the bloodstained labels attached to the coffins to see if . . . they could see the name of their relative or friend [but] most of the names were . . . (perhaps fortunately) indecipherable. . . . In the distance, against the grey scudding sky, a Spitfire wheeled and twisted; the sound of its engine came fitfully to us down the wind.

One hundred and seventy-two people were buried that day, followed by 250 more at a similar service on the following Saturday. Among them were two young children whose cousin, then a schoolgirl herself, can remember asking, 'as we looked down on the coffins one on top of the other in the communal grave, "Which is Muriel and David?" but no one knew. Most were covered in wreaths and you just placed them anywhere.' She was conscious of the 'deep mourning and tears' of the children's mother, her aunt, whom they had to support and the futility of her cousins' deaths – they had been killed by the same delayed-action bomb, while the fourteen-year-old was taking her one-year-old brother to the lavatory.

Another woman, then aged thirteen, found the whole episode puzzling. It took her, she admits, 'a long time' to accept that one of her classmates had been killed. 'It was the first time I realized that this wasn't just a "grown-ups'"' war. Olive had been a thin meek girl and I couldn't understand why anyone should want to kill her, or why God should allow it.'

No doubt similar doubts troubled many adults, but the Bishop of Coventry, who spoke at the first service, and Provost Howard, who delivered the address at the second, refused to refer to 'a holy war', or preach the gospel of revenge. They spoke instead of the nation-wide reaction to the raid, which had brought 'hundreds of letters . . . from all over the country' expressing 'sympathy, admiration and trust' for the people of Coventry. 'Let us vow before God,' said the Bishop, 'to be better friends and neighbours in the future, because we have suffered this together and have stood here today.'

One of the busiest places in Coventry at this time was the office of the Registrar of Births, Marriages and Deaths as the then Miss Lucy Moseley remembers:

We were snowed under with work once order was slowly restored. Some staff came over from Birmingham Register Office to help out just as the first batches of requisite forms were coming through from the Public Health Department. From these we registered the deaths. This help ended abruptly when Birmingham itself was the second target on the German Air Force list with a thirteen-hour raid. We had no light, heat and water. My colleague and I moved into an upstairs office that captured more daylight – and had a candle in a clay flower pot on the desk to warm our fingers for a few moments.

In these conditions they had to carry out such tasks as taking statements from a whole range of witnesses to establish beyond all question that some missing individual had been blown to pieces without trace, like a group of men who had tried to move a landmine to allow an ambulance to pass. 'These cases were distressing even to us, requiring statements from many other people,' this informant admits, 'but it had to be done.'

All too often such sad scenes wrote the final chapter to the story of someone who was officially 'missing', but sometimes there were happier sequels, as in the case of the fourteen-year-old girl described earlier, who had been evacuated from the Coventry and Warwickshire Hospital the morning after the raid, when confusion was at its height.

As the days went by with no word of my parents I began to think they were all dead. After about a week one afternoon I looked up the ward and saw dad coming through the door. . . . He told me he had walked to Coventry to find me but no one knew anything about us. On the way he had met the mass funeral of people killed. He had stood and watched not knowing if I was one of them. But by chance someone had told him a few of us had been taken to Stratford and as a last resort he had gone there. . . . It was very strange later to find I had been presumed dead and to see my own name on the mortuary list outside the Council House.

Although those present at the two civic funerals must have been able to make their own estimates of the total death roll the figure was never publicly announced, prompting rumours that it had been enormous and that many bodies had simply been bricked up in the ruins.

The Rev. W. B. Sells was assured by some of his parishioners:

On the night of the blitz three shelters in The Butts nearby had been visited by Civil Defence and found to be intact, but everyone dead inside from blast. Another tale was that the workers at Courtaulds . . . had gone down to deep shelters, under the works, these had had a direct hit and been sealed off so that hundreds of workers were dead and buried alive.

The Birmingham sheet-metal worker previously quoted shared his table at the factory canteen with one supposedly well-informed workmate who

knew for a fact that when the Standard Co.'s enamelling shop had received a direct hit, over 400 people were killed in that building alone, and as it would have been impossible to retrieve their bodies, a burial service was conducted by three vicars, one at each end and one in the centre of a huge mound of rubble about sixty yards long. . . . This, he assured us, was by no means the only case of its kind.

The Mayor's daughter recalls her father being 'furious' when asked, while enjoying a drink in a pub at Milverton, 'if it was true that there were so many dead bodies under the Market Hall that it would just be sealed up', and it was perhaps this incident which prompted the issuing of an official denial in the *Midland Daily Telegraph* of 25 November:

In the last few days it has been widely stated that not only are many bodies still buried beneath piles of debris and that in some cases central shelters are being sealed up, but that a number of people trapped on the night of 14 November are still alive and being fed regularly by tubes. Such statements are authoritatively declared to be incorrect.

The paper revealed that it had that morning sent a reporter on a 'tour of the shelters about which rumour had been most rife' and had 'found . . . every compartment . . . undamaged and intact'. A few people, it admitted, were still missing, but 'the greatest number of persons killed in any one spot was . . . thirty-five, all of whose bodies had been recovered'. The *Coventry Standard*, by contrast, which resumed publication on 30 November, encouraged the stories of a massive death roll by estimating total casualties at 3000, one of the few such figures to prove too high.

When, late in December, the government released casualty figures for the United Kingdom for the whole of November speculation revived. The *Midland Daily Telegraph* pointed out that with 'intense' raids upon Birmingham, Bristol, Merseyside and Southampton' during the same period, as well as almost daily attacks on London 'those who have endeavoured to estimate local casualties in terms of "thousands" have been absurdly wide of the mark', but even the issue of the real figures, late in the war, did not finally still the rumours and some people in Coventry are still convinced that the true death roll was 'hushed up'.*

---

*I have found no evidence to support this suspicion. As the figures from Coventry were used in making plans to help other blitzed cities, and in predicting the likely death rate from R A F raids on German cities, it seems most unlikely that they were falsified.

18
MARKS AND SPENCER VERSUS
THE HUNS

*'Marks and Spencer . . . are playing their part in defying
the activities of the Huns by opening up in Whitefriars
Street.'*
The Midland Daily Telegraph, *21 December 1940*

'THERE was still chaos, but an organized chaos.' That is how one
AFS man from Birmingham pinpoints the difference between
Coventry on the morning after the raid and on the following
Monday. 'We were quite disorientated. Without landmarks how
does one find one's way about?' This was the reaction of one young
Civil Servant who, on that same Monday, 'walked into Coventry to
try to find the office site in case something was salvageable'. The
tinsmith from Birmingham, also quoted earlier, now found himself
forced to travel by train instead of driving to work and to walk
from the station:

Although all three of us knew the place well we halted at one corner
because we were lost. It was a dull morning at the end of November and
not a light was to be seen anywhere. Every building that we had known
was blasted into a mere shell and in whichever direction we looked, we
could not see a single recognizable building, be it house, office, factory,
warehouse, etc. Even the old oak tree which had stood on the corner for
donkey's years was leaning towards the middle of the road with a lot of
its roots, some as thick as my arm, pointing to the sky. What with the
gloom, the devastation, the complete and utter silence, we could have
been the first men on the moon and it affected us so much that we found
ourselves speaking in whispers.

On Monday 18 November the long haul back to something
approaching normality began. 'Several important factories had
resumed work,' Whitehall was informed in the local Situation
Report that evening, the output of electricity was back to 50 per
cent of the pre-raid figure, a number of telephone lines were in

service and some buses were running on all routes. Slowly, the business life of the city began to flow again. The experiences of the district manager of the Singer Sewing Machine Company, Mr F. K. Sheppard, of whose five branches only one had remained undamaged, were typical. On Monday both the shop and office staff reassembled, as previously instructed, at the home of one manageress. By the Wednesday a new temporary headquarters had been set up, to which car-loads of books and papers had been removed, some of the staff had been 'sent out to contact some customers' and Mr Sheppard had even given a pep talk to an 'outside salesman' who 'thought our prospects to be hopeless. . . . I stressed to him,' wrote Mr Sheppard in his business diary that day, 'that we now had even stronger selling points than before: (a) no shops with ready-made garments, hence greater need to have facilities for home-making, with their Singer machines; (b) ready-made garments taxable but not lengths of material.' That afternoon, he noted 'business now beginning to move at other branches' and the following day the formerly despondent salesman reported that he had 'secured sale of a machine put out on trial before the bombing'. On Saturday 23 November the first letters arrived since 14 November, and Mr Sheppard learned on 21 December that his company had been allocated a shop in the new temporary shopping centre. Although it was to be months before his shops had their windows restored, it had taken, he later noted, only about 'six weeks to get the business moving again'.*

This shop was one of thirty-eight erected in Corporation Street, and the hundred applications demonstrated that the city's tradespeople had not yet 'written off' Coventry as a shopping centre. The 'Co-op' – that 'old-established Coventry institution', as the local press called it – also replaced its main premises in West Orchard by new ones in the Corporation Street complex, while 'Messrs Marks and Spencer of Smithford Street,' reported the same newspaper, 'are playing their part in defying the activities of the Huns by opening up in Whitefriars Street' in part of a garage damaged in the raid. By Christmas even Owen Owen had reopened in cramped quarters in Trinity Street. 'I apologized to the customers,'

---

*The Singer company, having survived the worst the Luftwaffe could do, was to suffer soon afterwards from the elimination of 'luxury' trades. Many Singer shops were shut, and Mr Sheppard found himself redundant.

Leslie Worthington recalls, but 'many of them cried and said they were so grateful, as it was a boost to their morale.'

Coventry was also well served by its banks. One AFS man, in private life an accountant, who returned to Coventry on the Saturday found his 'bank manager . . . carrying on business on a bench outside the damaged premises' and 'drew some money with just a signature on an old envelope'. One by one other businesses reopened. One housewife living in Harris Road can still recapture 'the sheer luxury of having my hair shampooed and set' after 'going into town one Saturday and finding a hairdresser's open'. The spirits of a works chemist at a major factory were similarly raised by finding that, in spite of the twelve public houses destroyed, 'there was . . . no lack of beer, since such a large proportion of the population moved out every night', though so many glasses had been broken that 'we either took our own tankards to the pub or drank out of jam jars'. It was, more or less, also 'business as usual' at the Gulson Road Hospital as one nurse, then a student, remembers:

Work was done in the most extraordinary places. A kitchen became the theatre at one time, but the surgeons never grumbled, though they did, fortunately for our training, expect the same high standards of technique as they had in normal conditions. The equipment was a little Heath Robinson at times, such as a fish kettle in which to sterilize the instruments, and scrubbing up was often done with cold water.

While some of the staff of the Central Library were occupied trying to trace missing families, others tackled the weary job of salvaging more than 30000 volumes from the reference library. The only books from the gutted lending section to survive had been those 'out' at the time and an appeal was made for them to be returned to one of the other branches. For once those who had kept books out too long were popular, and no fines were levied when long overdue volumes reappeared.

Although it was the burning down of the Cathedral which had attracted international attention, four other Anglican churches had been destroyed and five others badly damaged. The congregations of St Luke's and St Paul's found shelter in nearby schools or institutes, while those who worshipped at St Nicholas and St Francis, the *Midland Daily Telegraph* reported, 'have adapted public houses to their needs'. The first substitute for the Cathedral itself was found 'in the drawing room of the Provost's House', but, as the Provost later wrote:

On the second Sunday we established our Cathedral chapel in the Wyley Crypt Chapel, with an 8 o'clock celebration of Holy Communion. . . . For many Sundays the rain dripped in from the ground above, now open to the sky. Two inches of sawdust was placed all over the floor to absorb the rainwater. But gradually the roof was waterproofed, with a concrete pavement on the floor of the ruins and a reasonable degree of comfort was attained.

Coventry also had a large Roman Catholic community. Two churches, St Mary's and All Souls, had been partially wrecked, while a third, the major Roman Catholic centre in the city, St Osburg's, had suffered £100,000 worth of damage including its brand-new schools, and a magnificent new hall. Its congregation moved in with that of the church of Christ the King, though its priest, the local paper reported, was 'hoping it may be possible to convert the school's air-raid shelter . . . for holding services'. The non-conformist churches had escaped more lightly, apart from the Congregationalists, whose main church, at Well Street, after being damaged, had been taken over as the site of the municipal cafeteria, and who had also lost their Bell Green church. Some of those bombed out of their own churches now moved in with other congregations, while many, returning to the tradition of the early church, met in private houses.

The educational system took longer to recover, for the whole of Coventry, directly after the raid, was declared a 'danger' area, from which evacuation was encouraged. For those who stayed, the majority, the aftermath of the raid provided some refreshing breaks from routine. One wartime schoolboy remembers how his school, King Henry VIII's, now offered a novel activity on games afternoon, 'filling in the bomb craters on the school pitches'. Barrs Hill Girls' School was even more affected. 'As we look back over the year,' acknowledged the next edition of the school magazine, 'the night of Thursday, November 14th stands out in strong relief . . . as the parting of the ways', for that night the whole of its new buildings, including the hall (opened only four years before) had been gutted by fire – though 'due very largely to the gallantry of our brave caretaker' the other buildings were saved. The school, only reunited at the start of the term, after a previous 'partial evacuation' to Leamington, was now split up again, most of the staff and pupils moving to Atherstone, about twelve miles away. By 2 December it had reopened in four patched-up classrooms and a makeshift hall, for the 164 girls still in Coventry, who clearly made the best of things. 'We had a picnic lunch in the hall and immediately, unimpeded by the task of "clearing away", the whole school danced, the Lower Third almost as assiduously as the Fifth, whose elegance won the admiration of all!'

Unemployment had been almost forgotten in war-booming Coventry, but in the second half of November there was a sudden upsurge of 3000 in the number out of work and at one time 15500 people were claiming 'emergency relief' in the local employment exchanges. Responsibility for deciding the order of priority for getting factories back into action rested with the Coventry Industrial Reconstruction and Coordinating Committee, set up directly after the raid as a result of Lord Beaverbrook's initiative. The chairman was a dynamic young local businessman, 'Billy' – later Sir William and later still Lord – Rootes, and the members included a personal representative of Lord Beaverbrook, spokesmen for local employers and trade unions, Army and RAF officers and Civil Servants. The Chairman of the Council's Emergency Committee, Alderman Halliwell, was in constant attendance. The Emergency Committee and the group of Army officers responsible for deploying the troops and other help sent from outside met in the same building, the Council House, at the same time, 10 a.m. each morning and managed to work effectively together, despite frequent, and sometimes bitter, arguments. It caused much wry amusement in Coventry when the Secretary of State for War told the House of Commons a few months later, 'those who . . . saw Alderman Halliwell sitting in the City Chambers in rubber boots and a pullover next to a big general in a brass hat and a "British warm" realized that the old city of Coventry had still something new to tell the world'. The Committee tackled its formidable job with vigour. 'We never knew whether it was Christmas Day or August Monday,' remembers a former director of one of the three family building firms in Coventry. 'We were too busy sorting out factories before they were knocked down again. Our only concern was to "Get a roof on and b—— them".'

Even before shattered roofs and walls had been replaced the employees were often back at their benches, like the sheet metal worker from Birmingham, who had spent Saturday cleaning up at his factory in Much Park Street.

The following day [Sunday] I found myself among a gang of my mates, sweeping up broken glass, nailing sheets of cardboard to window apertures and generally clearing up. And the atmosphere had completely changed.... Everybody was silent, grim and in deadly earnest. They had a job to do, and they were doing it. . . . I saw no horseplay, heard no repartee, no smutty stories. The sooner the clearing up was done the sooner we could go back into production again.

The firm resumed production on the Tuesday, though output was not back to normal for several weeks. At Coventry Climax, meanwhile, Len Dacombe had returned to his job as a toolsetter on Monday 18 November.

We had to work with tin hats and overcoats on as glass and asbestos kept falling from the roof. After about two weeks the roof was covered with tarpaulin and power was restored, so we started up production again. We had no lights or heating, so we worked from 9 a.m. to 4 p.m. and made braziers out of old oil drums, to try and keep warm. Although we still had to wear tin hats, overcoats and gloves, we managed to start production going. When it came around to Christmas the management gave us all £1 extra in our wages for working in such atrocious conditions.

At this time the gulf between 'works' and 'staff' was usually wide but at the Daimler No. 2 aero-engine factory at Allesley both now endured together for much of the roof had been blown off and with 'windows shattered and no heating' one woman, who was then a Hollerith accounting machine operator, remembers, 'it was bitterly cold'. The girls in her section, like the men on the work-benches, swathed themselves 'in coats, scarves and gloves' and were 'allowed to have frequent breaks to keep circulation going', soup and hot drinks being supplied from a field kitchen.

Ironically the constant tributes to the heroism of the people of Coventry actually resulted in some loss of production. 'The effects of the November raid on the working population,' concluded the Ministry of Home Security Research Department, 'were greater than expected from the observed behaviour in other cities. The explanation appears to be that the . . . publicity given to the raid and its damage resulted in slightly more absenteeism than the post-raid situation in the city really warranted.' It remained, however, very slight: an average of no more than 4·37 days per worker, of which just under two days was 'voluntary', i.e. lost for 'personal reasons' when a factory was working.

On the Monday after the raid more than one factory – like the Self-Changing Gear Co. in Lythalls Lane – was 'ready to start full production but lacking electric power', so that essential hardening processes were having to be 'farmed out' as far afield as Rugby. Thanks, however, to the loan of craftsmen by other electricity undertakings, production of electricity was back to nearly half the pre-raid figure four days after the raid, and to seven-eighths by 11 December, which meant that (allowing for reduced demand) nearly everyone requiring electricity was 'back on supply'. After the priority industrial consumers had been connected up the town was divided into twenty-one sections, through which repair teams worked systematically, defeated only by 'premises where it was not possible to gain access to meters and services, i.e. demolished'.

Restoring the gas supply proved far more difficult. The Gas Department faced what one official at Regional headquarters rightly called 'the stupendous task' of mending 374 fractures in the mains. Many essential works were crippled for lack of gas, among them the Alvis Motor Co., which made superchargers for Merlin aircraft engines, and Riley Ltd, which manufactured military vehicles. To meet the needs of such priority consumers a temporary cast-iron main was laid in the gutter, but the ordinary civilian had to wait his turn – and it was a long wait. For a week after the raid only a few households on the northern fringes of the city were receiving any gas at all. Even by the end of November the daily output was still only 8 per cent of normal, but then, with the arrival of parties of skilled fitters from London and Newcastle, the real improvement began, reaching 64 per cent by 11 December and, just before Christmas, achieving a sudden surge forward to 90 per cent, the work being completed early in the new year.

The factories also received priority in the restoration of the water supply. The 710 General Construction Company, Royal Engineers, were assigned to the Water Department and in the next few weeks they laid six miles of temporary water main for industrial use. To obviate 'difficulties arising from variations . . . in general service conditions', as the Water Engineer put it (that is, to avoid rubbing in the fact that the servicemen, although often 'well-trained municipal workmen' in civilian life, were being paid one-fifth of what civilians received for doing precisely the same job), the troops were assigned a separate section of the city.

The backbone of the whole effort was provided, however, by the local Water Department with the help of civilian teams from other Midland cities. The Water Engineer later remarked with professional pride that 'water becomes recognized as the main essential of communal life only when its availability is temporarily withdrawn', and to those affected the water supply seemed to be off for months. In fact, with the help of standpipes in the street, within eight days consumption was back to 60 per cent of normal and 95 per cent of homes already had some sort of supply nearby.

As people in one road after another again turned on their taps and, with delight, found them responding, friends and relations from districts still 'dry' became frequent visitors. 'Our water came on before my mother's in Earlsdon,' remembers one woman then living in Brookside Avenue, Whoberley, 'so I cycled there every day with a can of water on each handle-bar and another can in the basket on the front, till a stop tap was put in their road.' The Moseley family, in Kensington Road, relied for drinking on water fetched from 'a standpipe . . . in a nearby street', eked out by the carefully rationed contents of the 'two big covered barrels in which rain water was collected' in the garden. 'All the water we used from then until the mains were repaired,' remembers the then Miss Lucy Moseley, 'seemed to be used for more than one purpose. For instance, after washing we would wash through small articles of clothing – and then the water had to be used to flush the lavatory.'

Even when the taps began to flow again economy remained vital. 'Don't rush to the tap as soon as the supply is restored,' urged a Ministry of Information circular at the end of November. 'Remember that the supply is restarted primarily for essential domestic and sanitary purposes. . . . Wash only the absolute essentials. . . . A dirty collar is preferable to an empty kettle.' For the health authorities the repair of the mains brought a new anxiety: typhoid. On 17 December Dr Massey, the Medical Officer of Health, reminded readers of the *Midland Daily Telegraph* that milk and water should still be boiled although it was reported that 'there now remains no area in Coventry without water supplies . . . only isolated streets'. It was not, however, until January 1941 that the City Water Engineer was able to inform the impressively titled 'Waterworks and Fire Brigade Committee' that 'your undertaking may be considered to be functioning normally'.

'If anyone went hungry in the city it was their own fault,' Councillor Pearl Hyde told the Council on 3 December. The assertion was not strictly true, but in the first three chaotic days after the raid the WVS had, it was said, served 50000 meals, and within a week 'there were seventy canteens in action, distributing free food to approximately 20000 people a day', and at least sixteen field kitchens, attached to rest centres or providing substitute canteens for essential factories. Alderman Hodgkinson, visiting one at Foleshill School, found presiding over 'an improvised range in the open air . . . made of bricks and a metal grid . . . a chef from one of the big hotels in London. . . . He decided to come up to see what he could do and fitted himself in quite unsolicited on to this job of supervising the cooking of meals at an open fire in the school yard.'

The first step towards providing permanent catering facilities came with the opening, a few hours after the raid, of the students' refectory at the Technical College as a Communal Feeding Centre, which was soon serving 2000 meals a day and also supplying 'take-away' food to people who arrived with their own plates and basins. The meal provided was a bargain: 6d for a main course of meat and vegetables; 2d for a sweet, usually a comfortingly solid steamed pudding and custard; 1d for a cup of tea and 2d for coffee. Soon afterwards other centres were opened in Stoke and in a former chapel in Well Street, the later offering a continuous service from breakfast at 7 a.m. (bacon and sausage 6d) to high tea before 6 p.m. (steak-and-kidney pudding and 'mash' 6d).

The Emergency Committee recruited the former manager of Woolworth's café as their expert adviser and tackled the problem of obtaining scarce crockery and cutlery by direct approaches to Stoke-on-Trent and Sheffield, the country's crockery and cutlery 'capitals'. By early February 1941, though the immediate crisis had passed, the three municipal cafeterias were catering for 5000 customers a day, becoming the model for the British Restaurants soon familiar everywhere.

The Coventry skyline after the bombing and subsequent clearance. The clock tower of market hall still stands in the foreground, flanked by the spires of Holy Trinity and the ⟨cath⟩edral behind

⟨Abo⟩ve left: The King's visit. In the foreground, left to right, are Alderman Halliwell, King ⟨Geo⟩rge VI and the Mayor, Jack Moseley. Just behind them are the Minister of Home Security, ⟨Her⟩bert Morrison, and, in police uniform, the Chief Constable and ARP Controller, Captain ⟨Hec⟩tor

⟨Abo⟩ve right: The Prime Minister's visit. This photograph was taken in the Cathedral ruins in ⟨Sept⟩ember 1941. Provost Howard is on Winston Churchill's left

Getting back to normal

Above: A street scene some time after the bombing

Below: A residential street with the damage cleared and 'glass substitute' in the windows

ping. Temporary shops erected to replace some of those destroyed

king. Public houses enjoyed little priority for rebuilding but at least one temporary one opened

The new Coventry

Above: The ruins of the old cathedral. The site has been preserved as a war memorial and place for quiet meditation. The cross in the centre is made from roof beams rescued from the rubble

Below: The new Coventry Cathedral, consecrated in 1962

Most people, however, still ate mainly in their own homes. With cooking difficult, bread was in universal demand and one man then working for a Coventry building firm still remembers as the high spot of the morning after the raid the totally unexpected arrival in its yard of a baker's van bearing the name of a Stratford-on-Avon baker. The firm's owner having found the driver 'arguing at a police road block . . . had promptly bought the van-load' and, using his builder's pass, had driven it into the city. 'The next morning,' this observer remembers, 'I chalked up a notice at the yard entrance, "Bread for sale". People read it . . . couldn't believe it . . . walked on and then dashed back. It had all gone by 10.30 a.m.' The Ministry of Food, realizing the need for bread, was soon organizing emergency supplies. By Sunday 40000 2-lb loaves had already been delivered, and 'in one day,' recorded the *Coventry Standard* a little later, 'more than 100000 loaves were sold to the eager public' – with the result that in the six weeks after the raid consumption of bread per head rose to six times the previous figure.

Some women look back almost nostalgically on this period, for at midday on Friday, 15 November, all rationing in the Coventry area was suspended. One woman, then a fourteen-year-old schoolgirl, has not forgotten the thrill of 'cycling into Earlsdon Street and obtaining three succulent pork chops – off the ration. . . . My mother was thrilled.' Sometimes goods were cash-free as well. One member of the Ambulance Service recalls his wife's excitement at discovering in Earlsdon 'that they were *giving away* shin of beef and one onion per person'. Later, at a confectioner's in Whitchurch, when the shopkeeper heard that his customers were from Coventry he told his assistant, 'Give them all the cakes they want and don't charge them.'

The gastronomic gold-rush supposed to have followed the suspension of rationing has entered local legend. Angry councillors denounced the greedy visitors said to have descended from all over the Midlands with empty shopping baskets and tactless shoppers were said to have asked for rapid service as they had to catch a long-distance bus. With its customary efficiency, however, the Ministry of Food was soon back in control. Alternative supplies were arranged for 'registered' customers whose shops had disappeared, 20000 new ration books were issued to replace those declared lost or destroyed, and on Monday, 2 December, Coventry's two glorious weeks of coupon-free existence came to an end.

The absence of ration books was in any case a trivial bonus to set against the difficulty of cooking anything, rationed or unrationed. A Cheylesmore woman is proud of the results she achieved by placing 'the browning sheet from the oven over the coke fire. With some patience and a very red face I managed to cook a meal in the fish frying pan, which was deep, and took the meat and potatoes.' In Harris Road, one housewife remembers, a modest approximation to a Malayan 'long house' developed, the five families in her block taking it in turn to cook for each other on their open grates until her husband 'made a Dutch oven out of a biscuit tin and we cooked any bacon or meat or sausages we could get. I made a large steamed pudding and someone else custard and vegetables.' Later she became chief cook to the whole group, for her electric cooker was usable long before her neighbours' gas stoves.

Of all those who in the aftermath of the great raid faced seemingly insuperable tasks, none had a less enviable one than Councillor Harry Weston:

My first duty as Chairman of the Housing Committee was to contact the [city] architect, Don Gibson, to start . . . repairs. . . . Gibson and I met at his office at half-past nine that Saturday morning following the blitz. And from then he and I decided on a repair service which operated as follows. We decided to make the town into sixteen wards or divisions with a Clerk of Works in charge of each ward, with instructions to give any contractor with the experience and equipment as many streets as he could manage for temporary repairs to make the houses habitable. . . . No question of estimates; no question of how much it was likely to be, but we put the contractor and their men on their honour to report to us what they had spent and we would pay them 10 per cent on what they had spent towards the cost of whatever it was. . . . And it worked just like a miracle.

This imaginative policy, so contrary to the cautious traditions of municipal finance, was to have less happy repercussions two years later, when the final bills came in and with them unsympathetic auditors from the various ministries involved, but its effects on Coventry were heartening. Everywhere could be heard the clattering of hammers as broken doors and window frames were boarded up. The most urgent need was for tarpaulins and Councillor

Weston 'acquired', to use his own word, 30000, worth £32000, from an Army dump nearby – the subject of a nice little inter-departmental squabble later – and, for more permanent repairs, 'we sent lorries out to mid-Wales to collect slates'. Such items as doors and window-frames from houses past repair were 'cannibalized', and often, recalls Mr Weston, 'we had to sort the tiles to make one house complete out of two', so that one can still see houses where the roof resembles a patchwork quilt.'

The results of the Housing Department's efforts were beginning to be apparent within six weeks, when a report to the City Council revealed, with justifiable pride, that 'first-aid repairs' had already been completed to 12000 houses and that work was continuing at the rate of 532 houses a day, thanks largely to a vast influx of building workers from outside. These included many recently dis-charged servicemen, for the Forces had agreed to release anyone with tiling experience, a call to which former wall and floor tilers had eagerly responded – though Coventry needed only roof-tilers.

The effects of the great clear-up soon began to be apparent and within a few weeks most people were able to move back into their own homes. Among them was an inspector at Armstrong Siddeley engines, whose house in Glendower Avenue soon had electricity, but no water and a badly damaged roof, though he had managed to rent a house in Whoberly Avenue, five minutes' walk away, 'that had a complete roof and water but no electricity'. The daughter of the house remembers the curiously divided existence which followed:

My mother used to visit Glendower Avenue to cook meals on the electric cooker and then take them back to the other house. My father and I used to visit Glendower Avenue to empty the buckets, bowls and other containers in the loft, but the plaster boards were hanging with water in the back bedroom and we needed more containers there. . . . It was about six weeks before 'oilskin' was fitted to the windows and a tarpaulin put on the roof. This made it all very dark and noisy when windy, but . . . we moved back home.

The Moseleys, too, were soon back in Kensington Road, Earls-don, and also found that the 'oiled cotton put in place of windows' rustled eerily in the wind. The family huddled in two rooms. 'Our parents,' remembers the then Miss Lucy Moseley, 'slept on a mattress put down each night on the living room floor, my sister slept at a friend's house, I had a folding camp-bed in the kitchen.'

Thousands of houses were, of course, beyond repair, but finding a new home was not too difficult. Even before 14 November 8 per cent of the city's houses had, an official inquiry found, 'been left vacant by people evacuating' and directly after that date the number of absentees soared still higher. Dr Alan Ashworth, bombed out of his house in Leamington Road, found the real problem was not lack of property but that the owners of many empty houses could not be traced, while estate agents, usually so eager and efficient, had no up-to-date lists of vacant premises, for many of the 'desirable residences' on their books had become overnight very undesirable indeed. Even so, it took him only a fortnight to locate a suitable house in the same district, which he 'rented for £75 per annum, in spite of its lack of glass, etc., in the windows'.

Civil Defence Staff Officer Harold Tomley, after some uncomfortable nights sleeping in his temporary headquarters, a classroom at the Technical College, found a two-room home above the office where his wife worked in Queen Victoria Road. Before long, he had also found a new office, 'two old cottages with cellar kitchens' in Priory Street. 'They had been used by the Art School before the war for training pupils in painting and decorating, and I suppose,' he reflects, 'the various designs of ceiling moulding and different wallpapers on every wall were, if anything, stimulating.'

The Council also offered a home-finding service, and Mrs Megan Ryan and her husband, who had registered as homeless directly on returning from brief holiday in the West Country,* were rapidly 'offered and accepted the attic in a house just outside the city centre', formerly 'the servants' quarters'. Here for a rent of £1, plus an average of about 17s a week for gas and electricity, they enjoyed 'a room with two dormer windows, a bath with a geyser and a sink. We also,' Mrs Ryan remembers, 'accepted the first available form of furniture removing. This turned out to be two horse-drawn coster's carts. The horses picked their way through the rubble to the old shelter', where the couple had stacked and boarded up everything they had salvaged from their ruined flat. 'We

*Mrs Ryan's husband had been given two weeks' paid holiday by his employer in recognition of his services on the night of the raid.

stacked it on the carts and drove to our new home perched high on the seats behind the horses.'

One of the earliest memories of one woman than aged four is of the 'many weeks' her parents spent 'digging at the great mound which was once our home'. 'They salvaged quite a number of things,' she remembers, 'including mother's engagement ring. . . . The ring was in a box and this was found first but was empty. After more digging mother unearthed her ring.' The items rescued from another house, in Coundon, were, the sixteen-year-old daughter of house observed, a little more substantial, if not so valuable: 'A three-piece suite, a little torn but usable, the dining-room table and three chairs, a radiogram and cabinet. Nothing else.' But harder to bear was the fact that 'people had looted the house of most of the other usable and unbroken items'.

This was a common experience, though with so many houses abandoned some people may have reasoned that it was better for items exposed to the elements to be used by *someone* rather than left to deteriorate. Many offenders, however, were thieves pure and simple, even breaking in to steal property that had clearly been stored under cover. 'A pilferer,' Mrs Megan Ryan discovered, 'had been before us, stealing the best of what we had so painstakingly saved from destruction. What was left was dirty, torn or cracked, with burn or scorch marks.' A girl living in Cheylesmore remembers how a week after the raid 'we begged a lift back to the ruins of our house . . . looters had already preceded us, and sightseers were cutting the parachute from the land-mine into small pieces for souvenirs. My mother found her handbag but otherwise we retrieved nothing.'

Money usually proved an irresistible attraction: no fewer than 800 coin-in-the-slot electricity meters – a quarter of all those removed from damaged houses – were found to have been broken open.

By 7 December the worst was over. The *Coventry Standard* reported that day:

There is evidence of Coventry's revival. Slaters and tilers are busy repairing damaged roofs, post office workers are to be seen clinging to the top of old telegraph poles, fitting new wires to replace tangled lines. Broken windows are being covered with felt and laths. . . . The dominating thought about it all is that, badly as Coventry suffered, it is not knocked out.

What of the trekkers? People with their own cars, and able to
pay for out-of-town lodgings while keeping up their own homes
in Coventry, were slow to return, but the movement back, for
ordinary families with smaller incomes, was quicker. At first, a later
survey found, 'large numbers were taken in by people in the surrounding towns and villages' and 'the charge made for accommodation . . . seems to have been quite low, but the emotion of pity
does not seem to have lasted long. . . . As the billets grew more
permanent so the prices increased.' The County Rest Centres were
closed and 'people sleeping in village halls, etc. . . . drifted back to
Coventry'. How many returned by Christmas, which itself exerted
a powerful homeward pull, is uncertain, though the number must
be somewhere between the 70000–100000 who had 'slept out' in
the second half of November and the 15000–20000 who were still
doing so in October 1941. A few had gone for good. Another
survey, made in 1944, found that about 4 per cent of the working
population (i.e. about one in twenty-five) in the munitions industries had moved right away after November 1940, although their
place was subsequently filled by an even larger influx of new labour.*

One of those who left at this time was a woman who had lived in
Daventry Road. With two small daughters to keep her busy, she
found life in the Vale of Evesham village of South Littleton so
agreeable that, after staying with her parents for a time,

because of shortage of space we moved up the lane to a farm. . . . There
were eggs straight from the nest, milk warm in the pail, freshly baked
bread. Even our sweet supply was better than average, as great-granny
had the local store. . . . I went back one Saturday and between us we
packed up our belongings on to a potato lorry and for the duration of
the war they were stored in the local tithe barn.

Her husband was soon afterwards moved to a job in London; they
never went back to Coventry. Nor did the woman Civil Servant
bombed out of her hostel in The Butts, though when posted to
another government office in Leamington, 'I felt,' she confesses,
'almost ashamed to be out of the danger zone.'

Amid the evidence of death and disaster all round love still
flourished. One young woman at Nuneaton had lost on the night of

*Some of those who left Coventry moved with firms whose works had been des-
troyed and which now set up new plants in less vulnerable areas.

14 November, not merely her home, badly damaged by a bomb, but also the special licence for her wedding on 23 November, which had been burned in the Cathedral. The Bishop of Coventry wrote out another 'by hand in beautiful copper-plate writing' and so only a week late, on 30 November, 'I was married from a house with no roof and we spent our first night with a mattress thrown over two chairs and a sofa'.

19
CHRISTMAS IN THE RUINS

*'We are in brave spirits and can wish the Empire a
courageous Christmas.'*
Provost Howard broadcasting from the Cathedral ruins,
25 December 1940

CHRISTMAS 1940 was a strange one for the whole country and
nowhere stranger than in Coventry. In many homes the gas supply
was restored on Christmas Eve, this being regarded, to quote one
of those affected, as 'a smashing Christmas present'. Most families
in Coventry, with its high proportion of 'reserved occupations',
were spared the separation which millions of others had to endure,
but a Coundon woman remembers this as her saddest Christmas.
Her mother had been killed and her father badly injured in the
November raid, and her husband had just left for the Far East after
embarkation leave. The family were not to be back in their own
house until mid-January.

On 18 December my son and I went back to Coventry . . . and stayed
with my friend's friend. There were five adults and two children all
sleeping downstairs on the floor. . . . We spent Christmas there and managed to make it fairly happy for the children's sake.

The 'Round the Empire' programme between 2 and 3 p.m. on
Christmas Day was always the climax of the broadcasting year. In
1940 it was called *Christmas under Fire*, and opened with the chimes
of Coventry Cathedral's clock striking two and the voice of Provost
Howard:

I am speaking from the ruins of Coventry Cathedral. . . . Last Christmas
we had our wonderful carol services in the glorious building of pink
sandstone . . . with its tall, slender pillars, its wide arches and spacious
windows, every stone of it loved and treasured by twenty generations of
Coventry people. Six weeks ago the enemy came and hurled down fire
and destruction upon our city all through the long night. . . . Early this
morning, here under these ruins in the lovely little stone chapel built six

hundred years ago we began the day as usual with our Christmas communion, worshipping the Christ, believe me, as joyfully as ever before. . . .

We Coventry people do here and now wish all absent friends and relations, especially those in the Forces, a happy Christmas. What we want to tell the world is this. That with Christ born again in our hearts today we are trying, hard as it may be, to banish all thoughts of revenge. We are trying to brace ourselves to the tremendous job of saving the world from tyranny and cruelty, we're going to try to make a kinder, simpler and more Christ-child like sort of world in the days beyond this strife.

We are in brave spirits and can wish the Empire a courageous Christmas.

Behind the scenes, however, there was increasing friction between the local authority and the government. One of the first to suffer was the Minister without Portfolio, Arthur Greenwood, who made a well-meaning broadcast declaring that 'despite all that had been suffered by Coventry . . . the city had already recovered and the munitions industry was going along much as usual'. This tribute seems to have been regarded as a prelude to the withdrawal of government aid and at the first post-raid meeting of the corporation on 3 December Greenwood was publicly denounced for a 'crazy foolish speech. A more foolish statement,' thundered one alderman (surely guilty of exaggeration in his turn), 'could not have been made by a man in an important position.'

The day after this public rebuff had been reported in the local press another struggle began with the arrival at the War Office of requests to the Secretary of State for War 'to cancel', as he wrote to the Home Secretary that day, 'the movement from Coventry of any of the troops at present engaged there'. The city still contained two companies of Royal Engineers, two Home Defence Companies of the Pioneer Corps and '900 infantry soldiers', whose training was 'being seriously interfered with'. Was it not up to the local authority to mobilize 'local labour resources (particularly the unemployed) which would at any rate release the unskilled element in the Army troops?'

These arguments, powerful though they were, were not well received in Coventry. 'Dad,' remembers the Mayor's daughter, 'asked one high-ranking officer what would be the use of training if Coventry factories were producing no weapons for them to use?'

On New Year's Eve William Rootes and Alderman Halliwell

submitted a joint Report on behalf of the Coventry Reconstruction Co-ordinating Committee to the Regional Commissioner. It contained many useful recommendations applicable in other bombed cities, but also some disturbing revelations, for example the 'refusal of the bus drivers to work after 6.30 p.m. even after they had recovered from the first shock of the raid'. When 'with the assistance of the unions the bus drivers were induced to work late' some simply failed to turn up, with 'disastrous' results, for not merely did 'perhaps thirty men lose an hour or two of their work', but there was a general loss of confidence in the bus service. 'In our view,' concluded William Rootes and, far more surprisingly, that dedicated ex-trade unionist William Halliwell, 'government support must be given to transport undertakings to overcome the . . . lack of a sense of duty among certain of their employees and an absence of the discipline which is the only substitute for such a sense of duty.'

If what the working man needed was discipline, what Cabinet ministers required, it appeared, was flattery, to judge from the letter which Lord Dudley sent to Lord Beaverbrook two days later, forwarding the Coventry report.

As you appointed the Committee . . . I would like to take this early opportunity of expressing to you my deep gratitude for your wise and far-sighted action . . . I would like also to tell you what a happy and encouraging effect your early personal visit on the very morning after that cowardly attack had upon the citizens and industrialists of that stricken town. . . . The sympathetic and inspiring words which you and my Minister [i.e. Herbert Morrison] addressed to the chief citizen and his representatives in that historic scene in the Council House did much to put fresh heart into them, and strengthen them for the tremendous task of reconstruction which lay before them.

In an accompanying private memo to the Ministry of Home Security Lord Dudley struck a less fulsome note. 'I hope,' he wrote, 'the Minister will not think I have laid it on too thick. But I feel in these butterless days that a little overdose of fatty substance does nobody any harm.'

Beaverbrook ceased to be Minister of Aircraft Production five months later, and was thereafter little involved in the affairs of Coventry, something his colleagues must have envied, for it became increasingly notorious in Whitehall as the 'problem child' among bombed cities. Some of the arguments were about money. The government vetoed in January 1941, for example, the corporation's plan to recruit 2000 full-time, paid fire-watchers. Other arguments were about authority and there was a major row when in June, partly as a result of experience in Coventry, all the local fire brigades were merged into the National Fire Service and control of the Coventry brigade was transferred to Birmingham. But many disagreements seem to have resulted from the trade union tradition in which so many of the city's leaders had been reared, leading them to treat the ministers and Civil Servants with whom they dealt as particularly hard-faced and unreasonable employers. Something approaching a collective paranoia developed in the city, revealed in the widespread belief that its citizens were being deprived of their just share of the nation's resources, whether it was finance for rebuilding, or scarce items of food. When the Chairman of the Coventry Food Control Committee, a city councillor, defended Whitehall, he was sternly taken to task by the *Coventry Standard*. 'He denies,' protested an editorial on 15 March 1941, 'that other towns are freely selling what is practically unobtainable in Coventry. Yet many of us know it to be true. . . . Many lines of goods are indeed very short in comparison with the position in other parts of the country.'

Always responsive to criticism, the Ministry in November 1941 sent its own special investigator to Coventry, and his report was both frank and forthright:

Coventry labour has a minimum of civic sense. . . . Wartime wages in Coventry are probably the highest in the country, while war savings per head of population are somewhere near the lowest. The Coventry War Weapons Week of last winter was a failure. . . . The municipal organization of the city, comparable with the organization and leadership of Coventry trade unions, is a weak and feeble thing. Taking into account its importance as an industrial centre, Coventry is not adequately served by its local administration. After the severe raids of last winter, Coventry came into the news as . . . the example and proof of the proud claim that 'Britain can take it'. Royalty, foreign personages, politicians and journalists all flocked to the town, saw the ruins and made their speeches. Then the excitement died down, important visitors became fewer, and Coventry began to feel neglected. . . .

As the people of Coventry looked out on their ruined streets day after day a somewhat fantastic feeling grew up in the town. This feeling is apparently shared by . . . the Town Clerk, who considers that 'because Coventry is down and out there is a concerted desire on the part of various government departments and hostile interests to keep her so.' . . . In spite of proof to the contrary, the rooted belief persists that Coventry is not getting her fair share of food as compared with other towns. In spite of the ruins and the factories the war seems far away. There are few uniforms, no bands, no parades of tanks, no recruiting drives, few organized entertainments and a shortage of beer. . . .

At the Labour Exchange I saw the Manager . . . the Welfare Officer and the district organizer and secretary of the Transport and General Workers' Union. . . . All the usual complaints were made – that Coventry did not obtain her fair share of unrationed foods, that the canteens and British Restaurants took supplies intended for the retailer, and that Coventry was generally badly treated. . . . Those present were astonished when I produced as 'Exhibit A' half a pound of raisins which I had bought on my way to the meeting . . . at the first grocer's shop which I had passed. I also referred them to a letter received at [Ministry of Food] Divisional Headquarters only that morning from a woman in Kenilworth who said that she always came to shop in Coventry because there she could obtain unrationed foods without any trouble.

The survey concluded that 'shopping difficulties formed a convenient stalking horse for more fundamental grievances', and the report was therefore passed on to the Ministry of Home Security, where it raised a flurry of indignation. Why, Herbert Morrison's officials demanded, had not the Regional Commissioner been consulted before such a depressing document was allowed to circulate through Whitehall? – a line of complaint abandoned when Lord Dudley confirmed that the picture was true.

Within a month, however, there came more cheerful news, for the Ministry of Labour, not to be left out, made a follow-up inquiry of its own.

I am glad . . . to report [its Permanent Secretary wrote to his opposite number at the Ministry of Food on 3 December] that a senior officer in our Welfare Department visited Coventry about ten days ago and after an interview with the Town Clerk came to the conclusion that there was a considerable improvement in the local spirit and that the [local] authority and other bodies and organizations were now taking more active steps in meeting the situation in the town.

Relations between government and corporation remained strained, however. The Mayor's daughter recalls 'endless struggles with petty officialdom:

Dad would never take what he considered interference from outside. To him our city and the welfare of its people came first. He was more than outspoken in all these affairs and on more than one occasion had really heated arguments with higher authority. This we firmly believe was the reason he was the *only* Mayor or Lord Mayor of all heavily bombed cities in Great Britain whose name never appeared in the Honours List. But it never bothered him in the slightest.

If news of grim living conditions and poor morale in Coventry made unwelcome reading in most departments it was received with mixed feelings in the Air Ministry, which, having won the battle on behalf of the strategic bombing offensive, tended to regard Coventry as a 'test tube' showing how comparable places in Germany might react to similar attacks. Research into the effects of the November 1940 raid on the working population of Coventry was still being commissioned three and a half years later, and many German cities were to benefit, if that is the word, from experience painfully acquired there. The main lesson, concluded Sir Arthur ('Bomber') Harris, Commander in Chief of Bomber Command, was that 'Coventry was adequately concentrated in point of space, but . . . there was little concentration in point of time'. Attacks on German cities were therefore increasingly crowded into no more than an hour or so, even though some, the famous 'thousand bomber raids', involved twice as many aircraft as had bombed Coventry. The British planners learned, too, the destructive potential of fire, especially when used with high explosives, and the devastating results demonstrated at Coventry were soon visible in the gutted acres of Hamburg and the Ruhr.

In one respect Coventry did come up to the government's expectations. There had been, as described earlier, little call for reprisals directly after the November raid, but as the war went on bitterness increased and the mood began to change. Both the Bishop of Coventry, at the funeral of the victims, and the Provost, in his Christmas broadcast, had preached the virtues of forgiveness and when in May 1941 a man fighting the by-election at King's Norton on a 'bomb-reprisal' ticket, appealed to the Bishop for a declaration of support, the Bishop wired back, 'I am not a reprisalist.'* Jack Moseley, when similarly approached, responded very differently, declaring, according to the *Midland Daily Telegraph*, that 'he was personally in agreement' with the opinion, 'which he thought was shared by 90 per cent of the people of this country, that Britain should carry out reprisal raids on Germany for the mass slaughter by night bombers', though he later admitted that he 'had no idea' that his letter would be used 'for propaganda purposes'.

Among ordinary citizens opinion was also hardening. The Birmingham tinworker quoted earlier confesses that his feelings had undergone a sudden change on the morning after the raid when he saw the pitiful procession of refugees flowing out of Coventry. 'I felt . . . a blazing, white hot anger,' he admits. 'Had I, in that moment, had the power to annihilate the whole German race . . . I would have wiped them from the face of the earth.' He was delighted to witness a revealing incident in the canteen at Much Park Street, when, instead of the usual ENSA concert party, a clergyman attended to give an uplifting talk.

The vicar . . . said that 'the mills of God grind slowly, but they grind exceedingly small' and that 'God would surely punish the evil doer, but in his own good time', whereupon one of our number stood up and said in a very determined voice that 'The Germans will most certainly be punished, but we cannot wait for God, we ourselves will blast them to eternity and the sooner the better.' I shall never forget the terrific thunder of applause from us all. That roar from about 150 men and women . . . would have beaten the Wembley roar for fervour, and the meeting broke up.

As regards compensation for the loss they had suffered people in Coventry had perhaps some justification for feeling they had been let down by the government. At the Council meeting of 3 December a speaker had warned Whitehall not to drag its feet over assisting 'people whose livelihood had been lost through the destruction of property. . . . The Council should not tolerate the position whereby the government would not compensate these owners until after the war. We want something done immediately.'

The first steps in settling such claims were in fact taken promptly, and the daughter of the man previously mentioned whose sign-

*The candidate won only 1700 votes, and lost his deposit.

writing business had been burned out, remembers the valuer arriving while he lay ill on 12 December and interviewing him at his bedside. Like other claimants, however, he faced a long wait, the first payment of £250 not being made until eight years later, in December 1948 and the last not till March 1950. All told he received, after this ten-year wait, only £632 14s 2d, about a third, the family considered, of the real value of the business.

Compensation for the loss of one's private effects was slightly more generous. One family bombed out of their home in Cheylesmore received from the War Damage Commission, as one member of it recalls, '£30 for immediate necessities' during the week after the raid, and 'about three months later a further £180 to cover the total loss of our homes and clothes'. Payment for the house itself (which was rented) went to the landlord. Dr Alan Ashworth received, he recalls, '£90 war damage compensation for the contents of my house, car, motor-cycle, bicycle, etc.'

The city had hardly ceased to echo to the sound of unsafe buildings being demolished when the corporation began to raise the question of rebuilding. Only a few weeks after the raid it set up a City Redevelopment Committee, under the chairmanship of the Mayor, and including such other Council stalwarts as Alderman Halliwell, George Hodgkinson and Councillor Weston of the Housing Committee. Early in January the Committee went to London to see the new Minister of Works, Lord Reith, who later wrote:

These poor men were perplexed and dismayed. I would not allow this high-powered civic deputation to return to their battered city with a tale of Whitehall grunting and waffling, telling their wives it was all a waste of time. . . . I took them all to lunch in a private room at Claridges. . . . I told them that if I were in their position I would plan boldly and comprehensively: and that I would not worry at this stage about finance.

The Coventry delegation were delighted at this reception. Jack Moseley declared, 'I've been coming on deputations to Whitehall for twenty years but I've never had such treatment as this', and the councillors, at Reith's suggestion, went home carrying two or three daffodils each, taken from the lunch table. Unhappily, however, the episode ended in recriminations. Reith was reproved by the Ministry of Health, then responsible for local government, which felt the deputation should have visited them instead; and the advice he had given was to be constantly quoted in the years that followed as proof of the government's bad faith.

Talk of rebuilding was in any case clearly premature at this stage, for after some very minor, scattered raids, Coventry was again heavily attacked for six hours, on the night of 8 April 1941, and again on the 10th, for three hours, 360 tons of bombs being dropped in the two raids together (compared to the 500 tons of 14 November), producing a casualty list of 451 dead and 723 badly injured, many of them at the Coventry and Warwickshire Hospital, which the Germans seem to have mistaken for a factory.

Once again recovery was surprisingly swift, and April 1941 was really the end of Coventry's ordeal. In later raids only one or two aircraft were involved and the highest death roll was no more than six. The last bombs were dropped in August 1942: Coventry's forty-third raid, although the All Clear did not sound for the final time until 3 August 1944, marking the end of Coventry's 380th alert. By then all told 1253 people had been killed, 1859 had needed hospital treatment and 1999 had been treated at first aid posts.

V E Day on 8 May 1945 was celebrated as elsewhere, though beneath the surface gaiety there were widespread fears of returning unemployment, but a more important occasion for the city was perhaps Victory Day on 8 June 1946, when with great ceremony a stone inscribed with the already familiar theme of a phoenix rising from the ashes was laid in the centre of Coventry, from which it was intended that all levels should be measured during the rebuilding. The city architect had already produced a bold plan to give the city a whole new centre, with a network of broad roads and a large traffic-free shopping precinct, then a novel conception, even though some traditionalists protested that this meant sweeping away most of the few old buildings which had survived.

Alderman Hodgkinson, who had been Mayor in the last year of the war and was the driving force in the City Redevelopment Committee, enthusiastically supported the scheme but complained that at the authorized rate of £500000 worth of new building a year it would take a century before the job was finished.* He was also doubtful if Coventry could be adequately rebuilt under a capitalist

---

*This was almost exactly equal to the Council's budget for emergency services in 1941–2, though six-sevenths of this was reclaimable from the government.

order of society. Some tough bargaining with the government as well as developers and commercial interests followed. But the rebuilding programme was visibly under way in May 1948 when Princess Elizabeth opened the new Broadgate, around a grassy island where a statue of Lady Godiva now rides. In May 1953 the first major new building, Broadgate House, built on council land, was opened and that August the first large chain store, Woolworth's, welcomed its first customers. A year later the raid was recalled even more vividly when the new Owen Owen, which had cost £1 million, was opened close to the site of its predecessor, and within the next few years Coventry also acquired a major hotel, the first new theatre to be built in the country since the war, and a new art gallery and museum. There was a fierce debate as to whether a new £1 300000 municipal baths, later said 'to be among Europe's finest', or the new public library should have priority; the baths won.

What had made the name of Coventry synonymous with the wastefulness of war had been the destruction of the Cathedral, and as early as 1941 the Cathedral authorities had resolved to rebuild it on or near the original site. The first design, prepared by Sir Giles Gilbert Scott, was, however, turned down by the Royal Fine Arts Commission and eventually a competition was held, which attracted 219 entries, the winner, announced in 1951, being a young architect who had hitherto specialized in exhibition buildings, Basil (later Sir Basil) Spence.

Spence's designs provoked a great storm, clearly epitomizing for many people all that they disliked about modern art. The correspondence columns of the newspapers were full of protests against the 'concrete monstrosity', which, Spence insisted, was in fact to be built of pink sandstone. 'A horror', 'an aesthetic outrage', 'a super-cinema': these were some of the comments remembered by Provost Howard, who was one of Spence's staunchest advocates, and Spence himself received hundreds of letters which, as he later wrote, 'if not abusive or downright insulting were just plain critical'.

The City Council did not object to the Cathedral on aesthetic grounds but considered that labour and materials should be devoted to more urgent objects like houses and schools. Alderman Hodgkinson admired Basil Spence, whom he considered 'could sell ice cream to Eskimos' but he led a delegation to the Minister of Works,

the future Lord Eccles, to plead for the rebuilding of the Cathedral
to wait for at least ten years. This time, however, there was no
lunch at Claridges and no present of daffodils, and the Minister was
not convinced. He explained soon afterwards:

The Cathedral is not a building which concerns Coventry and Coventry
alone. The echo of the bombs which destroyed your city was heard
round the world. We cannot tell how many people are waiting in this
country and abroad for this church to rise and prove that English traditions live again after the Blitz.

The specialist labour force required, he suggested, need not en-
danger the housing drive and on 6 May 1954 a building licence was
issued 'at a total cost not exceeding £985 000'.

After eight years' work the Cathedral was consecrated on Friday,
25 May 1962, in a ceremony which brought to Coventry a larger
number of famous visitors than it had known since the bombing.
Among them was the Queen, whose father had twenty-two years
before visited the ruins which Spence had now incorporated into
his design. To Provost Howard the occasion seemed proof of 'the
recognition of God's miraculous power and undefeatable love in
creating out of such evil and sorrow such good and joy. It was a
moment of blazing glory.'

The Cathedral soon proved an enormous asset to Coventry. The
debt on the building (which had ultimately cost £1 385 000) was
paid off in seven months by donations from visitors, of whom
two and a half million arrived in the first year, the start of a continuing flood. The city which few visited when it was full of historic buildings is now, as a showplace of contemporary architecture,
on every tourist's itinerary.

Although as late as 1967 one engineering magazine voted Basil
Spence's creation 'the ugliest building in the Midlands . . . and the
sixth ugliest in the country', the passing of the years has lessened
hostility to it. Many, perhaps most, of those who remember its
predecessor would agree with the informant who wrote, 'The old
Cathedral for me every time', but this view is by no means unani-
mous. One woman, often quoted on earlier pages, who saw the new
building 'in all its stages of construction' and has 'spent many quiet
hours' in the finished edifice, regards it as 'a nearly perfect beauty of
today'.

As for the reshaping of the town centre, although one person at least now regards it as 'a concrete cold-hearted place', the view is more commonly expressed that 'the old buildings and alley-ways would have had to be cleared anyway, for modern traffic', and even the woman previously quoted, who recalls 'the warm friendliness' of the pre-war town ('Coventry,' she writes, 'was a "cosy" city'), admits, 'I don't remember how smelly and narrow the streets probably were in reality' and doubts if 'the old character could have been retained'.

More distasteful to her, as to many others, is the change in attitude towards the nation who destroyed the old city. Germans have been honoured guests in Coventry and civic delegations of Coventry councillors have been warmly received in Berlin and East Germany.

I do not like the policy of friendships with German towns. My father is a Great War veteran, my husband a Second World War veteran – the feeling that the Germans are a race to be wary of is instinctive. . . . Almost daily one still comes across someone whose life has been blighted by that one night. I worked for years with a widow of the Blitz. My hairdresser's father was blinded in the raid. . . . I can forgive but not forget.

Not everyone, perhaps – certainly not those too young to remember the war – will share these sentiments, but many surely will echo this Coventry citizen's conclusion: 'It doesn't seem like a nightmare looking back, it seems like another life. . . . But if it *had* to happen I am glad I saw it.'

APPENDIX A

*Did the British government receive prior
warning of the raid on Coventry?*

THE story that the British government received prior warning of
the air raid on Coventry on 14–15 November 1940, but deliberately
left the city to its fate rather than compromise a uniquely valuable
source of intelligence, has been given such wide currency that,
from mere repetition, it appears to be acquiring the status of proven
fact. Certainly it is becoming accepted as such in Coventry, where
it was referred to in the *Coventry Blitz Show* mentioned in the
Introduction. Even those who know nothing else about the raid
appear to have heard the suggestion, so that an event of exceptional
interest for many valid, historical reasons seems to be in danger of
being remembered for something that, in my opinion, never
happened. I say 'in my opinion' because, until, if ever, the ULTRA
papers are released to historians the matter cannot be conclusively
settled with 100 per cent certainty.

Something approaching certainty, however, seems to me not
unattainable. The 'prior warning' story has recently been repeated
in two books, both published while my own work was in the press,
William Stevenson's *A Man Called Intrepid*, about the British
Security Coordination organization, and Anthony Cave Brown's
Bodyguard of Lies, about Allied deception strategy. On the general
reliability and accuracy of these works the reader is referred to *The
Times Literary Supplement* for 28 May 1976, where both were
reviewed at length by authorities on their respective subjects, Sir
David Hunt, a former senior government official who served after
the war as a private secretary to Winston Churchill, and Michael
Howard, well known as a writer on this period and formerly
Professor of War Studies at Oxford.

The 'prior warning' story appears in its most colourful form on
pages 152–3 of *A Man Called Intrepid*:

Occasionally German orders did give the real name of a proposed target.
... In the second week of November in 1940, Bletchley [i.e. the British

code-breaking centre] obtained the German order to destroy Coventry. The name came through in plain text. . . . The name of the target was in Churchill's hands within minutes of Hitler's decision. . . . If the Prime Minister evacuated Coventry, as he so desperately wished to do, he would tell the enemy that he knew their plans. The value of Bletchley and all that ULTRA implied for the future would be lost. If the citizens were not warned, thousands would die or suffer.

Churchill chose wormwood, and did not warn them, beyond the customary alerting of fire-fighting and ambulance services, normal procedure in areas that might be logically assumed to have appeared on the German list of targets for the night. . . . Coventry was a foretaste of the dreadful dilemmas imposed by the need to conceal secret knowledge. . . . History does not record, because what then was secret has remained so until now, how the decision to let Coventry burn so moved the President that he initiated a flurry of actions, most of them directed to the training, support and expansion of guerilla forces in Europe.

Setting aside this final proposition as unverifiable – and there are, I believe, somewhat different reasons why 'history does not record' what Mr Stevenson claims to have happened – it will be noted that the revelation of the name of Coventry is here only stated to have occurred in 'the second week of November'. Anthony Cave Brown in *Bodyguard of Lies* is more specific, though offering an equally exciting, if far more verbose, version of events:

On the morning of November 12, 1940 a number of command directives began to issue from the headquarters of the Luftwaffe. . . . They were quickly unbuttoned by 'The Bomb' [i.e. the machine used in deciphering Enigma transmissions] and there emerged plans for what the Germans called 'Moonlight Sonata' – a raid in great strength for the night of November 14/15, 1940, against the cathedral and industrial city of Coventry. As Bletchley transmitted the Ultras through MI–6 to the Prime Minister's war bunker, it became clear that the Germans intended the same fate for Coventry as they had visited upon Rotterdam on May 14, 1940. . . .

The Ultra intercepts showed that, in addition to Coventry, two other major British cities – Birmingham ('Operation Umbrella') and Wolverhampton ('Operation All-One-Piece') – were to be attacked in the moonlight period of November 1940. They also showed in some detail what German tactics against Coventry would be . . . Ultra gave Churchill and his advisers at least forty-eight, possibly sixty, hours' warning of the devastating raid that was planned for Coventry. When the Luftwaffe intercepts reached Churchill's headquarters, he gave instructions that their contents were to be kept to the smallest possible circle as he and his advisers debated the defence options open to them. How important was the security of Ultra? Was it more important than the security of a major industrial city? It would be for Churchill alone to decide.

While the defences against night bombing attacks were then extremely primitive, there were several measures that could be taken to protect Coventry. The first was to frustrate the raid at the outset by using all available aircraft in an operation that was code-named 'Cold Douche'.... There was time to increase – even concentrate – anti-aircraft, searchlight and smokescreen defences, and fire-fighting and ambulance services around the city ... But that might compromise the security of Ultra ...

But if no extraordinary defensive measures could be taken to protect Coventry, might not a confidential warning that their city was about to be attacked on a large scale be given to civic authorities and to the fire-fighting, ambulance and hospital services? Should not the population of the inner city, together with the aged, the young, and those in hospital, who could be moved, be evacuated? To all these propositions, Churchill said no; there must be no evacuations and no warnings. To do so might cause panic among the population, panic that could result in far more casualties than the actual bombing; and, again, it would alert the German intelligence service to the fact that the British had foreknowledge of the raid. ... It was a tragic decision for Churchill to have to make but it was the only way to protect Ultra. ... *The Times* ... called Coventry a 'martyred city'. And indeed it was – martyred in part to Ultra.

A number of comments can be made upon detailed points in this dramatic account, from which I have omitted nothing of substance, though forced to cut it heavily for reasons of space. Thus all other authorities state that the code-name 'Moonlight Sonata' was only understood at first to refer to a major operation planned for mid-November, and that the name of Coventry only emerged later, if at all. The chief historian of ULTRA, whose work I discuss below, asserts that the name became known at 3 p.m. on 14 November, i.e. four hours before the raid began, not forty-eight or sixty. They cannot both be right, though both can be – and indeed, I believe, are – wrong. Mr Cave Brown refers to the RAF's spoiling operations as having the code-name 'Cold Douche'. The correct name is in fact 'Cold Water'. 'Cold Douche' was only one small part of the overall plan, namely an attack by two Whitley bombers on the main *Knickebein* transmitter at Cherbourg. Mr Cave Brown has also clearly missed the point of the German code-name for

Wolverhampton, which, as I point out on page 267, was derived from Woolworths and meant All-One-*Price*, not All-One-*Piece*. As for his central thesis, spelt out here in far more detail than by any other writer, I cannot improve on Michael Howard's comments in the review previously mentioned:

His allegations have been put forward as if they were established and incontrovertible facts in British newspapers . . . In spite of all that can be done to set the record straight, millions of people are now likely to believe, and hundreds of historians to repeat, that the Coventry raid was known about three days in advance but kept quiet. . . . Perhaps the damage done by such books as this and by the journalists who allow themselves to be taken in by them can never be completely undone. Mud is easy enough to throw and some of it always sticks.

The real originator of the 'prior warning' story is F. W. Winterbotham, now a retired Group-Captain, who in 1940 was head of the RAF section at SIS headquarters and was also responsible for the security of ULTRA material, the very existence of which remained unknown to the public until he published a book 'revealing all' in 1974. *The Ultra Secret* is in a different category from the books just mentioned, being a concise, soberly written account of events of which its writer had first hand knowledge, and, for these reasons, it merits detailed examination.

Group-Captain Winterbotham himself is, very understandably, sensitive to any tendency to link his work with that of the writers mentioned above, as he made clear, following the appearance of the reviews just quoted, in a letter to *The Times Literary Supplement* of 25 June 1976:

Unless there is some easing of the release to Public Records, at least of the most important signals I have referred to, we shall continue to get 'climbers onto the Ultra bandwagon' publishing books based on hearsay and each other's stories, and in this respect I feel I have a right to protest at being bracketed with them. Such releases might also temper the accusation of 'general unreliability'. Some inaccuracies there may be, my comments may not always agree with official reports; I wonder how many official reports presently available admit the elements of Ultra and their effect on our operations.
  At least I 'was there'. I knew most of the principal characters, even Hitler. I was personally responsible to Churchill through my chief for the security of Ultra in the field and operated a large organization to

ensure it. I read all the important German signals; nor was I likely to forget the substance of many of those which so vitally affected our operations.

What of the one, vital signal with which this book is concerned? Group-Captain Winterbotham is equally emphatic about this, too:

Coventry – I was not responsible, as Michael Howard suggests, for any of Cave Brown's remarks or paragraphs on this subject such as Churchill having forty-eight hours' notice and sacrificing the city for the sake of Ultra, nor do they reflect the views expressed in my book, and I am glad he contradicts the assumption by agreeing with my version regarding the four hours' warning. Sir David's [i.e. Sir David Hunt's] version is also in line with this. I do not know if either of these eminent historians have access to those signals which I sent to Downing Street, or the CWR [Cabinet War Room] . . . These signals were sent to Churchill in a red box in a blue van, and returned to me the same way, many with Churchill's comments. Among them there must remain the signal I sent over on November 14, giving the target for that night as 'Coventry' in clear. Whether this was done at Bletchley as a result of lower grade information I do not know, but the outcome was the same . . . . Despite official records I am unlikely to forget that signal: in the evening I went to my cottage west of London and counted the enemy bombers going overhead on their deadly mission.

Despite the wildly different 'facts' about the warning given by ULTRA published by other writers – which I have no doubt that Group-Captain Winterbotham is right in rejecting – and the scepticism about his own more modest claim for a four-hour period of notice expressed by two highly reputable authorities, whose conclusions I respect, he insists, therefore, on the trustworthiness of his own, unsupported, recollections. What is the real truth as it appears to me, as a historian knowing nothing of ULTRA except what F. W. Winterbotham has written himself, but, I hope, a good deal about the November raid on Coventry?

As I have made clear in Chapter 3 the British intelligence services believed in the autumn of 1940 that Coventry *might* be attacked in the near future and they *suspected* that a particularly heavy raid, probably on the Midlands, would take place during the period of full moonlight around 14 November. They also, in the person of the then Dr R. V. Jones, correctly *guessed* during the late afternoon of

14 November that Coventry was likely to be attacked that night, though, for the reasons I have explained, the radio counter-measures taken proved ineffective. I know of no evidence, however, other than the recollections of Group-Captain Winterbotham that anyone in authority on the British side knew definitely that Coventry was about to be heavily bombed; not do I know of any evidence of any kind that any prior warning was given to anyone connected with the active or passive defences of the city.

Group-Captain Winterbotham states in his book that 'at about 3 p.m. on November the fourteenth someone must have made a slip-up and instead of a city with a code name, Coventry was spelt out'. Two years later he repeated this assertion, equally categorically, in the letter quoted above. Professor R. V. Jones writes, however:

I have no knowledge of any signal such as Winterbotham describes. . . . It is just possible that for some reason a signal went to him and not to me, although the teleprint room was between his and mine, and I normally got repeats of all signals going to him as well as many more technical ones that came to me direct. I have therefore checked with the Head of the Air Historical Branch in the Cabinet Offices and find that he has been through the signals and there is not one such as Winterbotham describes, i.e. that Coventry was specifically mentioned in the afternoon before the raid.

Group-Captain Winterbotham also states that 'In the event it was decided only to alert all the services, the fire, the ambulance, the police, the wardens and to get everything ready to light the decoy fires.' I have made no inquiries about decoy fires, which were no doubt lit as a matter of course during any heavy raid anywhere, but I can state, as the first author to write a full-scale study of this raid, that whatever decision is said to have been made about giving a warning to the authorities in Coventry it was certainly not implemented, as the following facts confirm:

1 There is no reference to any preliminary preparations, such as would have followed a prior warning, in any of the Ministry of Home Security papers. On the contrary, all the documents I have seen suggest that the raid came as a surprise.
2 If by 'the services' the Anti-Aircraft Regiment manning the defences of Coventry is meant, they were *not* informed in advance.

Their commanding officer, who was one of my informants, is positive that his first information came when enemy aircraft were already approaching the Midlands, i.e. had been detected by normal means. The balloon barrage commander also seems to have received his first warning about the same time; certainly it was only at this stage that he was instructed to raise the balloons to their operational height.

3 If 'the fire' means the Coventry Fire Brigade, this does not appear to have had any prior warning. The first moves of appliances from outside only came after the raid had begun, following an appeal for assistance when the local brigade found itself overwhelmed.

4 As for 'the ambulance, the police, the wardens', the Director of Casualty Services is now dead. The Deputy Director, who was in fact in charge on the night of 14 November, is among my informants. *His* first knowledge of the raid came when the sirens sounded. The same is true of the staff of the Coventry and Warwickshire Hospital and of at least one First Aid Post. According to Anthony Cave Brown, whose evidence on this point presumably comes from first hand inquiry, Captain S. A. Hector, then Chief Constable and ARP Controller, confirmed that 'no warning was received by him and no special defensive precautions were taken to defend the city'. This, of course, bears out what I learned from everyone I consulted.

5 The then Chairman of the Coventry War Emergency Committee is now dead. His deputy, and successor, who is one of my informants, is emphatic that this committee, responsible for ARP services in Coventry and for immediate post-raid recovery measures, was *not* told that a heavy raid was expected.

6 The then Mayor is also dead. His daughter, however, also one of my contributors, insists that neither her father nor any other prominent member of the local authority was given prior warning. On the contrary the raid came to them, as to everyone else involved, as a complete shock.

Group-Captain Winterbotham is now in his seventies and is, of course, describing events which occurred thirty-four years before his book appeared. This does not by itself invalidate his memories: a similar lapse of time was involved before most of the contributions sent to me for this book were written down. In these cases, however, I have been able to check the memories of more than a hundred informants both against contemporary records (official and private, such as diaries) and against each other. Group-Captain Winterbotham, by contrast, admits in his foreword to *The Ultra Secret* that 'Unfortunately I have had no access to official records, and the book is written from my own recollections of the events described and of the hundreds of signals which I left locked in the vaults of Whitehall.'

On one point, however, Group-Captain Winterbotham's memory of the events of 14 November can be checked against material that is no longer secret. He states that on that afternoon he was sitting in his office 'a little weary after the sleepless bomb-torn night before'. He may, of course, have been unlucky enough to have been in a particularly heavily attacked area the previous night, but the night of 13–14 November was not particularly 'bomb-torn' – certainly not for anyone who had already lived through more than five weeks of the Blitz. On the contrary, according to the German records, which have been accepted by the official British historian Basil Collier (see *A Note on Sources*), only twenty-five enemy bombers were over London that night, compared to as many as 410 on one earlier night and an average for the whole period since 7 September of 163.

What really happened on the afternoon of 14 November 1940? Since the books quoted above were published, and indeed since I finished mine, this Appendix having been added at proof stage, a further piece of evidence has come to light, in the review of William Stevenson's book by Sir David Hunt, mentioned earlier. Sir David writes:

As for the great moral burden of decision which Churchill is supposed to have assumed so unflinchingly, he does not appear to have been aware of it at the time. I owe what follows to Sir John Colville, a friend and colleague at No 10 in later years, who was on duty at No 10 on the night of November 14. He is not only an excellent historian but also kept a diary for the relevant period. The Prime Minister set off that afternoon for Ditchley [the country house in Oxfordshire used in place of Chequers on moonlit nights] with another private secretary, John Martin* ... travelling

*The name of 'John Peck' appears in the original article, but was corrected by Sir David Hunt in *The Times Literary Supplement* of 9 July and in a private letter to the author.

with him in the car. On the way he opened his yellow Ultra box . . . and read the Ultra message announcing the heaviest bombing raid so far on a target not specified. It seems possible that he did not then have the X-Gerät indication of the Midlands, which would have reached him by a different method, being of lower security classification. . . . He immediately turned the car around and returned to Downing Street. Plainly, however, he expected the raid to be on London, because for the first time he ordered these two private secretaries to take refuge in the deep air-raid shelter, at Down Street Underground Station . . . telling them their young lives were valuable for Britain's future. He himself went up to the Air Ministry roof with [General Sir Hastings] Ismay and gazed through the clear moonlit air for the raid on London that never came.

This account fits in entirely with the recollections of Professor R. V. Jones, quoted earlier, and the evidence which supports it is overwhelming. First, the deciphering of the key message itself. In *The Times* of 31 August 1976 Mr Peter Lucas, of Cambridge, wrote as follows: 'On the afternoon of the raid, the watch of which I was a member read a low-grade cypher signal to the effect that the night's target was Korn. . . . Unfortunately we were not bright enough to guess that Korn might be Coventry.'

Second, the telephone call reporting ULTRA's revelations. Sir David Hunt revealed in *The Times Literary Supplement* of 9 July 1976 that he had made 'inquiries of the people then at No. 10, who have no recollection of such a telephone conversation'.

Third, the Prime Minister's alleged agony of mind. His then 'duty private secretary', now Sir John Martin, described in *The Times* of 28 August 1976 handing Churchill a top secret message just as they were leaving London for Ditchley, after reading which the Prime Minister 'immediately told his driver to return to Downing Street. My recollection', wrote Sir John, 'is that he explained that the German "beam" indicated the prospect of a heavy raid on London and that he was not going to spend the night peacefully in the country while the metropolis was under heavy attack.' Far from spending anguished hours over whether to sacrifice Coventry, *Winston Churchill did not even know on the afternoon of 14 November that it was likely to be attacked.* No citizen was left to die, no humble home left to burn, for reasons of high strategy. The traumatic 'to warn or not to warn' discussion never took place.

APPENDIX B

The official RAF report on the raid,
compiled at the time

1. *Note on German Operation* 'MOONLIGHT SONATA',
and Counter-plan 'COLD WATER'.

Intelligence

On the 11th November it was reported that a Prisoner of War, in conversation with a room mate, said that a colossal raid had been planned to take place between the 15th to 20th November, at the full moon, and that Coventry and Birmingham would be the towns attacked. Every bomber in the Luftwaffe would take part, and workmen's dwellings would be methodically attacked in order to undermine the working classes, who were believed to be near revolt. The prisoner thought that every Knicebein route would be used.

2. On the same day information was received from another source that the Germans were planning a gigantic raid under the code name 'Moonlight Sonata'.

3. On the 12th November Air Intelligence was able to amplify this information sufficiently to confirm that a heavy scale attack was probable at the full moon; that the Knicebein and V.H.F. beams (River Group) would be employed; that Air Fleets 2 and 3, together with KG—100 (amounting to some 1,800 first line aircraft) would be participating; and that the operation would be undertaken in 3 phases; and that there were 3 target areas which were alternatives. Finally, the Commander-in-Chief of the G.A.F. would be controlling the operation in person.

Air Staff Counter-Plan.

4. On receiving the above information the Air Staff issued a counter-plan (code name 'Cold Water'), the principal features of which were:-

    (a) Continuous watch on German radio activity, and maximum radio interference with enemy navigational beams and beacons:

(b) Security patrols by Bomber aircraft over the German aerodromes occupied by Air Fleets 2 and 3:

(c) A heavy scale of attack on the aerodrome at Vannes and St. Leger used by the specialist beam flyers of KG–100.

(d) A special bombing attack on the Knicebein and V.H.F. beam transmitters near Cherbourg by aircraft flying up the beams and dropping sticks of bombs in the silent zone, which has been discovered immediately above the transmitters:

(e) A heavy bombing attack on a selected city in Germany:

(f) The maximum scale of night fighter and anti-aircraft artillery to be concentrated against the enemy raiders.

5. The operation orders to implement this plan were issued at 0300 hrs. on the 14th November.

History of the Action.

6. At about 1300 hours on the 14th November German radio beam activity coupled with enemy reconnaissance reports, and the interception of messages from the Central Control for the operation at Versailles, indicated that operation 'Moonlight Sonata' was to commence on the night of the 14–15th November. An executive order to implement counter-plan 'Cold Water' was thereupon issued to all concerned.

7. By 1500 hours on the 14th November the Radio Countermeasures Organisation was able to report that the enemy 'River Group' beams were intersecting over Coventry. All R.A.F. Commands were informed, and Home Security and Home Forces put into the picture.

Action by Coastal Command.

8. One Squadron bombed Vannes aerodrome and started one large, and several small, fires. Bursts were also seen on the runways and in an aircraft dispersal area.

9. The aerodrome at St. Leger was bombed by 8 Blenheim aircraft, but results were not observed.

10. 8 Hudson aircraft attacked aerodromes at Rosendail, Gravelines, and the jetty at Calais. At Rosendail an Me. 110, which took off to engage our bombers, was shot down.

11. All Coastal Command aircraft returned from these operations.

Action by Bomber Command.

12. A heavy attack by 30 aircraft was delivered against military objectives in Berlin, during which 17 tons of high explosive bombs, 4,000 incendiaries, and 6 1,500 lb. land mines were dropped. A number of large fires and explosions resulted.

13. 43 bomber aircraft attacked aerodromes of Air Fleets 2 and 3. The results were good. For example. At Melun fires were started in the hangars and bursts were seen close to 14 aircraft on the ground. At Chartres an enemy aircraft was set alight on the flare path.

14. Our casualties during the night amounted to 10 bombers missing, 2 in the sea, and 1 crashed on return.

Action by special Radio Bombers.

15. 2 special aircraft and crews attacked the beam transmitting stations on the Cherbourg Peninsula, by dropping sticks of bombs in the silent zone immediately above the stations. One stick of bombs was observed to straddle No. IV Knicebein Beam which became silent and did not open up again during the night. An intercepted instruction to the V.H.F. Beam Station at Cherbourg, to switch to a new target, produced the reply that the apparatus was unserviceable. It is presumed, therefore, that these special bombing attacks succeeded in putting 2 beam transmitters out of action during the night.

Radio Counter-measures.

16. All radio counter-measures were put into effect. These included 'neconing' the enemy radio beacons and spoiling the beams. While these operations were technically successful they are unlikely to have contributed materially to the defence, since the night was so clear and bright that radio navigational aids were not essential.

Fighter Action.

17. A total of 121 fighter sorties were despatched during the night, consisting of 10 A.I. Beaufighters, 39 A.I. Blenheims, 22 Defiants, 45 Hurricanes, 4 Gladiators and 1 Spitfire. The fighter operations resulted in 11 A.I. detections, culminating in one enemy sighting: one sighting assisted by searchlights and 9 unassisted sightings. 2 engagements resulted from these sightings and one enemy aircraft was damaged.

18. The disappointing number of combats which followed on

the 21 interceptions or enemy detections is attributed, inter alia, to the exhaust glow from Hurricanes and Defiants, which has the double disability of interfering with the pilots' vision and acting as a warning beacon to enemy bombers. The poor vision through the perspex screens of Blenheims and Hurricanes is also a contributory cause.

19.   The fighter deployment provided for patrols over the target area, patrols across the beams and on enemy lines of approach, and also for vectoring on to specific enemy raiders.

Balloon Defence.

20.   The Coventry barrage of 56 balloons was reinforced on the 14th November by 16 further balloons, 8 of which were deployed on the night 14–15th. The barrage was flying throughout the enemy attack, and no enemy aircraft came below the level of the balloons. Balloon casualties resulting from the bombardment were slight.

A.A. Gun Defence.

21.   40 high angle guns were deployed for the defence of Coventry, and these remained in action throughout the bombardment. Although the Gun Operations Room was bombed it soon returned to action, and at the end of the operation was in control of all the heavy anti-aircraft except for 6 guns.

22.   The light anti-aircraft deployed in Coventry had been increased on the 12th November by 12 Bofors provided by Home Forces.

Enemy Action and Tactics.

23.   It is estimated that some 330 enemy aircraft were engaged in the attack on Coventry, which was opened by some 10 aeroplanes of KG–100, which flew up the beams and started fires in the target area. The remaining aircraft then bombed the fires. While earlier raids followed the beams they were soon abandoned by subsequent sorties, which took full advantage of the bright moonlight and approached the objective over a wide front.

D.D.H.O.

17.11.40.

Author's notes on:
Note on German Operation 'MOONLIGHT SONATA'

1. I have reproduced this document exactly as it appears in the Air Ministry files, including the mis-spelling of *Knickebein* and Gravelines and figures of doubtful accuracy (see pages 51–2 and 140–1). The statement that 'no enemy aircraft came below the level of the balloons' is not borne out by the evidence of eye-witnesses, British or German.

2. The word shown here as 'neconing' (paragraph 16) is not clear in the original text. I suspect the word intended was 'meaconing', the term used to describe blotting out the genuine German transmissions with masking beacons, i.e. 'meacons', and substituting a misleading signal from British radio stations (see pages 54–5).

3. 'A.I.' stands for air interception radar, as yet in its infancy. 'D.D.H.O.' is short for Deputy Director, Home Operations.

4. An exhaustive and authoritative analysis of 'Operation Cold Water' by Mr N. E. Evans of the Public Record Office appeared in *RUSI*, the Journal of the Royal United Services Institute, in September 1976. His findings bear out my account in Chapter 3; he also explains why the Air Staff failed to identify Coventry as the target for 'Moonlight Sonata'. The official appreciation was wrong on all counts, predicting that the raid would probably occur on 'a night between 15 and 20 November' and the likeliest target areas, 'probably alternative to each other', were 'Central London (not absolutely definite), Greater London, the area bounded by Farnborough–Maidenhead–Reading, and the area bounded by Rochester–Favisham [i.e. Faversham]–Isle of Sheppey'. This was almost certainly the document which caused Churchill's return to No. 10 on 14 November, though he seems to have disregarded the sentence in which the Air Staff hedged their bets: 'If further information indicates Coventry, Birmingham or elsewhere we hope to get instructions out in time.' Mr Evans is sceptical of Ultra's efficacy. 'Ultra', he wrote, 'gave advance notice of a large-scale aerial assault and of the radio messages which would signal its imminence. It made no further useful contribution.' German intentions were discovered, he points out, solely by 'conventional' radio intelligence, for 'Ultra failed to establish the date of Operation Moonlight Sonata and . . . actually diverted attention away from the true objective. A simple exercise in listening did no worse in the first respect and rather better in the second.'

A NOTE ON SOURCES

MOST of my material has been drawn from eye-witness accounts by informants, specially written for this book. I have also made extensive use of contemporary publications and of government archives in the Public Record Office, which have only recently become available to historians. Most of the papers I have drawn on are from the files of the Home Office and Ministry of Home Security, identified by the prefix HO.

GOVERNMENT PAPERS CONSULTED

An Investigation of Probable Air Raid Damage dated June 1940. (Reference: HO/195/7 X/L 02120)

Note on German Operation 'MOONLIGHT SONATA' and Counter-plan 'COLD WATER', dated 17 November 1940, in Air Ministry file Air/20/2419/00718, the full text of which is reproduced in Appendix B of the present book

Chart of Air Raids on the City of Coventry, 18 August 1940 to 3 August 1942 (HO/192/1167 X/J 5494)

A Narrative of the Major Features of the Coventry 'Blitz' Raid 14/15 November 1940, extracted from documents available in the file TL/5/2/4 No: 70, 18 March 1943 (HO/192/1159 X/J 5494)

Additional Notes to Narrative of the Raid of 14/15 November 1940, 9 October 1943 (HO/192/1167 X/J 5494)

Air Raid on Coventry 14/15 November 1940, by Eric L. Bird, 18 November 1940 (HO 199/178 X/J 5467)

Civil Defence (No. 9 Region) Air Raid on Coventry 14/15 November 1940, by R. A. Youll, 19 December 1940 (same file)

Admiralty Weekly Intelligence Report, 24 November 1940 (same file)

Ministry of Home Security Weekly Appreciation Report, No. 22 for period 0600 hrs 13 November to 1600 hrs 20 November 1940, Appendix (same file)

Ministry of Home Security Situation Reports, from No. 85, 1945 hrs, 14 November to No. 102 1950 hours, 18 November. (The numbering begins afresh at 0001 hours each day, and these reports are referred to later as *HSWR*) (File HO/199/178 X/J 5467)

Report and Recommendations of the Coventry Reconstruction Coordinating Committee, 31 December 1940 (*'Rootes Report'*) (HO/186/603 X/J 5464)

Repair of Air Raid Damage: Summary of Action taken by the Departments concerned on Matters Dealt With in the Reports of the Coventry Reconstruction Coordinating Committee, July 1941 (same file)

Coventry City Police: General Situation Report for the Two Weeks ended 23 November (HO/199/178 X/J 5467)

Working a Rendezvous Post, 22 November 1940, by C. H. le Grand, Regional Training Officer (same file)

Military Assistance at Coventry, by E. J. Hodsoll, 22 November 1940 (same file)

General Reports to Admiralty on RMS Operations in Coventry, 15–19 November, 1940, 20 November 1940 (same file)

City of Coventry Water Department: Report on Air Raid Damage 14/15 November and Subsequent Reconstruction, 4 January 1941 (HO/192/1164 X/J 5494)

British Waterworks Association: Notes on Procedure Adopted in the Light of Experience, undated (same file)

City of Coventry Gas Department: Notes upon Experience gained in Restoration of Gas Supplies, July 1941 (HO/192/1164 X/J 5494)

City of Coventry Electricity Department: Coventry Blitz, 14/15 November 1940. 1 January 1941 (File HO/192/1164 X/J 5494). (This document is paper number 5 in a *Report* dated 17 May 1943 in the same file)

German Reports on the Coventry Raid of the 14/15 November 1940, 10 December 1940 (HO/199/178 X/J 5467)

The Effects of the GAF [i.e. German Air Force] *Raids on Coventry based on the Results of a Social Survey,* Ministry of Home Security Research and Experiments Department, 8 September 1944 (HO/192/1657 X/J 5494)

Report of the Nightly Exodus from Coventry, by the Friends Ambulance Unit, Based on an inquiry carried out in October 1941 (HO/207/1069)

Report on the Shopping Difficulties of Women War Workers in Coventry, 3 November 1941 (HO/207/1069)

Letter from the Secretary of State for War to the Ministry of Home Security, 5 December 1940 (HO/186/556 X/J 5465)
Letter from Lord Dudley to Lord Beaverbrook and from Lord Dudley to the Ministry of Home Security, 2 January 1941 (HO/207/1068)
Telephone Message received at the Home Office, from the Acting Inspector of Constabulary, 10.25 a.m., 15 November (HO/199/178 X/J 5467)
Telephone Message received at the Home Office, from the Chief Constable of Coventry, 10.40 a.m., 15 November (same file)
Cabinet Minutes, 15 November 1940, (CAB 65/10 WM (40) 289) and 18 November (WM (40) 290).

NEWSPAPERS AND PERIODICALS

Birmingham Gazette
Coventry Standard (abbreviated in later references to *C S*)
Local Government Service, January 1941, for article, 'Coventry's Lessons for YOU'
London Calling, No. 63, 1941, (BBC, London), for transcript of Tom Harrisson's broadcast
Midland Daily Telegraph (*MDT*), later the *Coventry Evening Telegraph* (*CET*)
National Civil Defence Journal and ARP News, February 1945, for the very useful article, 'Coventry Survived the Terror'
Radio Times, November 1940

BOOKS AND PAMPHLETS

Anon., *One of His Own Trees*, publisher unstated, n.d., in Imperial War Museum
Bisset, Ian, *The George Cross*, MacGibbon and Kee, 1961
Briggs, Asa, 'The War of Words', in *The History of British Broadcasting*, vol. III, OUP, 1970
Brown, Anthony Cave, *Bodyguard of Lies. The Vital Role of Deceptive Strategy in World War II*, W. H. Allen, 1976
City of Coventry, After Raid Information Service, *Information Officers' Guide*, City Treasurer, Coventry, June 1943
Clark, Ronald W., *The Rise of the Boffins*, Phoenix House, 1962
Clitheroe, Rev. G. W., *Coventry Under Fire, by the Vicar of Holy Trinity*, British Publishing Co. Ltd, Gloucester, 1941

Collier, Basil, *The Defence of the United Kingdom*, HMSO, 1957
Coventry City Council, *The City We Loved*, Ed. J. Burrow and Co., Cheltenham, for Three Spires Publishing Co., Coventry, 1942
Donoughue, Bernard, and Jones G. W., *Herbert Morrison, Portrait of a Politician*, Weidenfeld, 1973
Fleming, Peter, *Invasion 1940*, Hart-Davis, 1957
Fox, Levi, 'Coventry's Heritage', *Coventry Evening Telegraph*, 1947
Harris, Air Chief Marshal Sir Arthur, *Bomber Offensive*, Collins, 1947
Harrisson, Tom, *Living through the Blitz*, Collins, 1976
Henze, Carl G. P., 'Experiences of the Crew of a Junkers 88 in Operations against England', in *War Books of German Youth*, vol. 84, translated by E. H. Dean of Coventry Technical College, 1945
Hobbs, Ernest, *The Battle of the Three Spires, Impressions of a Blind Citizen*, Coventry, publisher unstated, 1942, in Coventry City Library
Hodgkinson, George, *Sent to Coventry*, Robert Maxwell, 1970
Howard, Rev. R. T., *Ruined and Rebuilt, The Story of Coventry Cathedral 1939–1962*, Council of Coventry Cathedral, 1962
Hughes, Trevor, 'Autumn Convoy', in H. S. Ingham (Editor), *Fire and Water*, Lindsay Drummond, 1942
Lee, (General) Raymond E., *The London Observer*, Hutchinson, 1972
Marchant, Hilde, *Women and Children Last*, Gollancz, 1941
Newbold, E. B., *Portrait of Coventry*, Robert Hale, 1972
Parkinson, Roger, *Blood, Toil, Tears and Sweat*, Hart-Davis, MacGibbon, 1975
Pile, General Sir Frederick, *Ack-Ack*, Harrap, 1949
Price, Alfred, *Instruments of Darkness*, William Kimber, 1967
Reith, J. C. W. (Lord), *Into the Wind*, Hodder and Stoughton, 1949
Richardson, Kenneth, *Twentieth Century Coventry*, Macmillan, 1972
Roof Over Britain, The Official Story of the A.A. Defences 1939–1942, HMSO, 1943
Shelton, J. B., *A Night in Little Park Street*, Britannicus Liber Ltd, London, 1950
Smith, Frederick, *Coventry: Six Hundred Years of Municipal Life*, City of Coventry, 1945
Spence, Basil, *Phoenix at Coventry, The Building of a Cathedral*, Geoffrey Bles, 1962

Stevenson, William, *A Man Called Intrepid, The Secret War 1939–1945*, Macmillan, 1976

Taylor, A. J. P., *Beaverbrook*, Hamish Hamilton, 1972

Titmuss, Richard M., *Problems of Social Policy*, in the official *History of the Second World War* series, HMSO, 1950

Wheeler-Bennett, Sir John W., *King George VI, His Life and Reign*, Macmillan, 1958

Willis, Jerome, *It Stopped at London*, Hurst and Blackett, 1944

Winter, Dr Harry, 'The Man in White', in Allen A. Michie and Walter Graebner (Eds), *Lights of Freedom*, Allen and Unwin, 1941

Winterbotham, F. W., *The Ultra Secret*, Weidenfeld, 1974

DETAILED REFERENCES

(For full particulars of the sources mentioned see the list above)

Chapter 1: Too far inland to be bombed

The information about the city's early history and Lady Godiva comes from Newbold, the list of ancient monuments from *The City We Loved* and the description of the Cathedral from the radio programme mentioned in the Foreword. The deep shelter controversy, the account of anti-fire precautions, and the change-over to war production, including the quotation from Sir Alfred Herbert, are mentioned by Richardson. *An Investigation of Probable Air Raid Damage* includes a number of maps showing the predicted random distribution of the bombs and adopts the Cathedral as the likely aiming point in four of the six imaginary raids studied (consisting of three pairs of otherwise identical raids occurring respectively by day and night). (The most useful map, however, while correctly stated in the text as being on a scale of 25 inches to the mile, is wrongly identified in the legend at its base as 25 *feet* to the mile.) Although the paper contains at first sight a remarkable amount of detail, and many equations, impressive to a non-mathematician, I confess I am puzzled as to its purpose. I also share the doubts expressed by Professor Titmuss, the great authority on post-raid conditions, as to the accuracy of its forecasts. The document makes no reference at all to such foreseeable difficulties as the blocking of the roads, the interruption of public utility services, or the plight of trekkers and the homeless and while estimating the exact numbers likely to become casualties at home or in Anderson shelters does not mention people in public shelters or caught in the street. It is therefore almost impossible to compare the forecasts of these two eminent experts with what actually occurred. Most curious of all, they refer throughout only to 'casualties', although the distinction between those killed and injured was extremely important to those planning A R P and post-raid services as well as to the people directly affected. For conflicting views on *An Investigation* see Titmuss, p. 329 footnote.

Chapter 2: Jerry's late tonight

Newbold describes the landing of the first bombs, details of the early raids appear in the *Chart of Air Raids* and the *CS* quotations appeared on 14 October and 9 November 1940.

Chapter 3: A blow for Herr Churchill

Coventry's identification as a potential target in 1934 is mentioned by Clark, the account of pre-war defensive measures and the switching off of the searchlights in 1940, comes from Pile, details of the defences of Coventry appear in Basil Collier, p. 475, the *Knickebein* technique and the incident at Swanage are described by Price, the 38 A A Brigade Operation Order is in War Office file 199/502, and the quotations from Professor Jones are taken from an interview, and correspondence with, the author. The account of the piecing together of intelligence about the German intentions, and the description of British counter-measures, come from the *Note on German Operation 'Moonlight Sonata'*, the full text of which is reprinted in Appendix B. The German pilot was interviewed by Henze. It should be noted that the timings of the raid given by Price, p. 44 (which has K G 100 taking off 'soon after dark' but not crossing the Thames until 8 p.m., and not reaching Coventry until a quarter past midnight) are wrong. So is the statement by Ronald W. Clark, p. 122, that the raid began some time after 8 p.m. On the whole question of prior warning, and the claims of Winterbotham and others, see Appendix A.

Chapter 4: An ordinary winter's evening
The information in this chapter, including Colonel Lawrence's recollections, came from individual contributors, apart from the description of the scene in the Barrage Control Office which appeared in *Roof over Britain* and the material from *MOT.*

Chapter 5: Tonight he means it
The police constable's account is in the Imperial War Museum (Manuscript K.6.066) and the description of the incendiaries on Greyfriars Green appeared in the *CET* on 16 November 1967 in a series of articles about the raid.

Chapter 6: The Germans seem strangely persistent
I used extensively the Ministry of Home Security Situation Reports, from No. 83 for 14 November onwards. The sources disagree (very understandably in the circumstances) about the number of fires; the figure of 240 appears in *Coventry Survived the Terror.* I drew heavily, at points evident from the text, on Clitheroe, Shelton, Winter, Howard (both his book and the subsequent radio interview) and the account of the attack on the Daimler factories comes from St John C. Nixon, *Daimler 1896–1946* (G. T. Fowkes and Co., n.d., but *c.* 1946).

Chapter 7: Like a gigantic sunset
Donoughue and Jones describe supper at Himley Hall, Wheeler-Bennett the view from Windsor Castle, Marchant conditions in Birmingham, and R. A. Youll the sending of outside assistance to Coventry.

Chapter 8: Too busy to be afraid
Apart from Dr Winter, J. B. Shelton and private informants, I drew on the *Narrative* on the general course of the raid, R. A. Youll on First Aid Posts in general, and for events at No. 4 FAP on an account specially written directly after the raid for Dr Alan Ashworth.

Chapter 9: Just waiting and praying for morning to come
Apart from Dr Winter, on conditions at his hospital, Provost Howard, on the movement of shelterers from the Cathedral crypt,

and *Coventry Survived* on the land-mines, all the material was from private informants.

Chapter 10: Having it all their own way

The German account comes from Henze, the fire situation message was No 14 of 15 November, Dr Winter and Mr Shelton described conditions at the hospital and in Little Park Street. Night-fighter operations are described by Collier, p. 264, and Portal's statement to the Cabinet is recorded in Cabinet minute CAB 65/10 WM (40) 289 of 15 November. The 'official Ack-Ack Command account' is quoted by Pile pp. 177–8 and the experiences of 916 Squadron (apart from those at No 33 Balloon Site, which came from a private informant) are described in *Roof*.

Chapter 11: Mummy, where's our house gone?

The description of the 'morning after' was broadcast by the BBC Home Service at 1.15 p.m. on Sunday 24 November and is now in the BBC Sound Archives. I also quoted from Howard and Hodgkinson.

Chapter 12: Closed, but not for long

CS, 30 November, described the reaction of the banks to the raid. Peeping Tom's survival is mentioned by Newbold, p. 188. On the history of Coventry's trams I used an interesting article in *The Tramway Review* vol. 4, no. 30, 1961, though the description quoted here came from a contributor.

Chapter 13: A good night's sleep

The misleading figure of 300 evacuees appears in the *Admiralty Weekly Intelligence Report*, the 'special inquiry' mentioned was the *Report of the Nightly Exodus*. The reporter who encountered streets apparently 'covered with ice' was Marchant.

Chapter 14: The balance sheet

The chapter epigraph cames from the *Narrative*, which also gives details of the bombs dropped and mentions the escape of the two shadow factories. The 'inspector's report' was *Air Raid on Coventry*. Richardson, p. 84, attributes to Lord Rootes the estimate that 'nearly 75 per cent' of the city's industry had been damaged, and

Hodgkinson, p. 160, refers to seventy-three factories being destroyed. Statistics about housing appear in *Additional Notes* and about council houses in *MDT*, 4 December. Damage to the water supply is mentioned in *Air Raid*, but on the public utilities I mainly used the three *Reports* by their respective chief engineers. Hodgkinson, p. 157, described the gas-holder burning, damage to the railways is set out in the *Narrative* and to the bus fleet in *Additional Notes*. The *'Rootes Report'* and *Repair of Air Raid Damage* describe the troubles of the postal and telephone services, the criticism that their restoration was 'too slow' appearing in paragraph 21 and 22 of the latter. The reaction of public shelters to bombing is decribed in the *Narrative, Air Raid on Coventry* and *Additional Notes,* which mentions the destruction of records and the abandonment of some public shelters. The casualty estimates I used appear in *HSWR No. 58*, 15 November; *Admiralty Weekly Intelligence Report,* the Police *General Situation Report*; and, the final, authoritative figures in *Additional Notes*. Casualty figures for the United Kingdom as a whole appear in my *How We Lived Then* (Hutchinson, 1971), but see note on page 284 for my reservations about the ratio of casualties to population in Coventry.

Chapter 15: Go round the back, Your Majesty
On the despatch of the Regional Officer see *Working a Rendezvous Post*; on police assistance see *HSWR No. 78*, 15 November, and *Telephone Messages received at Home Office*. On the use of troops I consulted *Military Assistance, HSWR No. 155*, 16 November and *HSWR No. 38*, 17 November. *General Report to Admiralty* desccribes the mine disposal operations and *HSWR No. 134*, 17 November, includes the UXB return and describes conditions generally. Alderman Halliwell's personality is described by Richardson, pp. 203–4, and Hodgkinson's life in his autobiography. Donoughue and Jones, p. 292, describe the classic meeting at the Council House, A. J. P. Taylor quotes Beaverbrook's untimely metaphor, Richardson describes the setting up of the Rootes Committee, the Water Department *Report* recounts the provision of emergency supplies. Basil Collier, p. 265, gives details of German operations on the night of 15–16 November and the improvement in conditions during the weekend is made clear from the *Admiralty Weekly Intelligence Report* and the Ministry of Home Security

Weekly Appreciation Report, which gives details of the reduction in the number of fires. *CS,* 30 November, describes the suspension of rationing, the AFS man fed on jam sandwiches and corned beef was Trevor Hughes, improvements in food supplies are described in *Narrative,* p. 13 and *HSWR No. 134,* 17 November, and Pearl Hyde by Richardson, pp. 80–1. The King's decision to visit Coventry and his reflections on his experiences are in Wheeler-Bennett, pp. 477–9, Newbold, pp. 29–30, described the scene in the rest centre, Howard, p. 20, that at the Cathedral, and *CS,* 30 November, explained Pearl Hyde's absence.

Chapter 16: A most depressing broadcast

The chapter epigraph and subsequent quotations from enemy broadcasts are from *German Reports.* Peter Fleming, p. 112, described the background to *Workers' Challenge.* The text of the BBC news bulletins is filed at the BBC Written Archives Centre and the recordings used in *They Went To It* are in BBC Sound Archives. Sir John Anderson's report is in Cabinet minute WM (40) 289 of 15 November. The text of Tom Harrisson's broadcast is in *London Calling,* No 63, 1941, the War Cabinet's reaction in CAB 65/10 WM 290 (40) for 18 November, and its attempts to control the BBC in Reith, p. 438 and Briggs, p. 332. I also relied heavily on private information from Tom Harrisson. The heroes' welcome to the AFS at Rugby is in Trevor Hughes, the course of the Blitz later in the year is described by Basil Collier, and the *Evening Standard* journalist was Jerome Willis. Ian Bisset, pp. 35–6, gives details of Brandon Moss's bravery and the other medals awarded are reported in *MDT,* 14 and 16 December 1940 and 18 January 1941. Newbold, p. 30, mentions some goodwill messages, and those from HMS *Coventry* and Coventry, Rhode Island, appear in Frederick Smith. *MDT,* 5 December, reported the letters of condolence, and, on 14 March 1941, the Mayor's Fund, of which details also appear in *CS,* 7 December and Newbold, p. 33. *CS,* 30 November, chronicles some of Coventry's distinguished visitors, one of whom was General Lee. See also Ernest Hobbs, *The Battle of the Three Spires, Impressions of a Blind Citizen* (Coventry, publisher unknown, 1942), which is in Coventry City Library, and Anon., *One of His Own Trees* (publisher unknown, n.d.), in the Imperial War Museum. The verse at the end of the chapter appears in *The City We Loved.*

Chapter 17: A grim task

Most of the information came from private informants. The quotations from George Hodgkinson are from a recorded interview, not from his book. The two notices quoted are now in the Coventry City Library. The figures for unidentifiable bodies and fears of a timber shortage are in R. A. Youll, p. 4. *MDT*, 21 November, described the digging of the graves and the account of the funeral, by the Rev. Leslie E. Cooke, is taken from *The City We Loved*, though I have somewhat edited the original text. *MDT* reported the addresses at the two ceremonies on their respective days and, on 21 December, warned against believing rumours about the death-roll. I also consulted, on burial procedure generally, the *Information Officer's Guide*.

Chapter 18: Marks and Spencer versus the Huns

The partial restoration of electricity is mentioned in *HSWR No. 152*, 18 November and the dispersal of machine tools and evacuation of schoolchildren in *Weekly Appreciation Report*; revival of business life generally and the re-opening of the libraries in *CS*, 30 November and *MDT*, 21 December, the latter, on 5 December, reporting how the churches were coping, though on the Cathedral crypt I consulted Provost Howard. On Barrs Hill School I used the admirable *Barrs Hill School Magazine* for July 1941, which gives a vivid picture of the whole period. The number of people claiming relief appears in the '*Rootes Report*', the work of the Reconstruction Committee is described by Richardson, p. 85 and the quotation from the Secretary of State appears in *MDT*, 17 March 1941. On the restoration of public utilities I used the *Reports* previously cited, and on the effect of the raids on factories the *Weekly Appreciation Report*, R. A. Youll and Hodgkinson. *CS*, 30 November, carried the warning about typhoid and the shortage of water and a reference to the restoration of supplies is in *MDT* for 17 December. The same paper reported Pearl Hyde's boast about the adequacy of food supplies on 4 December. *Coventry Survived* gives details of the meals served, *Weekly Appreciation Report* provides information about canteens, George Hodgkinson gives an interesting and detailed account of the development of municipal catering, *Local Government Service*, for January 1941, supplies details of meals and their prices and *MDT*, 14 February 1941, re-

counts the progress of the civic cafeterias and visits from representatives of other boroughs. Details of bread supply are given in *CS*,
7 December, *Admiralty Weekly Intelligence Report* and Hodgkinson.
The work of the Housing Committee was described in a recorded
interview by Mr Harry Weston, and by *MDT* for 21 December,
while Richardson, p. 86, mentions the famous tarpaulins, *Local
Government Service* the influx of building labour and Hodgkinson,
p. 159, the fortunate floor-tilers. An account of the number of
houses vacant before the raid, and of movement after it, appears in
The Effects of the GAF Raids. The thefts from slot-meters are
mentioned in the Electricity Department *Report*, p. 4. The post-
raid account of trekking from *Report of the Nightly Exodus*.

Chapter 19: Christmas in the ruins

The text of Provost Howard's broadcast comes from a recording
in the BBC Sound Archives. The criticism of Arthur Greenwood
is in *MDT*, 4 December. *MDT*, 15 March 1941, and Richardson,
p. 87, refer to the city's arguments with Whitehall. The findings of
the Ministry of Food investigator are in *Report on the Shopping
Difficulties* and the Ministry of Labour's subsequent comments,
dated 3 December 1941, are in the same file. The research on Coventry's experiences referred to is described in *The Effects of the GAF
Raids* and Sir Arthur Harris's view is on p. 83 of his book. *MDT*
reported concern about compensation on 4 December 1940, the
creation of the City Redevelopment Committee on 16 January 1941
and the Mayor's attitude to reprisals on 8 May. Reith, p. 424,
describes the meeting in London. Later raids are described in
Coventry Survived and by Richardson, p. 88, and details appear
in the *Chart of Air Raids*. Arguments over rebuilding are described
by Richardson, pp. 295–6, Newbold, pp. 46–9, and Hodgkinson.
Figures for the Civil Defence budget appeared in *MDT*, 14
March 1941. On the Cathedral the main source was Spence, but I
also consulted Hodgkinson, on the Council's opposition, Newbold,
pp. 73–5, who describes the flood of visitors and quotes the engineering magazine's verdict, and Provost Howard.

Appendices

The books consulted are mentioned in the text, and details appear earlier in this bibliography. The articles and letters mentioned appear in *The Times Literary Supplement* for 28 May, 25 June and 9 July 1976, and *The Times* for 28 and 31 August 1976. Another relevant letter, from Sir Herbert Marchant, was printed on 27 August – the writer concerned having served in 'Hut 3' at Bletchley – prompted by an article by the paper's Defence Correspondent, Henry Stanhope, published on the previous day under the significant headline 'Churchill could not have known the truth about the Nazis' plan'. This is principally a summary of the article by Norman Evans entitled 'Air Intelligence and the Coventry Raid' on which I have drawn in Appendix B, published in *RUSI*, the Journal of the Royal United Services Institute for Defence Studies, in September 1976.

AUTHOR'S NOTE

The population of Coventry

Because of different ways of defining the area covered and the constant turnover in population, no two sources agree on how many people were living in Coventry on 14 November 1940. Not merely does the Ministry of Food figure for the total 'ration strength' differ from the Ministry of Home Security's, but both are different from that of the local authority estimate, and frequently different totals appear in the same file. The figures from all these varying sources range from 190000 to 250000. For the sake of consistency I have adopted the figure used in the document I have consulted most, the main Home Office *Narrative* of the raid, i.e. 238400. I suspect, however, that this may be significantly too high, which means, of course, that the ratio of casualties to population given on p. 190 is too low.

LIST OF CONTRIBUTORS

(This list does not include contributors already mentioned in the Foreword, or those who asked for their names to be omitted)

Mrs E. M. Anwyl, Solihull, Warwickshire; Dr Alan Ashworth and Mrs E. Ashworth, Brisbane, Australia; Miss Ruth Ashworth, Southampton; Mrs Jo Ault, Coventry; J.B., Birmingham; A. J. Bagshaw, Stratford-upon-Avon, Warwickshire; Mrs L. Baker, Stratford-upon-Avon, Warwickshire; Robert H. Baker, Stratford-upon-Avon, Warwickshire; Stephen L. Barnacle, Coventry; Mrs D. Barnett, Chilliwack, British Columbia, Canada; F. W. Barton, Bridlington, Yorkshire; R. Baxendale, Keresley, Coventry; A. Beach, Ancaster, Warwickshire; Mrs Elsie Beaufoy, Solihull, Warwickshire; A. A. Berry, Weston-super-Mare, Avon; J. Bingley, Coventry; Mrs J. Binns, Scarborough, Yorkshire; Mrs I. Blount, Panania, New South Wales, Australia; Mrs H. K. Bowler, Bedford; John Bowles, Yardley, Birmingham; W. E. Box, Harborne, Birmingham; J. Gordon Bramwell, Leamington Spa, Warwickshire; T. H. Brew, Leamington Spa, Warwickshire; Mrs Lilian E. Brown, Minehead, Somerset; Mrs M. Burgess, Hall Green, Birmingham; Mrs J. Bushnell, Earlsdon, Coventry; Mrs A. Carter, Burbage, Leicestershire; Mrs H. C. Chapman, Birmingham; Frederick A. Clarke, Lillington, Leamington Spa; Mrs K. D. Colwill, Leamington Spa; R. Coucham, Macclesfield, Cheshire; E. A. Cox, Barwell, Leicester; W. H. Cox, Coventry; W. J. Cox, Warwick; F. Cromblehome, Birmingham; L. A. and Mrs Cecilia Dacombe, Lillington, Leamington Spa; W. W. B. Davies, Sheldon, Birmingham; Mrs D. M. Drybrough, Newnham, Daventry, Northamptonshire; Miss L. F. M. Dunnicliffe, Kirby Muxloe, Leicester; Mrs B. Emms, Solihull; Les Engleman, Stoke, Coventry; Mrs M. Evans, Penzance, Cornwall; Mr and Mrs F. Farnell, Coventry; W. Feltham, Radford, Coventry; Rex W. Fray, Hinckley, Leicestershire; N. H. Freeman, Rugby, Warwickshire; Mrs G. Greening, Lutterworth, Leicestershire; Mrs E. M. Greenwood, Rugby; Mrs A. Golby, Bedworth, near Nuneaton, Warwickshire; K. R. Griffiths, Solihull; Walter Groom, Coventry; L. W. Hall, Four Oaks, Sutton Coldfield; Aubrey Hammersley, Tile Hill, Coventry; Mrs O. M. Harris, Tamworth, Staffordshire; Mr and Mrs B. Harrison, Meriden, Coventry; Mrs Lilian Hartley, Exhall, Coventry; Mrs C. Harvey, Birkenhead, Cheshire; E. H. Hemming, Birmingham; Mrs L. E. Hibbins, Hinckley, Leicestershire; Mrs F. E. Hoare, Rowley Regis, Warley, Worcestershire; G. E. Hodgkinson, Coventry; Frederick Hotton, Coventry; The Very Rev. R. T. Howard, Horsham, Sussex; Mrs Maud Ingrams, Coventry; Mrs Alice Jackson, Coventry; Mrs M. K. Johnson, Exhall, Coventry; T. N. Jellis, Macclesfield, Cheshire; Mrs A. E. Kendall, Leamington Spa; A. J. King, Ledbury, Herefordshire; C. W. King, Hinckley, Leicestershire; G. Kyrke, Stratford-upon-Avon, Warwickshire; Mrs M. Lewis, Shirley, Solihull; Michael Logan, Coventry; Mrs Mary Lock, Bilton, Rugby; C. E. Locker, Washwood Heath, Birmingham; Mrs Winifred Mabbott, London E17; J. McCann, Bishop's Stortford, Hertfordshire; Mrs Pamela Marks, Coventry; Mrs O. Matheson, Huddersfield, Yorkshire; F. E. Moore, Bishop's Itchington, Leamington Spa; Mrs Eileen Morris, Fen End, Kenilworth, Warwickshire; Miss Hilda Moss, Four Oaks, Sutton Coldfield, Warwickshire; Mrs G. Muckley, Warwick; E. R. Nicks, Birmingham; Mrs G. B. Ollerenshaw, Marston Green, Birmingham; Mr and Mrs W. Parnell, Lydney, Gloucestershire; Mrs May Patterson, North Fitzroy, Victoria, Australia; Ken Pittaway, Stratford-upon-Avon; H. J. Poulter, Radford Semele, Leamington Spa; A. John Probert, Tyn-y-Gongl, Anglesey, Wales; W. H. Prue, Birchmoor, near Tamworth, Staffordshire; J. Quimby, Keresley, Coventry; J. Quimby (junior), Appleby Magna, near Burton-on-Trent, Staffordshire; Mrs M. Restall, Rugby; W. H. Reynolds, Warwick; Mrs R. Richardson, Birmingham; W. Robinson, Hinckley, Leicestershire; Mrs. P. M. Rodwell, Oldbury, Warley, Worcestershire; Mrs V. E. Rose, Halesowen, Worcestershire; Mrs M. J. Ryan, Charing, near Ashford, Kent; Mrs Ethel Scrannage, Bron-y-More, Twywyn, Merioneth, Wales; Mrs E. E. Scrivin, Birmingham; The Rev. and Mrs W. B. Sells, Southsea, Hants; W. H. Sharpe, Northampton; E. Sheasby, Allesley Village, Coventry; F. H. Sheppard, Shipston-on-Stour, Warwickshire; Mrs Vera Skeoch, Warwick; Miss O. M. Smith, Cubbington, Leamington Spa; Mrs R. E. Smyth, Solihull;

A. W. Staniland, Coventry; Mrs C. Strange, Solihull; J. W. Strange, Yardley, Birmingham; A. Swaby, Claverdon, near Warwick; Mrs Florence Sweet, London NW3; E. W. Tasker, Sheldon, Birmingham; Miss D. W. Taylor, Worthing, Sussex; H. L. S. Taylor, Kenilworth, Warwickshire; Miss D. C. Tipple, Fenny Drayton, near Nuneaton, Warwickshire; Mrs B. Tomkins, Nuneaton; Harold Tomley, Lowestoft, Suffolk; Mrs Doreen Treadwell, Foleshill, Coventry; F. Tunstall, Leamington Spa; Mrs A. Turner, Belgrave, near Tamworth, Staffordshire; Mrs E. Walker, Warwick; W. J. Ward, Burbage, Leicestershire; Harry Weston, Holbrooks, Coventry; Mrs W. Wheatcroft, Barston, Solihull; Mrs Marjorie Whittaker, Coventry; H. H. Wolfe, Kenilworth, Warwickshire; Mrs M. Wolfe, Weddington, Nuneaton; Mrs Millicent Wood, Sutton Coldfield; Miss Nanci Wood, Buxton, Derbyshire; Mrs Lilian Woollard, Coventry; Mrs J. Woolnough, Styvechale, Coventry; J. Leslie Worthington, Westdene, Brighton, Sussex; Mrs Frances E. Wright, Chesterton, Peterborough.

GENERAL INDEX

Compiled by Gordon Robinson

INDEX OF PLACE NAMES

Compiled by Gordon Robinson